College Student Retention

PART OF THE AMERICAN COUNCIL ON EDUCATION, SERIES ON HIGHER EDUCATION

Susan Slesinger, Executive Editor

Strategic Leadership: Integrating Strategy and Leadership in Colleges and Universities
by Richard L. Morrill

Leadership Legacy Moments: Visions and Values for Stewards of Collegiate Mission
by E. Grady Bogue

The Indispensable University: Higher Education, Economic Development, and the Knowledge Economy
by Eugene P. Trani and Robert D. Holsworth

Peak Performance for Deans and Chairs: Reframing Higher Education's Middle
by Susan Stavert Roper and Terrence E. Deal

Presidential Transitions: It's Not Just the Position, It's the Transition
by Patrick H. Sanaghan, Larry Goldstein, and Kathleen D. Gaval

Changing Course: Making the Hard Decisions to Eliminate Academic Programs
Second Edition
by Peter D. Eckel

Searching for Higher Education Leadership: Advice for Candidates and Search Committees
by Jean A. Dowdall

Other Duties as Assigned: Presidential Assistants in Higher Education
Edited by Mark P. Curchack

Leaders in the Crossroads: Success and Failure in the College Presidency
by Stephen James Nelson

International Students: Strengthening a Critical Resource
edited by Maureen S. Andrade and Norman W. Evans

Faculty Success through Mentoring: A Guide for Mentors, Mentees, and Leaders
by Carole J. Bland, Anne L. Taylor, S. Lynn Shollen, Anne Marie Weber-Main, Patricia A. Mulcahy

Leading America's Branch Campuses
edited by Samuel Schuman

Beyond 2020: Envisioning the Future of Universities in America
by Mary Landon Darden

Out in Front: The College President as the Face of the Institution
edited by Lawrence V. Weill

Community Colleges on the Horizon: Challenge, Choice, or Abundance
edited by Richard Alfred, Christopher Shults, Ozan Jaquette, and Shelley Strickland

Minding the Dream: The Process and Practice of the American Community College
by Gail O. Mellow and Cynthia Heelan

College Student Retention

Formula for Student Success

Second Edition

Alan Seidman

Published in participation with the

American Council on Education™

Leadership and Advocacy

ROWMAN & LITTLEFIELD PUBLISHERS, INC.
Lanham • Boulder • New York • Toronto • Plymouth, UK

Published by Rowman & Littlefield Publishers, Inc.
A wholly owned subsidary of The Rowman & Littlefield Publishing Group, Inc.
4501 Forbes Boulevard, Suite 200, Lanham, Maryland 20706
www.rowmanlittlefield.com

Estover Road, Plymouth PL6 7PY, United Kingdom

British Library Cataloguing in Publication Information Available

Library of Congress Cataloging-in-Publication Data
College student retention : formula for student success / [edited by] Alan Seidman.
— 2nd ed.
    v. cm.
  Summary: "Although access to higher education is virtually universally available,
about 50% of students who start in a higher education program drop out before
completion of the degree. As enrollment and retention remain top priorities for
universities, colleges, governments, parents, and students themselves, this book
offers a formula for student success to retain and graduate students. Updates to
this edition include chapters on community college retention, on-line programs,
and retention theories"—Provided by publisher.
  Includes bibliographical references and index.
  ISBN 978-1-4422-1252-7 (pbk.) — ISBN 978-1-4422-1253-4 (electronic)
  1. College attendance—United States. 2. College dropouts—United States.
3. Academic achievement—United States. I. Seidman, Alan.
  LC148.2.C65 2012
  378.1'619--dc23

                                                                    2011041695

For my wife, Barbara,
who continues to inspire me

Contents

Introduction

Why should we care about college student retention? We should care about student completion of academic and personal goals for many reasons, including student development and financial issues (those of both the college and student). The development of critical thinking skills is very important. The ability to critically analyze an issue, whether deciding on a political candidate or what kind of merchandise to buy, is essential in today's multimedia experience extravaganza. Being able to wade through the jargon, images, and the like is an important skill indeed. Bombarded from all sides—newspapers, television, radio, web, cell phones—it becomes almost impossible to ascertain the story behind the story. As a society we demand that our citizens participate in healthy debates and discourse on vital issues. If people believe what they hear and what they see indiscriminately, misinterpretations may affect decision-making and our country's quality of life. Therefore it is important that students learn critical thinking skills. College is where this learning usually takes place, a forum in which critical thinking skills can be honed without judgment.

We also want those who follow us to contribute to society. Nowadays it is difficult for individuals without college degrees to acquire wealth and happiness or to prepare for the world of work. The training a student receives at a college should prepare her for a chosen career area. In our fast-paced world there is continuous change within our areas of expertise. Inventiveness is a way of life and within the workplace process changes daily. We want our students to know where to obtain the latest information in their career areas and to keep up with the latest trends in their chosen fields. We want our students to be catalysts for change, both within their fields and in society in general.

Vital information can be obtained though periodicals, professional associations' conferences, books, and skill enhancement through education, whether on-site, off-site, or through the Internet. A student who is turned off to the educational system may not avail himself of these learning opportunities. A negative college experience can make a person shy away from formal learning approaches in the future. This is a great hindrance to job advancement.

Additionally, in many instances, a person who wants to apply for another job will need a reasonable amount of knowledge in the area of interest. The move up the employment ladder often takes into account experience in a particular endeavor. Sometimes the upward move is within the current company or institution. A student turned off to the education system may not take advantage of the opportunity to learn new skills through education; without learning new and varied ways of doing things, stagnation and deflation may occur, even in a person's current employment situation. Working in a job of little or no enjoyment creates poor employees, which in turn causes productivity to plummet.

There is also the loss of time, a non-renewable resource, when a student leaves formal education without meeting academic and/or personal goals. Time is the great equalizer. Each of us has 168 hours per week to do with what we desire. No more, no less. Attending a college but leaving prematurely wastes that precious commodity. It cannot be retrieved or replenished; it is gone.

There are many financial consequences of early student departure from college, for both the student and the college. The student may be left with loans that must be repaid. This can affect future borrowing and credit rating and may dash hopes for a certain level of personal security (type of home and car, etc.). For a college, the financial loss can be quite substantial. For instance, if tuition and fees are $5,000 per term, the loss of only ten students is $50,000 per term. The loss for three terms is $150,000, while for seven terms it is $350,000—a significant amount of revenue for most colleges. This does not even count the lost revenue for auxiliary services such as residence halls, cafeteria, college bookstore, and attendance at college events. The revenue lost to local businesses—off-campus housing, restaurants, and the like—can also be substantial.

Probably an important sidelight to all of this is that unhappy students tell their friends about their unhappy experiences, often through social media. Nowadays this form of word of mouth can reach a great number of people very quickly, and accounts of negative experiences in a particular college can impact recruitment efforts.

It can be said, then, that education is also the great equalizer. No matter what economic strata a person is born into, she can acquire the skills necessary to succeed through education. A strong, vibrant, varied, and expanding national economy is due in part to the educational attainment of its citizens. A nation that values and promotes the educational attainment of its citizens is concerned with its ability to compete in the global economy.

In a technological society, with ever-increasing use of the Internet and other modes of communication and commerce, it behooves us to continually enhance our skill sets if we want to remain knowledgeable and competitive. Those unwilling or unable to obtain the necessary skills to compete in an increasingly complex workplace are doomed to stay in low-skill, low-paying jobs. When our nation has to look abroad for workers skilled in mathematics, quantitative reasoning, and the sciences, it is a sign that perhaps our education system is failing to provide those skills at the level necessary to continue to move our country forward. Those turned off to education, not willing to continue their growth both culturally and intellectually, will surely become a burden to society later on. We cannot afford to waste our precious human capital.

Having come to realize that education is important to the vitality and success of our country, the federal and state governments have virtually mandated the accessibility of higher education for all. This mandate has been demonstrated for more then one hundred and fifty years by cooperation between the federal and state governments, from the development of the land-grant college of the nineteenth century to the development of the open admissions, low-cost community college in the beginning of the twentieth century. The opportunity for higher education is available for most citizens who want to take advantage of it.

Even though access to higher education is becoming universally available, many students who start in a higher education program drop out prior to completing a degree or achieving their individual academic and/ or social goals. This is not a recent phenomenon. For years, some students who entered the education enterprise were not successful in completing their academic and personal goals. In response to student attrition, colleges have developed intervention programs and services to try to retain students and have spent vast amounts of money setting up programs and services for a variety of groups who may be in need of extra services to develop the necessary skills to graduate. There are special programs for the economically disadvantaged, programs for underrepresented students (minorities), and programs and services for students with disabilities, women, and older adults re-entering college or beginning college for the first time. Counseling programs have been strengthened to try to meet the needs of students. Job and career centers have been established to help students decide on career options and provide a place for potential employers to come and meet students. Federal and state governments have made financial aid more readily available to a wider range of students, even though aid is now provided as loans rather than outright grants, except to the neediest students.

In spite of these additional programs and services, neither retention from first to second year nor graduation rates have improved over time. Logic dictates that the addition of programs and services should help improve the retention of students, but this seems not to be the case.

The knowledge of student behaviors and ways we can alter them will help students achieve their academic and personal goals and, we hope, develop a thirst for lifelong learning. To remain competitive in the ever-changing and challenging world, people will have to take it upon themselves to seek out educational opportunities. A person turned off to the education system because of a poor experience may never be inclined to avail herself of the opportunity to advance with additional education and, in turn, may not encourage others to take advantage of additional education. As we move ahead at a breakneck speed technologically, we must go on encouraging our citizens to continue learning new and different things.

This book examines a number of areas critical to the retention of students. Chapter 1 explores the history of the retention movement in the United States. Although we think of retention research, going back over eighty years, as old, in the scheme of the United States educational history it is very new indeed. In fact, the reader may be surprised to learn when the retention movement began and when we started to measure attrition and graduation rates and develop theories. Chapter 2 gives us measures of persistence from a number of perspectives. The reader will note that the data set used by researchers to study retention varies and can create different results for the same problem studied. We look at the various retention theories, models, and concepts in chapter 3 and at expanding our currently accepted theories to match the different avenues students use to pursue education. Exploring our definitions of retention in chapter 4 is very important. Without a standardized definition of retention, we may not be able to establish comparisons within the educational system. Additionally, the argument can be made for a nationally accepted definition for some types of comparisons, but local definition may be best when a college looks at its own retention. Chapter 5 examines the finances and trends and implication of retention; chapter 6 explores pre-college and institutional influences on degree attainment. Chapter 7 looks at community college retention. This chapter was added to this second edition of the book since the community college is such an important part of the educational system of higher education. How students choose pathways to achieving a four-year degree is explored in chapter 8. This chapter reaffirms our knowledge about college student retention, showing how complicated the path to earning a four-year degree truly is for some students. The focus of chapter 9 is online student retention issues. As for-profit online degree institutions proliferate and brick and mortar institutions offer more online courses, it is becoming a significant part of the educational enterprise. Hence the addition of this chapter. Chapter 10 looks at the little-studied area of retention and graduation beyond the first year. Most colleges front-load—that is, put most of their retention programs and services into the first term and year—and have seen some positive results. But what happens after the first year? Chapter 11 tells us the direction we must go to truly help retain students through academic and personal goal completion. Tying all this information together is chapter 12 and the Seidman formula and model for student success. This formula and model create an action plan and explain what colleges can do now to effect change and retain students until they complete their academic and personal goals. Perhaps it is now time for action to help our populace achieve its academic and personal goals instead of trying to come up with additional theories that try to tell us why students leave college.

This book could not have been completed without the enthusiasm of the chapter authors. Each worked tirelessly to develop a chapter that is meaningful, educational, and reflects his or her latest thinking on the topic. These are truly the most influential teachers and practitioners in the field today. I am grateful to them for their willingness to contribute to this endeavor when asked. I cannot thank Susan Slesinger, editor at the American Council on Education (ACE), enough for her comments, suggestions, and encouragement through the publication process. I would like to thank the folks at the American Council on Education for permitting me to go forward with this book from an idea to completion. And to my wife Barbara who never stops believing in me and my abilities and commitment to college student retention: I dedicate this book to her.

1

Past to Present

A Historical Look at Retention

Joseph B. Berger, Gerardo Blanco Ramírez, and Susan Lyons

This chapter examines the history of retention with an emphasis on how our understanding of and attention to retention has changed over time. After reviewing historical antecedents, this chapter describes the beginnings of concern with retention in American higher education and its changes over time through the present. More specifically, this chapter answers questions such as:

- When did retention first become an issue and an interest to colleges?
- How has the view of retention changed over time?
- What is the current thinking about retention?
- What is the future for studying retention?

This chapter begins with an overview of the various contextual issues that have shaped the nature of retention and the ways higher education has addressed the issues. The chapter then moves to a brief discussion of the different ways in which retention and related terms are defined (see chapter 4 of this volume for a more thorough treatment of these definitions). The remainder of the chapter then covers the historical overview of retention in a substantive chronological narrative and concludes with some closing thoughts on the nature of retention over the years.

CONTEXTUAL INFLUENCES ON RETENTION

The main purpose of this chapter is to provide an overview on the historical development of retention. The history of retention is presented in a chronological fashion through the identification of major eras, each of which is characterized by different issues, concerns, and approaches to retention. However, before proceeding to the historical overview, it is important to set the context by summarizing some of the key definitions, assumptions, issues, and sources of influences on the ways educators have thought about, studied, and addressed student retention in higher education. These contextual factors—students, campuses, educator roles, socioeconomic conditions, policies and interventions, knowledge bases, and the conceptualization of retention—have all evolved over time, and within each era are intertwined in ways that define the unique stage of development for retention at different points in time. The following discussion provides a concise overview of these factors and their relationship to the historical development of retention in American higher education.

Students.   First and foremost, retention is about students. The supply of and types of students served by colleges and universities in our country has changed over time, moving from a small, selective, generally homogenous group of privileged individuals to a diverse spectrum of individuals numbering in the millions. As the student population has grown and diversified, so have retention issues. In the early history of American higher education, student demand for higher education was low, as were aspirations for earning degrees. As a result of a lack of student interest in higher education and in earning a postsecondary degree, retention was unimportant until the last few decades of the twentieth century. Once demand increased and student bodies diversified, college leaders responded by paying more attention to retention. Such interest was general at first, but increasingly became more nuanced and complex as campuses focused on retaining a more diverse range of students. Levels of preparation, motivations, and other individual characteristics shape the reasons why students attend college and directly impact the chances that students will be retained at particular types of institutions and ultimately persist to earn a postsecondary degree.

Campuses.   Retention is also a campus-based phenomenon. By definition, retention focuses on the ability of a particular college or university to successfully graduate the students who initially enroll at that institution. The number and types of campuses that comprise the loosely coupled system of higher education in America have changed over time as well, resulting in a diversified contemporary collection of campuses composed of more than 3,600 institutions. Moreover, specific kinds of campuses tend to attract different types of students. Some campuses, such as highly selective private institutions that are considered more prestigious, recruit and enroll students who are more likely to be retained given their family backgrounds, exposure to the expectations of college, and level of educational preparation. In contrast, less selective institutions tend to attract students that are less likely to be retained given the backgrounds of their students. It is also well documented that most students who enroll in courses at community colleges do not intend to earn degrees, so retention varies widely by program within this type of campus. Some campuses do a better job of retaining certain types of students—women's colleges and Historically Black Colleges and Universities (HBCUs) have been shown to be more successful at retaining female and Black students, respectively. Differences in retention rates are a function not only of the types of students attracted by certain kinds of institutions but also of the type of environment provided by the institution and how well that particular environment is designed to fit the needs of students enrolled at that institution (Astin, 1990). As the concept of retention has evolved over time, so has the recognition that one size does not fit all in terms of retention rates and the policies and interventions needed to improve retention on any one campus. Hence, as the study of retention has developed, so too has awareness that each institution must tailor retention to fit the specific needs of its students and the context of that particular environment.

Educational Roles. The roles of faculty and other educators, such as student affairs professionals, have also evolved. These changes have impacted and been impacted by retention issues. Early campuses were comprised entirely of faculty members (sometimes one or two individuals) who were generalists that were responsible not only for all instructional activities, but for all other professional roles and activities on campuses as well. As campuses grew and disciplinary fields became more specialized, so too did the roles of the professionals on campus. Faculty became more specialized and administrative roles became distinct. In particular, the growth of student affairs administrators, admissions officers, and enrollment management specialists was driven by and helped develop retention efforts across the spectrum of American higher education. However, more recent trends have seen retention increasingly recognized as the responsibility of all educators on campus—faculty and staff—even when there are specialized staff members solely dedicated to improving retention on campus.

Socioeconomic Conditions. The larger social, economic, and political contexts in which higher education is embedded have also played a key role in affecting the development of retention. As mentioned in several places throughout this chapter, the sociocultural context of American society has shaped who has been served and in what ways they have been served during different points in history. The demands placed by society on higher education and the need for college graduates with earned degrees have grown over time. This pattern of increasing importance for individuals to possess a college degree has led to increased concern about retention as higher education has grown on one hand and become a more competitive market for students on the other.

Demographic and economic shifts have accounted for much of the increased attention to retention over the last thirty years or so. For example, the relative stabilization (or even the anticipation of stagnation or decrease) of traditional pools of high school graduates increased concern about how to keep students who had already enrolled, rather than focusing solely on recruiting new students, to maintain desired student body sizes and tuition revenue. The economy has had similar effects, with economic downturns creating larger college enrollments and times of economic prosperity leading to more value being placed on the attainment of a college degree in the competitive workforce market. More specifically, the soaring costs of higher education in conjunction with decreased ability of institutions to raise tuition and fees creates more pressure for institutions to retain students already enrolled instead of spending their resources attracting pools of new students. State-funded public postsecondary educational systems have also been paying more attention to retention as policymakers have increased demands for publicly funded systems and institutions to strive for and document better performance on key outcome indicators such as retention. Material resources have not been the only source of resource dependency for postsecondary institutions. The symbolic prestige of high rankings in nationally known publications such as *US News & World Report* has increasingly created greater public awareness about and institutional responsiveness to retention rates of institutions. As a result, campuses around the country have become increasingly concerned about retention rates as a source of prestige that can be converted into other kinds of symbolic, material, and human resources—particularly in the competition for more and better students.

Policies and Interventions.   Policies and interventions have arisen in response to concerns about retention and have shaped the development of retention, as well as impacting retention and trends in campus interventions at the federal and state levels. The federal government has initiated a number of policy initiatives over time—such as the Morrill Acts, GI Bill, Civil Rights Act, and financial aid—that have increased the importance of and access to higher education. As a result, the cumulative effect of policies designed to increase access has been to further the importance of college degree attainment: as higher percentages of individuals went to college, the value of earning a degree increased, as postsecondary success shifted over time from merely attending college to earning a degree. As the completion of a college degree became more important for individuals, it also became more important for postsecondary campuses to demonstrate that they could help individual students realize those goals.

The role of state-level policy initiatives has also increased over time. While states historically have played a limited role in this regard, the end of the twentieth century and beginning of the twenty-first century have seen many states implement accountability systems in which retention is a key criterion for success and often a driver for at least partially determining funding for state campuses.

Knowledge Base.   Our base of empirical and conceptual knowledge about retention has grown and shaped retention efforts throughout higher education. While the earliest studies on student mortality, as it was originally conceptualized, began in the 1930s, it was not until the late 1960s that a more systematic knowledge base began to emerge. Prior to the 1960s the study of retention, and even the higher education enterprise as a whole, was still developing; in the early 1960s the first syntheses of existing studies began to emerge. However, it was a series of studies in the late 1960s—notably Feldman & Newcomb's (1969) pioneering work on the impact of college on students and more specifically the work of Alexander Astin and William Spady—that spurred a more systematic study of what came to be known as retention. Building upon these earlier works, Vincent Tinto published his interactionalist model of student retention in 1975, and this model spurred tremendous interest in the study of retention. Other important contributions included Astin's (1977, 1985) theory of involvement and the work of Kamens (1974) and Bean (1980, 1983), which made additional noteworthy contributions to the theoretical foundations of the study of retention. The emergence of a theory-base spurred a proliferation of studies that now number in the thousands, making undergraduate retention one of the most studied areas in higher education as a field of study. The development of brand new theories has slowed as the number of studies has expanded—but knowledge has continued to be refined and further developed. Many studies have applied the existing models to the examination of retention in different types of postsecondary institutions and for different types of students. There has also been a movement to integrate various theories to develop more comprehensive models, while others have used constructs from other disciplines and theories to elaborate upon the existing retention models.

Early retention studies focused primarily on single-institution studies and the growth of theory-driven research initially emphasized more generic models that could explain causes of attrition and suggestions for retention as a general phenomena. Many recent studies now focus on how specific types of students (e.g., students from different racial/ethnic backgrounds, socioeconomic statuses, etc.) fare in terms of retention at specific types of institutional settings (e.g., community colleges, selective institutions, etc.). Berger (2000) has proposed, for example, that students who come from different socioeconomic strata are more or less likely to be retained at different types of campuses and that future research should focus on a number of mid-range theories that explain the interaction between specific types of student and specific types of campuses, rather than continuing to search for more macro-oriented theories that try to explain retention for all types of students at all types of campuses.

Conceptualization of Retention. Finally, the ways in which retention and its related issues have been conceptualized and defined is important to understand as a contextual issue that must be considered in any historical analysis of retention. Therefore, before moving to the substance of this chapter, it is important to understand that the ways in which retention has been conceptualized have not been consistent across space and time. While various aspects of student departure from college have been a topic of great interest to educators and researchers for some time, the terminology used to explain this phenomenon has changed and includes descriptors such as student mortality (McNeely, 1937, Gekowski & Schwartz, 1961), college dropouts (Summerskill, 1962; Spady, 1971; Tinto, 1975), student attrition (Sexton, 1965; Panos & Astin, 1967; Pantages & Creedon, 1978; Tinto, 1993), college retention (Iffert, 1957; Tinto, 1990; Berger, 2002; Braxton & Mundy, 2002), and student persistence (Berger & Milem, 1999; Berger, 2002). While these terms are closely related, they are not synonymous; given the centrality of these key concepts to the phenomena being studied, each is briefly defined below:

- *Attrition* refers to a student who fails to re-enroll at an institution in consecutive semesters.
- *Dismissal* refers to a student who is not permitted by the institution to continue enrollment.
- *Dropout* refers to a student whose initial educational goal was to complete at least a bachelor's degree, but did not.
- *Mortality* refers to the failure of a student to remain in college until graduation.
- *Persistence* refers to the desire and action of a student to stay within the system of higher education from beginning year through degree completion.
- *Retention* refers to the ability of an institution to retain a student from admission through graduation.
- *Stopout* refers to a student who temporarily withdraws from an institution or system.
- *Withdrawal* refers to the departure of a student from a college or university campus.

When discussing student departure, it is important to distinguish between *voluntary* and *involuntary* withdrawal as well as *institutional* and *system* departure. *Voluntary* departure occurs when the student decides not to re-enroll; *involuntary* departure occurs when the institution does not permit the student to re-enroll. *Institutional* departure describes the process of leaving a particular institution; *system* departure refers to departure from the higher education system.

The contextual issues—student trends, diversity of campuses, educator roles, socioeconomic external conditions, policies and interventions, and bases of knowledge—are interwoven throughout the remainder of the chapter as key considerations in each of the nine historical eras described below.

HISTORICAL OVERVIEW

American colleges have existed for over three hundred years and continue to be among the most well respected postsecondary institutions across the world. Throughout the course of its life, American higher education has withstood changes in mission, curriculum, students, and financing. These changes have affected the nature of retention in terms of patterns of retention, institutional concern about retention, the ways in which retention has been conceptualized and studied, and the range and types of strategies that have been used in attempts to improve retention.

An examination of published reports and articles on the historical development of retention provides a basis for identifying distinct historical stages that serve as a map for understanding how retention has evolved over time in American higher education. The historical eras described below are one of many possible ways to organize the ways in which we view and understand important developments in retention. The time periods that comprise each era are not uniform in terms of the number of years within each chronological segment. Rather, each era represents common themes that evolved over time.

For the purposes of this chapter, we have divided the development of retention into nine eras, as follows:

1. Retention Pre-History (1600s–Mid 1800s)
2. Evolving Toward Retention (Mid 1800s–1900)
3. Early Developments (1900–1950)
4. Dealing with Expansion (1950s)
5. Preventing Dropouts (1960s)
6. Building Theory (1970s)
7. Managing Enrollments (1980s)
8. Broadening Horizons (1990s)
9. Current and Future Trends (Early Twenty-First Century)

The first four eras cover the precedents that led to the emergence of retention as a distinct issue to be addressed, studied, and improved throughout higher education. These first four eras cover almost 330 years, most of which is covered by the era labeled "Retention Pre-History," as there was little concern with retention in any systematic way until the beginning of the twentieth century. The last five eras cover the last thirty years or so, the period of time in which retention became a universal concern across the spectrum of the higher education landscape and in which the practical, theoretical, and knowledge bases became more fully developed. Each of the nine eras is discussed in chronological order throughout the remainder of the chapter. The subsection covering each of the eras includes an overview of each of the contextual issues discussed above and summarizes the key advancements that characterized these time periods.

Retention Pre-History (1600s–1900)

For many centuries there was no need to consider retention as an important issue because there were so few students attending colleges and very few students interested in graduating. Indeed, colleges in colonial America struggled to maintain even small enrollments and were primarily interested in attracting students with little or no concern about persistence toward and graduation with a degree. College degrees had little or no importance in early American society and higher education was such a small enterprise that there was no reason to consider persistence toward a degree as an issue. Moreover, these early postsecondary institutions catered to very specific populations. For example, the earliest American colleges, Harvard (1636), William and Mary (1693), and Yale (1701) were established as extensions of their respective churches with the goal of educating young men to satisfy the local demand for pastors and missionaries. Over two-thirds of the graduates during the seventeenth century became ministers (Geiger, 1999). As demand for ministers lessened and a need for more professionally trained men emerged, colleges expanded their curriculum to prepare men from elite families for vocations in law and public life. The continued demand for ministers was filled primarily by farmers' sons, and this fueled the growth of numerous extremely small colleges serving rural boys and young men. These institutions were not very stable; most did not even stay open long enough to develop a graduating class. It might be said that campus survival needed to be established in most cases before college officials could even begin to worry about issues of student mortality. This trend would continue well into the mid-nineteenth century.

Throughout this period of time, the massive expansion of the American frontier brought instant material gratification, which afforded the opportunity to prosper to many. It was difficult for families to forgo this material reward to allow their sons to attend college. For the majority of colonial families, college was a luxury, not a necessity. In addition, the distances that needed to be traveled to attend these institutions served as barriers to attendance. The largest class to graduate from Harvard prior to the American Revolution was the class of 1771, with a total of sixty-three graduates (Rudolph, 1990). By 1776, colonial colleges enrolled nearly 750 students: over half were sons of farmers destined for the ministry; the others were sons of elite gentlemen with aspirations of careers in law and public life (Geiger, 1999).

After the American Revolution, colleges were chartered in the newly free states including Maryland, South Carolina, North Carolina, and Vermont; however, it would be years before the infrastructures of either these institutions or the colonial colleges would be organized well enough to attract significant numbers of students. Between 1775 and 1800 there was actually a decrease in college attendance. The overall number of male students attending college and graduating was still so small that any thought of retention was premature.

The early 1800s was a time of rapid expansion of the American college. Private denominational colleges emerged and enrollments grew by over 80 percent (Geiger, 1999). By 1820 enrollments outpaced the population growth and male enrollments were back up to 1 percent. The number of men enrolling in college continued to rise significantly with the establishment of denominational colleges (Geiger, 1999). This period was also a time of great turmoil as institutions struggled to define what they were and whom they served. The Yale Report of 1828 restored to universities the notion of classical instruction, which focused on providing students with a foundation for learning. The report also called for an examination of admissions standards to distinguish a college from an academy.

Expansion in college enrollment was dramatic throughout the 1820s and 1830s. The rapid rise of denominational colleges was responsible for enrollment increases of nearly 80 percent in each of these decades. This rapid growth continued until the 1840s when hard economic times changed the outlook of the country in relation to college education. The crash of 1837 sparked discourse with the current state of education, as it was viewed to cater to the professional class and ignore working-class families.

Evolving Toward Retention (Mid 1800s–1900)

As noted in the previous section, retention did not exist as a concept in early American colleges because actual degree attainment was rare. While retention was still not a concern in the late nineteenth century, this period of time was marked by increases in degree attainment and by expansion of curricular and co-curricular options that provided a more complete collegiate experience. The development of a more comprehensive collegiate experience occurred in response to external conditions that stimulated the increased importance of degree attainment and helped make the completion of college a more desirable option as academic offerings and campus life improved.

By the mid-nineteenth century, colleges admitted men of all religious denominations across a wide range of ages. The most well established early institutions educated young men ranging in age from their early teens through late twenties, mainly children of elite families with goals of attaining skills comparable to those of their fathers. The curricula of these early colleges were developed to provide students with a liberal education that included classical languages, ethics, metaphysics, and natural philosophy or science. The student body at these early colleges did not take their studies seriously and a majority did not graduate. There is no evidence that progress toward the attainment of a degree was even expected by the faculty at these colleges. The time spent at college was idiosyncratic, depending more on the wishes and needs of the students' families than on the requirements of the institution.

In addition to academics, college life became an important part of the student experience during this time. Students created college life as a way to test authority. At Harvard, for example, students participated in organized social events, and it was customary for men to be found playing card games, drinking, and "stealing the turnkeys of their Cambridge neighbors" (Horowitz, 1987) as a bonding ritual. At William and Mary and Yale, literary societies were used as supplements to classroom learning. Students would participate in open debates and writing competitions, which provided a forum for further expansion of the mind.

With the rise in number of students attending college, the importance of student life began to be realized. Institutions created programs and promoted a well-balanced academic and social curriculum for differentiation and recruitment purposes. The role of student affairs took on importance as student life changed dramatically. During this time, extracurricular activities emerged and were used as an instrument to create loyalty to the campus. There is no evidence that such efforts were successful in improving retention, although retention rates were not tracked and higher education was still decades away from such concerns.

By 1850, the average size of a college was 174 students. Collegiate education continued to expand from an elite institution serving only privileged white males to a more diverse student body, which included women. Oberlin College was the first college to admit women, although very few in number. The majority of women were educated in academies at this time, as colleges resisted pressure to admit women until the second half of the nineteenth century. Between 1850 and 1900, over forty women's institutions were chartered, including Vassar, Smith, and Wellesley. The primary goal of women's colleges at that time was to prepare women for their eventual roles as housewives, mothers, and elementary school teachers.

One of the most defining moments for American higher education occurred in 1862 with the signing of the Morrill Land Grant Act. The act was responsible for massive expansion of number of institutions as it called for at least one college in every state to offer programs in agriculture and engineering. This act, along with the influence of German models that emphasized research and specialization, transformed the "college" into the "university." The Morrill Act, however, was not predicated upon student demand, and enrollments actually decreased at the same time that the number of universities dramatically increased. The shrinking demand for college reflected the fact that earning a college degree was not yet a widespread priority for students or postsecondary institutions.

The first 250 years in higher education focused more on institutional survival than it did on student persistence and retention. While there are many factors that contributed to this situation, two main sources of influence are particularly noteworthy. First, most colleges were small and campus openings and closings were a constant. Second, students generally were not going to college in order to earn degrees. As we will see in the next section, these trends changed, leading to the first embryonic movements toward retention.

Early Developments (1900–1950)

It was not until the early 1900s that the number of institutions opened remained constant, while enrollments increased. In 1895, the largest institutions recorded enrollments of two thousand students; in 1910 that number had doubled to four thousand, and by 1915 the number grew to five thousand students (Geiger, 1999). Across the country there were 110,000 students attending just over 1,000 institutions (Goodchild, 1999). The growth and stability of institutions was the result of the convergence of another set of larger societal issues. The nation had become firmly industrialized and increasingly urban, both of which contributed to increased need for college education as a means of producing managers and professionals to help run the increasingly organized and complex work of the nation.

The rapid growth in college enrollments allowed institutions to create selective admissions policies. For the first time in history colleges had enough interest from prospective students that some campuses could afford to start being more selective about the type and quality of students who attended their institutions. Students from elite families were given preferential treatment and were used as a tool to help create the image of elite institutions. As these institutions began to define themselves as elitist, national recruitment efforts increased in order to attract the best students from across the country to these institutions. The rise of selective admissions policies developed not only to ensure that students were academically qualified but also as a way to weed out "undesirables." Increased desire to attend college, coupled with increasingly selective admissions policies, led to the creation of many new institutions. Many were coeducational or women's colleges as women became an increasingly large part of the undergraduate student population. Institutions were also created, some with substantial financial backing, to serve Jewish, Catholic, and African-American students who were prohibited as undesirables in many of the well-established institutions. Many less selective colleges, including large numbers of private and public junior colleges, also arose at this time to serve students who otherwise would not have access to a postsecondary education.

Antecedents of retention began to emerge out of this growth in the undergraduate population and the increasing numbers of diverse types of colleges and universities. The enhanced nature of student differentiation across the different types of institutions greatly exacerbated existing differences across institutions with regard to the extent to which students would be likely to complete their studies and earn a postsecondary degree. This trend was further fueled by slowly increasing expectations that, in the competition for entry into higher-paying professional positions, a college degree was a valuable asset compared to merely a high school diploma along with some college education. The more selective end of the institutional spectrum began to view a certain amount of attrition as a hallmark of institutional success; that competition for academic success would inevitably lead to failure for some students. However, the vast majority of institutions continued to be more concerned with attracting students than with keeping them.

The increasing importance of the college degree along with the increased awareness of different attrition rates led to the first documented studies that clearly focused on what would come to be called retention. In fact, the first studies of "student mortality" emerged in the 1930s. One of the first widespread studies to examine multiple issues related to the departure of students at multiple institutions was conducted by John McNeely and published in 1938 on behalf of the United States Department of the Interior and the Office of Education. This study, entitled "College Student Mortality," used data from sixty institutions across the country and examined the extent of attrition, average time to degree completion, points in the academic career in which attrition was most prevalent, impact of institutional size, impact of other factors (gender, age at entrance, location of home, type of lodging, participation in extracurricular activities, and engagement in part-time work), and reasons for departure (academic dismissal, financial difficulties, illness/death, lack of interest, and being called home by parents). This pioneering work was remarkable for the breadth and depth with which it covered the extent of and patterns of student attrition. McNeely's work was clearly a forerunner of the more comprehensive studies that would become common some thirty years later. However, the effects of the Great Depression and the impact of World War II turned the nation's resources and interests away from postsecondary education for the next ten years. The post-World War II boom began higher education's golden age of expansion and provided the genesis for renewed interest in student access and degree attainment.

Dealing with Expansion (1950s)

Despite two world wars and an economic depression, enrollments would largely stay constant and even grow. The end of this period saw an American society that was sending over two million students to over 1,800 colleges. Most of the growth in student enrollments occurred in the last few years in the post-World War II period of the late 1940s. The growth in students had begun occurring in the early part of the century as college became increasingly desirable in an ever more industrial and technologically oriented society. However, government policy, in response to key events such as the Great Depression and World War II, was a major contributor to the enrollment boom that began at the close of the 1940s and shaped the rapid expansion of the 1950s. Immediately prior to this period, the National Youth Administration was developed in 1935 to help counter the effects of the Depression; it funded postsecondary educational opportunities to hundreds of thousands of students who otherwise would not have gone to college. The GI Bill had an even bigger impact, creating a tremendous surge in enrollment as soldiers returned home from war to attend college en masse. The primary purpose of the GI Bill was to help returning soldiers acquire skills necessary to reengage in civilian life. Over 1.1 million ex-GIs took the opportunity to further their education. Harvard received over sixty thousand applications (Geiger, 1999) and enrollment numbers exceeded capacity at many institutions. Finally, the launch of Sputnik was a trigger for the passage of subsequent federal policy interventions such as the National Defense Education Act of 1958 and the Higher Education Act of 1965. These acts encouraged college attendance and promoted education as necessary for the stability of the United States. These acts also defined the role the federal government would play in financially supporting higher education.

Expansion created the need to persist as a high school degree became less valuable for future economic and social attainment. Students became more committed to their studies and to graduating with the hope of bettering themselves. The explosion of higher education offered different avenues of access to the masses as well. During this time, community colleges grew in importance. These institutions, open to all high school graduates, served a diverse student body and were often used as a means to gain access to more selective four-year institutions. The importance of the community college continued through the 1960s and is evident by the rapid growth of and enrollments in this type of institution.

As the number of students enrolled across many types of institutions increased, institutions of higher education began to think about the retention issue, although it was not until predictions of a decrease in enrollment in the early 1970s that retention became a major focus of educators, researchers, and institutions alike. However, attention was increasingly being paid to getting a better understanding of why some students were not successfully earning their college degrees. Most of the emphasis, in practice and in the study of these issues, focused on understanding patterns of academic failure.

Preventing Dropouts (1960s)

By the beginning of the 1960s higher education was dealing with a myriad of consequences that arose from the post-World War II expansion of higher education. The rapid growth of student enrollment—not only in terms of larger enrollments, but also in terms of increasingly diverse student bodies—created many challenges for the expanding roster of college and university campuses across the country. The movement toward access that had begun in the late 1940s and continued throughout the 1950s included the Civil Rights movement, which created postsecondary opportunities that had not previously been widely available for African Americans and other racial and ethnic minority groups. Attempts to promote access and diversity on college campuses led to many challenges, some directly associated with the retention of students. Many campuses were unprepared to deal with a more diverse student body and many were unable or unwilling to create supportive environments for students of color. Additionally, many students from underrepresented minority groups that were now allowed greater access to higher education had not been provided adequate educational preparation given the inequities in school systems throughout America. As a result, retention rates were quite low for minority students.

Lack of preparation was not limited to students of color. The great expansion of the 1950s permitted greater access to higher education for increased numbers of middle- and lower-class students to attend college. It was during this time that students began to move away from learning as the primary goal of their education to making the grades that would help them in their future. This thinking was unsettling to many on campus and students expressed their dissatisfaction with the new direction of the curricula, protesting and demanding a return to "intellectual challenge, flexibility, and the recognition of individuality" (Horowitz, 1987).

Growing student discontent with the political and functional aspects of campus life grew as the higher education enterprise expanded in size and scope throughout the 1960s. This decade was a period of change for higher education, marked with student unrest. There were many simultaneous events during this time that caused dissention, beginning with the Civil Rights movement and culminating with the Vietnam War. These events coincided with growing recognition that student satisfaction with and departure from college was more complicated than a simple matter of academic fit and success. The early 1960s focused on individual characteristics associated with academic failure, but the latter part of the decade saw some initial efforts to understand the role of affective characteristics and social contexts in student departure. In response to growing concerns about college completion, and given growing recognition of the impact of greater student diversity, the early 1960s were characterized by a number of studies that began to look at individual student characteristics.

While individual campuses had begun to regularly monitor enrollments in the 1950s, there had been only limited attempts to systematically assess patterns of student persistence. Mostly psychological approaches were used in any studies that attempted to do more than report existing patterns of departure or look at demographic characteristics as sources of variation in departure patterns. Many of these early research studies on college student departure were conducted through the psychological lens (Summerskill, 1962), which focused on the personality attributes (maturity, motivation, disposition) of students as the main reasons for persistence or non-persistence.

Spady (1971) notes that there were six major types of studies—philosophical, census, autopsy, case, descriptive, and predictive—conducted up through the late 1960s, most of which were conducted at the tail end of the 1950s and throughout the 1960s. Philosophical studies (also known as theoretical studies) were usually built on assumptions that dropout from college should be prevented and consisted of recommendations for preventing this type of attrition. Census studies attempted to describe the extent of attrition, dropout, and transfer rates within and across institutions. Autopsy studies provided self-reported data regarding the reasons students left college. Case studies generally tracked students identified as at-risk upon entry to see what led to their success or failure to graduate from college. Descriptive approaches provided overviews of the characteristics and experiences of students who dropped out. Finally, predictive studies attempted to identify admissions criteria that could be used to generate forecasts about the potential for students to succeed in college. Despite all of these studies, Spady noted an absence of what he called analytical-exploratory studies that synthesized existing knowledge in order to systematically develop a coherent body of empirically based knowledge that could better inform efforts to understand and improve undergraduate retention. As we shall see in the next section, Spady's initial model and call for this type of knowledge development was the beginning of an ongoing movement in which retention would become a major focus of theory, research, policy, and practice throughout American higher education.

Spady's (1971) model emphasized the interaction between individual student characteristics and key aspects of the campus environment. Moreover, this model was derived from existing empirical evidence and designed to be a conceptual framework for developing a more coherent understanding of the student departure process. Spady's work was notable for several reasons. First, it was the first attempt to synthesize existing empirical work into a cohesive conceptual framework. Second, most of the previous studies had been grounded in psychology rather than sociology. Third, it served as a precursor to Tinto's model that would soon become "near-paradigmatic" (Braxton, Sullivan, & Johnson, 1997) in the study of research.

It was worth noting that Spady's contribution was made possible by an emerging body of work that provided him with the evidence that served as the foundations for his observations and synthesis. In fact, earlier attempts (e.g., Knoell, 1960; Marsh, 1966) to synthesize early dropout studies were acknowledged precursors to Spady's work. Additionally, by the late 1960s a few large-scale studies (e.g., Panos & Astin, 1968; Bayer, 1968; Trent & Medsker, 1968) had emerged and had begun a shift toward a more comprehensive and systematic examination of college withdrawal and persistence. However, these studies were either largely atheoretical or focused primarily on demographic and psychological characteristics. While these studies were improvements on the body of single-institution studies that had begun to be conducted on campuses in the 1950s, there was little emphasis placed on the interaction of student and campus characteristics and no real attempt made to collectively build knowledge on attrition and retention in a systematic manner.

Building Theory (1970s)

By 1970, retention had become an increasingly common topic within and among college and university campuses. The concerns about student dropout and satisfaction became increasingly crystallized throughout the 1960s and the 1970s dawned with greater efforts to systematically identify causes of and solutions to the challenge of retention. There were enough studies and published reports at this time to begin to construct a knowledge base that could inform retention concerns and issues throughout most of higher education.

In many ways, this era really began with the publication of Spady's seminal article, "Dropouts from Higher Education: An Interdisciplinary Review and Synthesis" (1971). His sociological model of student departure begins to explain the process as an interaction between the student and the college environment. Throughout this interaction a student's attributes (values, interests, skills, attitudes, etc.) are exposed to norms of an environment (faculty, peers, administrators). If the student and the environment are congruent in their norms, the student will assimilate both socially and academically, increasing the likelihood of persistence.

Not long after, Vincent Tinto built upon and enhanced Spady's model and other emerging sources of evidence about the nature of the student departure process. Tinto's interactionalist theory of student departure became one of the best known, and most often cited, theories relating to student departure. In its basic form, it incorporates elements of both the psychological and organizational theoretical models. It purports that a student's entry characteristics, coupled with his or her initial commitment to the institution and to graduation, influence student departure decisions. The theory also suggests that early and continued institution commitment will impact academic and social integration within the university, both important factors in college student retention (Tinto, 1975, 1993).

Another early sociological perspective comes from the work of David Kamens (1971; 1974). Kamens (1971) uses multi-institutional data to demonstrate how institutions with greater size and complexity, along with a superior capacity to place graduates in prestigious social and occupational roles, have lower rates of attrition than do other types of postsecondary institutions. He provides an open systems view of organizational behavior in higher education and emphasizes how colleges and universities with highly institutionalized social charters (Meyer, 1970) are able to use their elevated role in the field of higher education to enact a stronger influence on student persistence. In a later work, Kamens (1974) introduces elements of the symbolic dimension as he demonstrates how the use of legitimized myths in postsecondary institutional settings helps to reinforce the social charter of an institution, thereby strengthening the ability of an institution to retain students.

Alexander Astin and his colleagues at UCLA had also been studying retention since the late 1960s using large national databases collected from hundreds of colleges. Astin concluded from extensive analysis of these data that involvement was the key to retention. Simply put, the more students were involved in their academic endeavors and in college life, the more likely they were to be retained. Astin (1977; 1985) suggested that the amount of physical and psychological energy a student invests in the collegiate experience (both social and academic) directly influenced departure decisions. The simplicity of this model made it easily used and it served as the basis for many retention interventions on campuses throughout the country.

By the end of the 1970s, theory was well established and Tinto's work in particular was driving a more rigorous and systematic examination of retention. Most of the early empirical studies were conducted by Ernest Pascarella and Patrick Terenzini. They developed operational measures of the core constructs (relating to academic and social integration) from Tinto's models. This empirical work was a noteworthy contribution as it provided a foundation of research that led to an explosion of studies and a more systematic understanding of the nature of retention. This developing knowledge base would become the basis for a wave of studies and more systematic approaches to studying retention in the following decade and beyond.

Managing Enrollments (1980s)

The study of retention really took off in the 1980s. This was fueled in part by the conceptual and empirical contributions to knowledge made in the 1970s, but the practical realities of demographic shifts were the main drivers of sustained and expanding interest in retention. By the mid 1970s enrollments in higher education had exceeded 11 million; however, this growth was becoming stagnant. The anticipation of a leveling off of the supply of students led campus leaders at colleges and universities to further explore better ways for attracting and retaining students on their campuses. Previously, only limited connections had been made between efforts to recruit and enroll new students through the admissions process and efforts to retain those students once they were successfully enrolled. This separation between admissions and retention changed rapidly after the mid 1970s as campuses became increasingly aware that the enrollment boom of the previous few decades was about over.

In an effort to more effectively maintain optimally sized student bodies, in terms of quality and quantity, the concept of enrollment management was born and quickly spread throughout the country. The roots of enrollment management had begun in the early 1970s, but the first known use of the term came in 1976 when Jack Maguire, the dean of enrollment at Boston College, began disseminating information about efforts on his campus to align efforts across the admissions, financial aid, registration, and institutional research areas in order to better control enrollment. Maguire used the term "enrollment management" (Hossler, 2002). The concept spread rapidly throughout higher education and gradually became institutionalized throughout the American higher education system.

More specifically, enrollment management can be defined as:

> . . . both an organizational concept as well as a systematic set of activities designed to enable educational institutions to exert more influence over their student enrollments. This is accomplished by the use of institutional research in the areas of student college choice, student attrition, and student outcomes to guide institutional practices in the areas of new student recruitment and financial aid, student support services, as well as curriculum development and other academic areas which affect the enrollment and persistence of students. (Hossler, 1988)

Although the term enrollment management is a critical concept and formal in definition and theory, colleges and universities have implemented its practice to varying degrees. The enrollment management classifications typically employed by universities fall into one of the following four categories: the enrollment management committee; the enrollment management coordinator; the enrollment management matrix; and the enrollment management division. Each of these categories gets progressively more formal in terms of structure, authority, and effectiveness (Kemerer, Baldridge, & Green, 1982).

While the emergence of enrollment management dominated the practice of retention at this time, advances in the study of retention were being built on the successful contributions of the previous decade. For example, Bean (1980, 1983) offered a new theoretical perspective on retention that used concepts adapted from organizational studies of worker turnover (Price & Mueller, 1981) that were helpful in explaining student departure and that were subsequently used in other studies of undergraduate persistence (Braxton & Brier, 1989; Berger & Braxton, 1998). Bean's model examines how organizational attributes and reward structures affect student satisfaction and persistence and studies using this model have found that student perceptions of organizational routinization, participation, communication, and rewards influence levels of student satisfaction, which in turn affect student persistence.

By the end of the 1980s a number of models and theories had become well established in the literature and a substantial body of empirical studies had been conducted across a wide range of institutional settings. This continually developing body of work provided a foundation for a new generation of models and studies in the 1980s and 1990s that used existing theories and concepts as the basis for theory elaboration and integration that synthesized concepts from various existing frameworks and studies. Scholars have elaborated on Tinto's theory from a number of different perspectives (Braxton et al., 1997), including psychological, environmental, economic, and organizational. These attempts at theory elaboration provide evidence that Tinto's model, as initially conceptualized, benefited from the addition of constructs from other theoretical perspectives that can help improve the explanatory power of the model and provide information about sources of social and academic integration for undergraduate students.

The spread of knowledge through increased writing and research was also being matched by increased communication across campuses and major associations concerned with admissions, and student life began to feature retention as a major theme at regional and national conferences. The expanding knowledge base provided a stronger basis for professionals on campuses concerned with retention and enrollment management to be more intentional about their efforts to improve retention. The development of a variety of campus-based initiatives in turn provided campus professionals with a wealth of strategies and interventions that could be shared across campuses as part of a national dialogue. The study and practice of retention had grown into a topic of national attention. The emergence of a wider variety of more specific programs also created a growing body of literature on the evaluation of the effectiveness of these efforts. As a result, in addition to the growth in theory-driven studies, more research was being published about the wide variety of campus-based practices that were being implemented on campuses across the country.

At the same time, retention was becoming increasingly diversified in terms of the types of students and institutions concerned with the issue and the types of students that campuses were trying to retain. More studies were being conducted on campuses, and campus-based strategies were being implemented for different types of students from varying racial and ethnic backgrounds, first-generation college students, and non-traditionally-aged students. Retention was becoming a concern at a wider range of campuses, a trend that was coming to include community colleges to a greater extent than ever before. Additionally, the concept of retention even moved into graduate student retention after a long history of focusing only on the retention of undergraduates.

Broadening Horizons (1990s)

The 1990s were a continued expansion of research, knowledge, and strategies that continued the trend in which retention had become a dynamic and full-fledged area of study and had become permanently established as an educational priority throughout American higher education. It was also a time at which retention as a field of study had become well enough established to begin taking stock of the vast amounts of knowledge that had been amassed through thousands of published and unpublished studies.

Although many future researchers studied retention using Tinto's interactional model, very little empirical evidence existed relating to the internal consistency of each of these propositions. In an attempt to assess the internal consistency of Tinto's theoretical model, Braxton et al. (1997) empirically tested its fifteen propositions. Based on results of single-institution research studies, four propositions were found to be "logically interconnected." The four propositions are defined as (Braxton, 2000):

1. Students bring to college different entry characteristics, which will impact their initial commitment to the institution.
2. Students' initial commitment to the institution will impact their future commitment to the institution.
3. Students' continued commitment to the institution is enhanced by the level of *social integration* they realize early on.
4. The greater the level of commitment to the institution, the higher the likelihood of the student being retained through graduation.

These data suggest that social integration, not academic integration, is key to understanding student departure. Braxton et al. (1997) recommended that future researchers explore additional psychological, social, and organizational influences that impact both social integration and commitment (institution and graduation) as a way to improve upon Tinto's theory. Subsequent studies have begun to take on this challenge and other studies continued the quest to search for other explanatory factors that might help solve the departure puzzle.

While the need for financial aid and its important role on campus had been well established in practice for years, the significance of finances in retention was one of the areas that began to receive more attention as a field of study in the 1990s. A series of earlier studies by Alberto Cabrera, Amaury Nora, Edward St. John, Michael Paulsen, and others laid the groundwork for increasing recognition that the ability to pay for college was increasingly important and the growing recognition of financial barriers was an essential part of studying ways to improve retention.

There was also a re-emphasis on academics and student learning. It was increasingly recognized that greater emphasis was needed not only on retention but on student learning. Initiatives such as the Student Learning Imperative were developed by student affairs professionals to emphasize the centrality of learning as the primary goal of college. Many retention efforts reflected the renewed emphasis on student learning through the development of learning communities in which students who lived together also took classes together. These trends emphasized the overlap between involvement in the academic and social spheres of campus rather than focusing on them as separate sources of influence on retention.

Greater attention was also being paid to student diversity and the challenges of retaining students of color and students from disadvantaged backgrounds. Many critiques emerged of the dominant cultures on predominantly white campuses that created additional challenges for students of color and others to succeed. Some of these same critiques questioned much of the theory base that had been developed on assumptions that students must adopt the values and norms of a particular campus in order to succeed. Laura Rendon and others developed alternative models focusing on ways in which college campuses could validate the experiences and knowledge of students of color as an effective means for improving the retention and academic success for these students who had traditionally been marginalized in mainstream higher education.

The 1990s might also be called the era of the emergence of "persistence." Recognition that persistence and retention are distinct concepts began to fully emerge in the late 1990s. More and more, scholars and practitioners had begun to realize that while retention is an important concept for many students and for campuses themselves, many students attend more than one college as a means for earning an undergraduate degree. Increasingly, student success has been recognized as the ability to persist to the completion of a degree at one or more colleges.

Current and Future Trends (Early Twenty-First Century)

The early twenty-first century has dawned with retention fully entrenched as a major policy issue in higher education as well as a well established professional realm that has brought researchers and practitioners together in widespread efforts to better serve and retain college students throughout the country. Retention efforts are well established on virtually every campus in the nation, retention is used as a key indicator of institutional effectiveness, there are literally thousands of studies on this topic, and the field has even recently developed its own academic journal, *The Journal of College Student Retention: Research, Theory & Practice*, devoted solely to this important topic.

Yet there are many unresolved issues. Retention rates remain lower than most campus officials would like on the majority of campuses across the country. A report by American College Testing states that, nationwide, 25.9 percent of freshmen at four-year institutions do not return to school the following year. At highly selective institutions, the dropout rate is 8 percent and, at less selective institutions, it is as high as 35 percent. At open enrollment institutions, the departure rate is nearly 50 percent (Devarics & Roach, 2000). The numbers are worse when one considers the retention rates for students from underrepresented minority groups, first-generation college students, and those from lower socioeconomic backgrounds. Efforts to improve these patterns are essential to the success of individual students and campuses. As higher education becomes increasingly important for success in a society that has become knowledge- and technology-oriented, retention and persistence are more important than ever. The large number of studies and initiatives that have developed over the past few decades are a strong foundation for furthering this important work.

Building on trends that emerged in the late twentieth century, college campuses in the United States continue to become more diversified, and retention of underrepresented student populations has accordingly gained attention during the first decade of the twenty-first century (Seidman, 2005). This increased attention leads not only to the study of retention among specific underrepresented groups, but also to the study of retention in different institutional contexts. Three areas of focus for institutional contexts have been: 1) racial/ethnic oriented campuses such as Historically Black Colleges and Universities (HBCUs) or Hispanic Serving Institutions (HSIs); 2) campus racial climates on predominantly white campuses; and 3) the impact of organizational behavior on different groups of students. Racial/ethnic oriented institutions constitute an important context for the study and promotion of retention because they attract students of color, which also are students likely to come from lower socioeconomic status and to be first-generation college students (Merisotis & McCarthy, 2005). Many of these institutions have also proven successful at promoting the academic success and retention, in particular, of underrepresented students. The impact of racial campus climates on retention has been explored further. It is now understood that campus climate affects retention of all groups, not only students of color (Fischer, 2007).

These trends impact the study of retention by recognizing the need for taking a closer look at group differences and at the interactive influence between organizational contexts and the individual and collective characteristics of students; particular attention is given to how the dominant traditional organizational patterns have affected access and retention for students from underrepresented groups—including students of color and those with lower socioeconomic status. This emerging area of inquiry also brings into question the applicability of mainstream retention models among underrepresented groups. We can anticipate that the scholarship in this arena will continue to grow as will the search for institution-specific strategies to increase retention among underrepresented/underserved students. In fact, there is growing recognition that successful retention of underrepresented groups may require that campuses move away from the assumption that successful retention requires integration as a one-way street, and may become more successful as campuses find better strategies for adapting to the increasing diversity of their student populations. This is particularly important as institutions of higher learning of all types continue to struggle to retain racial minorities (Maldonado, Rhoads, & Buenavista, 2005).

The increasing trend toward accountability in higher education also has important implications for the future of retention. The past fifteen years have seen accountability become a more important mandate in higher education. Retention rates have been mandated as a core indicator by accrediting agencies for some time, but most states now review the retention rates of public institutions, and some states even tie resource allocations to such indicators. On a related note, most national rankings, such as the *US News & World Report* and others, use retention numbers to help rank institutions. These rankings are increasingly serving as a source of information to guide families in choosing colleges for their children, which creates a consumer-driven form of accountability. These trends appear to be here to stay and they make paying attention to retention more important than ever before. The continued increase of competition for resources in higher education will make retention crucial in the future.

New issues continue to arise as well. The emergence of distance learning and alternative modes of instructional delivery provide new opportunities and new challenges for promoting access to higher education and opportunities for degree attainment. Despite the fast growth of online and e-learning distance courses, the issue of retention in this educational modality has emerged as an important issue. It seems clear that e-learning courses have lower retention rates than on-campus modalities, which leads to an increased interest in understanding online dropouts (Levy, 2007; Park & Choi, 2009; Xenos, Pierrakeas, & Pintelas, 2002). While important advances have been made regarding some of the factors that influence student departure from online courses, there are many concerns about how these new instructional strategies impact retention in the larger institutional context. Thus far, most studies have focused on retention within distance-learning courses, not on how these courses promote institutional retention. This focus has led to a rapid expansion of knowledge regarding the factors influencing retention in e-learning courses, which include locus of control–related internal factors, course and tutor aspects, and student demographic characteristics (Xenos, Pierrakeas, & Pintelas, 2002). However, more research is needed on how online learning impacts persistence toward a degree. In fact, thus far little attention has been paid in the mainstream higher education literature about programmatic retention for online learning or to the ways in which online and blended courses affect retention and persistence toward degree attainment. This will become increasingly important as online learning continues to grow in traditional and nontraditional sectors of higher education.

It is also clear that how students are able to access higher education has profound affects on their ability to succeed. One of the elements that has influenced the understanding of college student retention during the twenty-first century is the concept of pathways to degree attainment. Cabrera, Burkum, and La Nasa (2005) indicate that pathways vary substantially according to socioeconomic status. Additionally, it is more and more common for students to transfer during their undergraduate education from two- to four-year institutions, or to earn credits at multiple institutions. This changing reality has led to new efforts for tracking and understanding patterns of student progression throughout a course of study (e.g., Robinson 2004). It is reasonable to expect that these changes will continue to influence the study of retention.

In conclusion, while little attention was paid to retention in American higher education during the first few hundred years, the subject has evolved over the last thirty-five years at a rapid pace. Retention has become one of the core indicators and major fields of study within higher education. As higher education and the earning of a college degree have become more important to society, retention also has become more important. A review of the history of retention clearly indicates that we should expect that the more we study and learn about this subject, the more we will recognize the complexities involved in helping the diverse array of students succeed in our equally diverse system of higher education. The future of retention promises to be as important and dynamic as its past.

REFERENCES

Astin, A. W. (1977). *Four Critical Years*. San Francisco: Jossey-Bass.

Astin, A. W. (1985). *Achieving Academic Excellence*. San Francisco: Jossey-Bass.

Astin, A. W. (1990). *Assessment for Excellence: The Philosophy and Practice of Assessment and Evaluation in Higher Education*. New York: Macmillan.

Astin, A. W. (1997). *What Matters in College: Four Critical Years Revisited*. San Francisco: Jossey-Bass.

Bayer, A. (1968). "The College Dropout: Factors Affecting Senior College Completion." *Sociology of Education*, 41: 305–316.

Bean, J. (1980). "Dropouts and Turnover: The Synthesis and Test of a Causal Model of Student Attrition." *Research in Higher Education*, 12: 155–187.

Bean, J. (1983). "The Application of a Model of Turnover in Work Organizations to the Student Attrition Process." *The Review of Higher Education*, 6: 129–148.

Berger, J. B. (2000). "Optimizing Capital, Social Reproduction, and Undergraduate Persistence: A Sociological Perspective." In J. M. Braxton (Ed.) pp. 95–126 in *Rethinking the Departure Puzzle: New Theory and Research on Student Retention*. Nashville: Vanderbilt University Press.

Berger, J. B. (2002). "Understanding the Organizational Nature of Student Persistence: Empirically-Based Recommendations for Practice." *Journal of College Student Retention*, 3(1), 3–21.

Berger, J. B. & Braxton, J. M. (1998). "Revising Tinto's Interactionalist Theory of Student Departure through Theory Elaboration: Examining the Role of Organizational Attributes in the Persistence Process." *Research in Higher Education* 39(2): 103–120.

Berger, J. B. & Milem, J. F. (1999). "The Role of Student Involvement and Perceptions of Integration in a Causal Model of Student Persistence." *Research in Higher Education,* 40(6), 641–664.

Braxton, J. M. (2000). *Reworking the Student Departure Puzzle.* Nashville, TN: Vanderbilt University Press.

Braxton, J. M. & Brier, E. M. (1989). "Melding Organizational and Interactional Theories of Student Attrition: A Path Analytic Study." *Review of Higher Education,* 13(1): 47–61.

Braxton, J. M. & Mundy, M.E. (2002). "Powerful Institutional Levers to Reduce College Student Departure." *Journal of College Student Retention,* 3(1), 91–118.

Braxton, J. M., Sullivan, A. S., & Johnson, R. (1997). "Appraising Tinto's Theory of College Student Departure." In J. S. Smart (Ed.) *Higher Education: Handbook of Theory and Research,* Volume XII. New York: Agathon.

Cabrera, A. F., Burkum, K. R., & La Nasa, S. M. (2005). "Pathways to a Four-Year Degree." In A. Seidman (Ed.). *College Student Retention: Formula for Student Success.* Westport, CT: Praeger.

Demitroff, J. F. (1974). "Student Persistence." *College and University,* 49, 553–557.

Devarics, C. & Roach, R. (2000). "Fortifying the Federal Presence in Retention." *Black Issues in Higher Education,* 17(3): 20–25.

Feldman, K. A. & Newcomb, T. M. (1969). *The Impact of College on Students.* San Francisco: Jossey-Bass.

Fischer, M. J. (2007). "Settling into Campus Life: Differences by Race/Ethnicity in College Involvement and Outcomes." *The Journal of Higher Education* 78 (2), 125–156. DOI:10.1353/jhe.2007.0009

Geiger, R. (1999). In P. G. Altbach, R. O. Berdahl, & P. J. Gumport (Eds.), *American Higher Education in the Twenty-First Century: Social, Political and Economic Challenges.* Baltimore: The Johns Hopkins University Press.

Gekowski, N. & Schwartz, S. (1961). "Student Mortality and Related Factors." *Journal of Educational Research,* 54, 192–194.

Goodchild, L. F. (1999). "Transformations of the American College Idea: Six Historic Ways to Learn." *New Directions in Higher Education,* 27(1): 7–23.

Horowitz, H. L. (1987). *Campus Life: Undergraduate Cultures from the End of the Eighteenth Century to the Present.* New York: Random House.

Hossler, D. (1988). "Admissions and Enrollment Management." In Rentz & Saddleman (Eds.), *Student Affairs Functions in Higher Education.* Springfield, IL: Charles C Thomas.

Hossler, D. (2002). "Enrollment Management." In J. J. F. Forest & K. Kinser (eds.) *Higher Education in the United States: An Encyclopedia, Volume 1.* Santa Barbara, CA: ABC-CLIO.

Iffert, R. E. (1957). *Retention and withdrawal of college students.* U.S. Office of Education, Bulletin 1957, no. 1. Washington, DC: US Government Printing Office.

Kamens, D. H. (1971). "The College 'Charter' and College Size: Effects on Occupational Choice and College Attrition." *Sociology of Education,* 44(summer): 270–296.

Kamens, D. H. (1974) "Colleges and Elite Formation: The Case of Prestigious American Colleges," *Sociology of Education,* 47 (summer) 354-378.

Kemerer, F. R., Baldridge, J. V., & Green, K. C. (1982). *Strategies for Effective Enrollment Management.* Washington, DC: American Association of State Colleges and Universities.

Knoell, D. M. (1966). A Critical Review of Research on the College Dropout. In L. A. Pervin, L. E. Reik, & W. Dalrymple (Eds.) *The College Dropout and Utilization of Talent.* Princeton: Princeton University Press.

Levy, Y. (2007). "Comparing Dropouts and Persistence in E-Learning Courses." *Computers and Education 48,* 185-204. DOI:10.1016/j.compedu.2004.12.004

Library of Congress (1975). *The Charter of the President and Fellows of Harvard College.*

Maldonado, D. E. Z., Rhoads, R., & Buenavista, T. L. (2005). "The Student-Initiated Retention Project: Theoretical Contributions and the Role of Self-Empowerment." *American Educational Research Journal 42* (4), 605-638. DOI: 10.3102/00028312042004605

Marsh, L. M. (1966). "College Dropout: A Review." *Personnel and Guidance Journal,* 44: 475-481.

Meyer, J. W. (1970). "The Charter: Conditions of Dffuse Socialization in Schools." In W. R. Scott (ed.), *Social Processes and Social Structure: An Introduction to Sociology.* New York: Henry Holt.

McNeely, J. H. (1937). *College Student Mortality.* U.S. Office of Education, Bulletin 1937, no. 11. Washington, DC: US Government Printing Office.

Merisotis, J. P., & McCarthy, K. (2005). "Retention and Student Success at Minority-Serving Institutions." In G. Gaither (Ed.) *Minority Retention: What Works?* San Francisco: Jossey-Bass.

Milem, J. F. & Berger, J. B. (1997). "A Modified Model of College Student Persistence: The Relationship between Astin's Theory of Involvement and Tinto's Theory of Student Departure." *Journal of College Student Development,* 38(4): 387-400.

Panos, R. J. & Astin, A.W. (1967). "Attrition among College Students." ACE Research Reports, 2(4).

Pantages, T.J. & Creedon, C.F. (1978). "Studies of College Attrition: 1950-1975." *Review of Educational Research,* 48(1), 49-101.

Park, J. H. & Choi, H. J. (2009). "Factors Influencing Adult Learners' Decision to Drop Out or Persist in Online Learning." *Educational Technology & Society 12*(4), 207-217.

Price J. L. & Mueller, C. W. (1981). "A Causal Model of Turnover for Nurses." *Academy of Management Journal,* 24: 543-565.

Robinson, R. (2004). "Pathways to Completion: Patterns of Progression through a University Degree." *Higher Education 47,* 1-20.

Rudolph, F. (1990). *The American College and University: A History.* Athens: The University of Georgia Press.

Seidman, A. (2005). "Minority Student Retention: Resources for Practitioners." In G. Gaither (Ed.) *Minority Retention: What Works?* San Francisco: Jossey-Bass.

Sexton, V.S. (1965). "Factors Contributing to Attrition in College Populations: Twenty-Five Years of Research." *Journal of General Psychology,* 72, 301-326.

Spady, W. (1971). "Dropouts from Higher Education: An Interdisciplinary Review and Synthesis." *Interchange,* 1, 64-85.

Summerskill, J. (1962). In N. Sanford (Ed.) *The American College.* New York: Wiley.

Tinto, V. (1975). "Dropouts from Higher Education: A Theoretical Synthesis of Recent Research." *Review of Educational Research,* 45, 89–125.

Tinto, V. (1990) "Principles of Effective Retention." *Journal of the Freshman Year Experience,* 2 (1), 35–48.

Tinto, V. (1993). *Leaving College: Rethinking the Causes and Cures of Student Attrition.* Chicago: The University of Chicago Press.

Trent, J. W. & Medsker, L. L. (1965). *Beyond High School.* San Francisco: Jossey-Bass.

Xenos, M., Pierrakeas, C., & Pintelas, P. (2002). "A Survey on Student Dropout Rates and Dropout Causes Concerning the Students in the Course of Informatics of the Hellenic Open University." *Computers and Education 39,* 361–377.

2

Measurements of Persistence

Thomas G. Mortenson

Voluntary school or college enrollment is not capricious—students (or their parents) must consciously decide and act to maintain student status in education—and it gets ever more costly to do so. Because of these costs, those who choose voluntary school or college enrollment must see school enrollment benefits outweighing these costs if they are to persist in education when no longer required to do so.

This student-initiated decision is persistence, or, from the institutional perspective, retention. It is measured through a series of status-to-status ratios. These may be called transition ratios, persistence rates, retention rates, completion rates, cohort survival rates, or graduation rates. They may also be used to measure dropout rates, transfer rates, and other measures of change in student status. These data are gathered to assess educational performance: How well are students moving through the education pipeline? Who is doing well and who is doing poorly? Are students persisting longer? Where does student persistence need to be improved?

To answer these questions data are gathered on the enrollment status of specific groups of students at successive points in time. Educational progress, or lack thereof, is measured and noted. This student persistence measurement activity is essential to understanding the progress of groups of students in the education pipeline. Cohorts of students are tracked from one status through transition to the next status level. The resulting rates describe the proportion of the original cohort reaching whatever the future status point happens to be: typically the next year or level of school or graduation.

The measurement of student persistence in education is complicated by the many ways students move through the education pipeline in the United

States. Quite likely very few or none of the millions of voluntarily enrolled postsecondary students pursue education in exactly the same way. Thus measurement systems struggle to define and count student progress in ways that provide useful information to users. Among the major persistence/retention measurement problems are student transfers between institutions, student progression at different rates, and stopouts.

Users are likely to have their own particular uses for persistence data.

- Institutional users are most likely to be interested in institutional retention and graduation rates: how well admitted cohorts of students succeed in their institutions. Have rates increased or decreased? How well does one institution compare to peer institutions?
- State users may be more interested in data cumulated to the state level, particularly for performance-based budgeting purposes. How many of those who start high school or college eventually graduate? Inter-institutional transfers may be irrelevant at the state level, although they reduce institutional graduation rates. Can persistence rates be used to project high school enrollment? High school graduates? College freshmen? College graduates?
- Users at the national level may be indifferent to institutional and state persistence and be satisfied with gross measures of high school and college graduation and attainment.
- Most users will be interested in population disaggregation by race/ethnicity, geography, gender, family income, and other demographic characteristics as well.
- All users should be interested in population disaggregation by academic characteristics of students: high school grades and class rank and other measures of academic preparation, ACT or SAT test scores, credit loads, etc.
- In experiments, data users are likely to want to control for institutional interventions believed to influence persistence such as where and with whom a student lives and academic support services used.

Here we follow students through the education pipeline along baselines of time and age to observe and measure their progress and persistence behaviors. There are a very few simple but essential guidelines to follow and we begin with these concepts and definitions.

KEY TERMS

The three foundations for the measurement of student persistence are definitions for cohorts, denominators, and numerators.

Cohorts.   Persistence measurement begins with the careful identification of a clearly defined group or cohort of students at one point in time, place, and with specific demographic and enrollment characteristics. Examples might be all ninth-grade students in a particular high school in the fall of a particular year, or all black male first-time, full-time degree-seeking freshman athletes beginning college at a particular institution in a particular term.

Because persistence and graduation rates are often descriptive and comparative, defining cohorts is especially important. Among the demographic cohort descriptors are: gender, race/ethnicity, age, and geographic location (state, county), etc. Academic descriptors might include: year of matriculation, academic (high school grades, class rank, ACT or SAT test scores), credits accumulated/college GPA, academic majors, etc.

Denominators.   The identification of a cohort of a certain number of students in time, place, and with specific demographic and enrollment characteristics fixes the denominator of whatever rate is being studied.

It is important that this number remain fixed in subsequent use. The most egregious misuses of persistence and graduation rates occur when this number is subsequently revised (always reduced) to adjust for some student enrollment behaviors, such as student transfers out of the school, institution, or system being monitored. Doing so amounts to manipulating the data to inflate and overstate results. These discredited adjustments have consequences when exposed.

Numerators.   As the original cohort is tracked over time the numbers shrink. All students eventually drop out, stop out, transfer, die, graduate, or in some way leave the original group. This attrition occurs over time. The measurement of the survivors at subsequent points in time provides the numerator for the persistence, retention, or graduation rate. While the primary objective of the data collection is to measure these rates for cohort survivors, collecting data on departures may be more important than is collecting data on persisters, particularly if these data are gathered to measure educational performance and success with an eye toward improvement.

HIGH SCHOOL PERSISTENCE AND GRADUATION

In nearly all states school enrollment is compulsory through a student's sixteenth birthday. Thereafter attendance is voluntary and attrition begins. Figure 2.1 shows the proportion of the United States civilian noninstitutional population enrolled in a formal school or college by age in 2009.

The measurement of high school student persistence and attrition is often badly understood because it is so poorly recorded and misleadingly reported. Figure 2.2 shows that high school graduation rates in the United

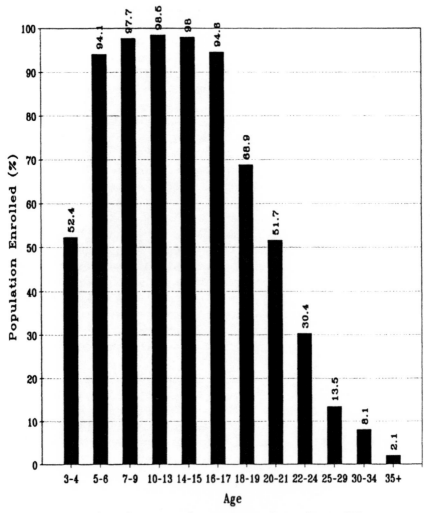

Figure 2.1. **School Enrollment Rates by Age.** *Source:* Census Bureau CPS

States may be increasing, stable, or decreasing over the last thirty years, depending on the data source used. The widely used Census Bureau data include as graduates high school dropouts who completed a GED test or other form of "equivalent" certification. This combined rate rises with age as young adults who did not complete high school and receive their diploma instead take and pass the GED test some time after leaving high school. The Census Bureau's reported high school graduate rate among twenty-five- to twenty-nine-year-olds has risen, from 78 percent in 1970 to 88.8 percent by 2010.

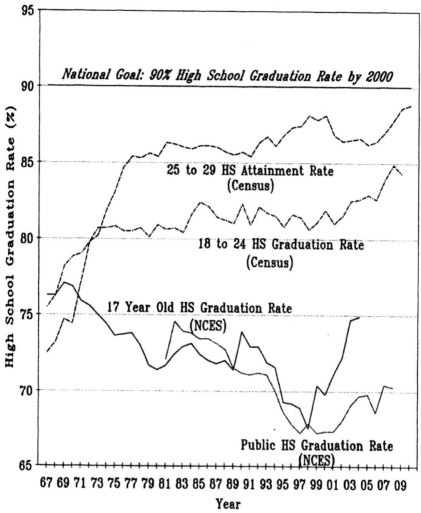

Figure 2.2. Various High School Graduation Rates 1967–2010.

However, if one looks at the high school graduation rate among seventeen-year-olds this rate has declined from 77.1 percent in 1970 to 74.9 percent by 2004. And the ratio of public high school regular diploma recipients to ninth-graders four years earlier has declined from 74.5 percent in 1982 to 70.3 percent by 2008.

One measurement problem is the shifting form of high school completion, from persistence through twelfth grade culminating in the award of a regular high school diploma to dropping out of high school and passing the GED test. But other problems are developing also. One of these is the shifting of reported data from high school graduation (with specific definition) to high school completion that may not include graduation (i.e., certificates of completion for those who do not complete course requirements for graduation, IEP diplomas). Another is home schooling, without graduation. A third results from immigration: interpretation of foreign education credentials.

In 1982 the report *A Nation at Risk* recommended significantly strengthening the high school curriculum to prepare students for college and work. States then added considerably to high school graduation requirements. As states added public high school graduation requirements, the share of public high school ninth-graders meeting these higher graduation standards has steadily declined.

For recent studies and tabulations on high school graduation rates for the United States and for states see:

Census Bureau.   Includes GEDs as high school graduates. Data collected in the October *Current Population Survey* and available at:

> http://www.census.gov/population/www/socdemo/educ-attn.html
> http://www.census.gov/population/www/socdemo/school.html.

Postsecondary Education OPPORTUNITY.   Using data collected by the National Center for Education Statistics on public school, graded enrollment and regular high school graduates. Divides regular high school diplomas by ninth-graders four years earlier.

> *http://www.postsecondary.org/archives/Reports/Spreadsheets/HSGradRate.htm*

> *Manhattan Institute.* Published a series of reports on urban public high school graduation rates. Available at:

> *http://www.manhattan-institute.org/html/ewp_03.htm*

COLLEGE FRESHMAN-TO-SOPHOMORE PERSISTENCE RATES

Student persistence and graduation in higher education is measured in two ways: *institutional* persistence and graduation, and *summary* persistence and graduation. The difference is the result of student "swirling"—enrollment in more than one institution between matriculation and graduation. The sum of institutional graduation rates in particular will be lower than summary graduation rates because of student transfers between institutions and to some degree this affects persistence measurement as well.

Freshman-to-sophomore persistence measurement is important both because of student vulnerability at the beginning of college and because institutions can react quickly with interventions. Figure 2.3 shows mean freshman-to-sophomore persistence rates for equally weighted four-year public and private colleges and universities since 1983 based on data collected by ACT. Institutional freshman-to-sophomore persistence rates have

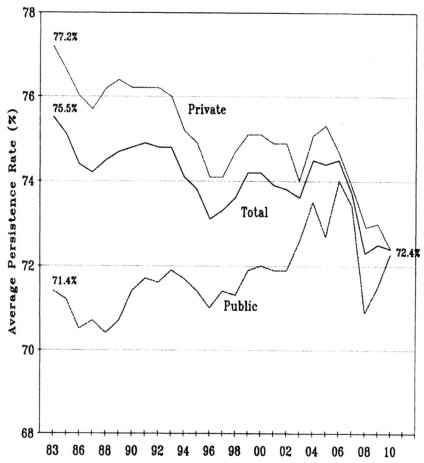

Figure 2.3. Freshman-to-Sophomore Persistence Rates at Public and Private 4-Year Institutions 1983–2010. *Source:* **ACT**

declined between 1983 and 2010. Figure 2.4 shows these data for public and private two-year colleges, also using data collected by ACT.

Figures 2.3 and 2.4 also show that institutional persistence rates vary by institutional control. Persistence has been somewhat greater in private institutions than it is in public colleges and universities, although that gap closed by 2010. Persistence rates also vary between two-year and four-year institutions.

Of critical importance, institutional persistence rates also vary directly with the academic selectivity of the institution: institutions that practice more selective admissions tend to have higher freshman-to-sophomore persistence rates than do colleges that practice less selective admissions.

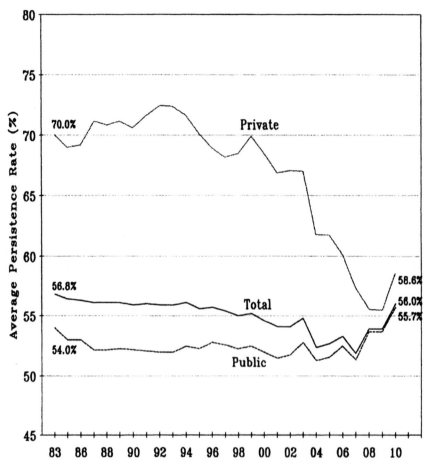

Figure 2.4. Freshman-to-Sophomore Persistence Rates at Public and Private 2-Year Institutions 1983–2010. *Source:* **ACT**

Students with the most successful academic records in high school are also most likely to be academically successful in college. And colleges that enroll these students are more likely to have higher persistence rates than do other colleges that are less academically selective in their admissions. Figure 2.5 shows average freshman-to-sophomore persistence rates at public and private four-year colleges and universities in 2010 according to their admissions selectivity. In 2010 first- to second-year persistence rates ranged from 59.6 percent at the liberal admissions institutions to 92.4 percent at the highly selective institutions. Figure 2.6 shows how these persistence rates have changed between 2000 and 2010.

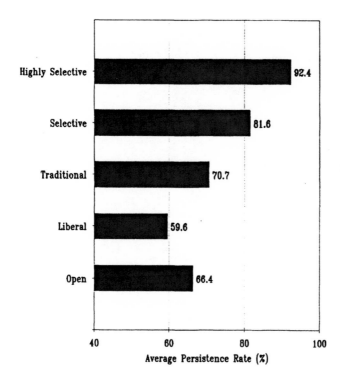

Figure 2.5. Freshman-to-Sophomore Persistence Rates by Admissions Selectivity at 4-Year Institutions 2010. *Source:* ACT

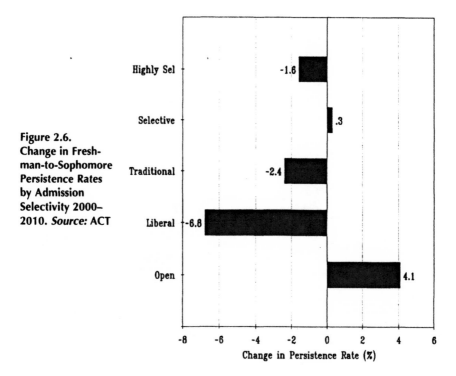

Figure 2.6. Change in Freshman-to-Sophomore Persistence Rates by Admission Selectivity 2000–2010. *Source:* ACT

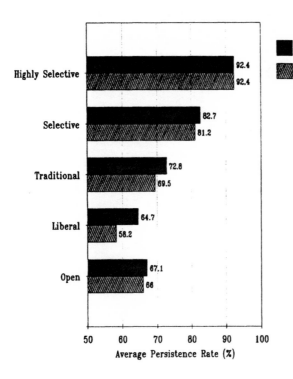

Figure 2.7. Freshman-to-Sophomore Persistence Rates by Admissions Selectivity and Control at 4-Year Institutions 2010. *Source:* ACT

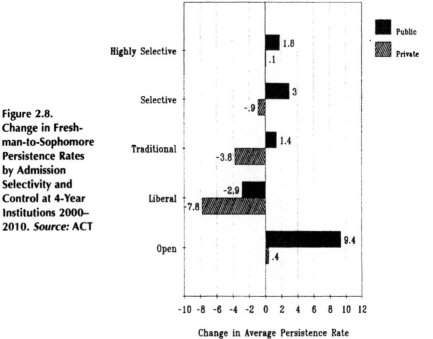

Figure 2.8. Change in Freshman-to-Sophomore Persistence Rates by Admission Selectivity and Control at 4-Year Institutions 2000–2010. *Source:* ACT

As shown in Figure 2.7, private institutions generally have a small edge over public institutions in freshman-to-sophomore persistence rates when admissions selectivity is controlled. However, between 2000 and 2010 public colleges had some success increasing freshman persistence in highly selective, selective, traditional, and open admissions institutions. In private institutions, by contrast, persistence rates declined slightly at most levels of admissions selectivity, as shown in Figure 2.8.

Over the last ten years of these ACT-collected and -reported data there have been changes in freshman-to-sophomore persistence rates across lev-

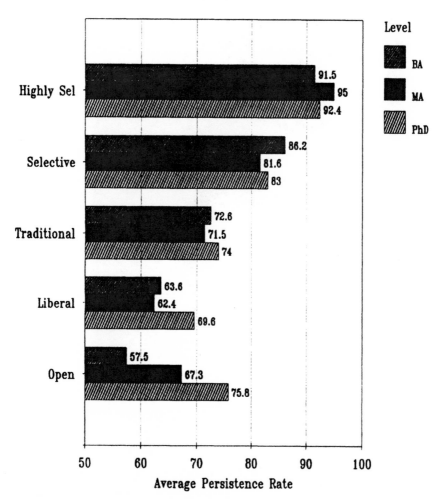

Figure 2.9. Freshman-to-Sophomore Persistence Rates at Public 4-Year Institutions by Level and Selectivity 2010.

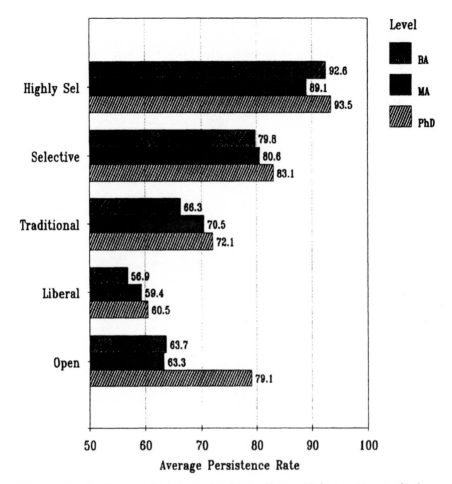

Figure 2.10. **Freshman-to-Sophomore Persistence Rates at Private 4-Year Institutions by Level and Selectivity 2010.** *Source:* ACT

els of admissions selectivity. The most obvious finding in Figure 2.6 is that persistence rates have declined the most at the least selective institutions.

When *political control* and *highest degree offered* are added as controls, doctoral granting institutions have a slight edge over institutions offering the bachelor's or master's as their highest degree offerings, as shown in Figures 2.9 and 2.10.

BACHELOR'S DEGREE GRADUATION RATES

College graduation rates for those who start college may be either decreasing or increasing, depending on the data set used. Or, if one uses the longest data set (from the Census Bureau) college graduation rates may be unchanged over the last fifty years. The answer depends on the data set referenced and the particular definitions associated with each data set. These data are particularly affected by lengthening time to degree and student enrollment at multiple institutions during their undergraduate careers.

Figure 2.11 shows how two important data sets can yield conflicting results.

- The ACT data gathered from public and private four-year colleges and universities show declining five-year institutional graduation rates,

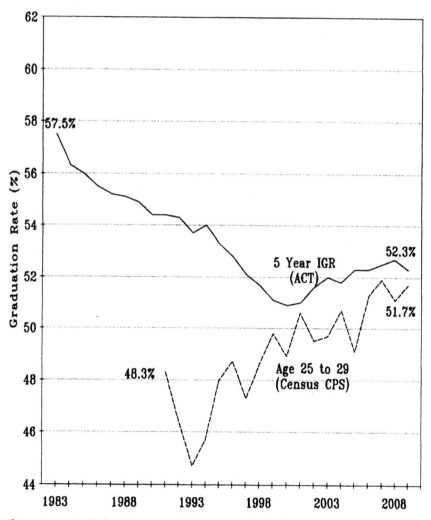

Figure 2.11.   Bachelor's Degree Graduation Rates 1983–2010.

from 57.5 percent in 1983 to 50.9 percent by 2001, then increasing to
52.3 percent by 2010.

- The Census Bureau's data gathered from a national sample of about
  sixty thousand households show a graduation rate increasing from
  48.3 percent among twenty-five- to twenty-nine-year-olds in 1992 to
  51.7 percent by 2010.

Not only are the results different, but so too are the trends evident in these
relatively short time spans. The census data show increasing graduation
rates, while the ACT data show decreasing rates since 2000. When older
census data (with different data definitions) are used, the 2010 graduation

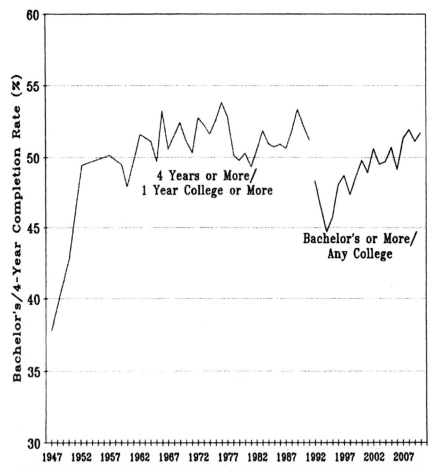

**Figure 2.12. Bachelor's Degree Completion Rate by Age 25 to 29 for Those Who En-
tered College 1947–2010.** *Source:* Census Bureau

rate of 51.7 percent shows little improvement compared to the 50.2 percent reported in 1957. This trend is flat, as shown in Figure 2.12.

The details of these different calculations explain some of the differences, although the explanations still fall short of a consistent and satisfactory answer. In these three widely used data sets there are differences in time frames, definitions, samples, methods of data collection, units of measure, and perhaps reliability of reported status data.

- The ACT data have been collected in an annual survey from public and private four-year colleges and universities since 1983. At that time

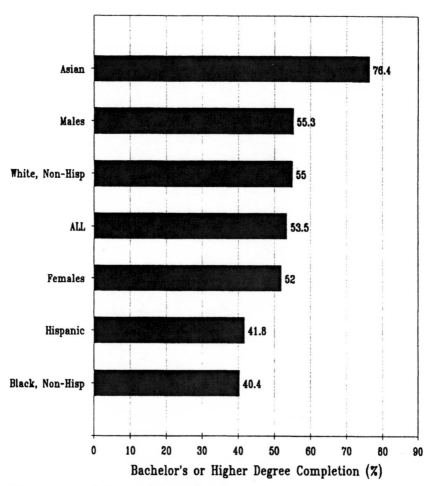

Figure 2.13.   Bachelor's or Higher Degree Completion by Age 25 to 29 for Those Who Entered College 2010. *Source:* Census Bureau

Thomas G. Mortenson

a five-year graduation rate was requested from institutions and for consistency ACT has continued to ask for five-year data. However, as time to degree completion has lengthened among undergraduates this measure has been replaced elsewhere by the six-year graduation rate. Even that now falls short as a NCES study reported that only about two-thirds of all bachelor's degrees were awarded by age twenty-four.

- The Census Bureau data are collected each March in the Current Population Survey. This is a sample of about sixty thousand households and the reported data are limited to the civilian, non-institutional population. The most useful reported data are on twenty-five- to twenty-nine-year-

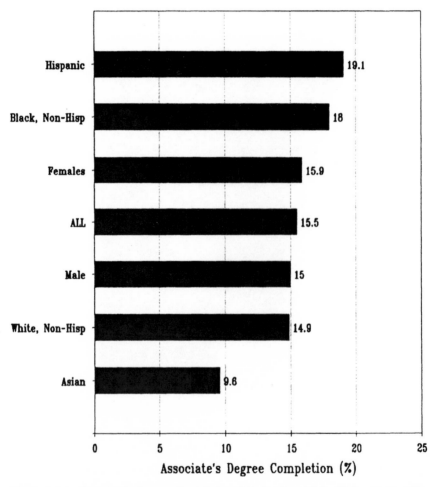

Figure 2.14. Associate's Degree Completion Rate by Age 25 to 29 for Those Who Entered College 2010. *Source:* Census Bureau

olds, after most students have completed their bachelor's degrees. These data capture the transfers that started out in one institution and graduated from another and thus are lost to institutional graduation rates.

Each data set offers useful insights into college graduation rates although no individual data set provides all or definitive answers. The major advantages and disadvantages of each data set include the following:

- The unit of analysis for the ACT data is the institution. ACT gathers additional data on institutional characteristics that make its detailed

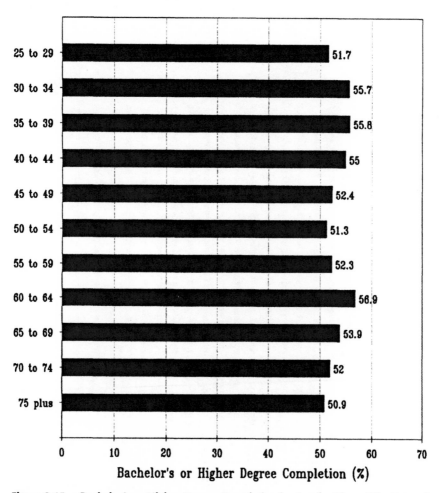

Figure 2.15.   Bachelor's or Higher Degree Completion by Age for Those Who Entered College 2010. *Source:* Census Bureau

reports especially valuable. In particular ACT's tabulation and reporting of average institutional graduation rates by admissions selectivity, highest degree offered, and control, along with standard deviations of cell means since 1983, makes these reports unique. The major drawback to the current ACT report is five-year institutional graduation rates.

- The Census Bureau data, while based on a population sample, have the advantage of capturing students who start out at one institution but graduate from another.

The following charts illustrate some of the stories told about college graduation rates in data reported by the Census Bureau for twenty-five- to

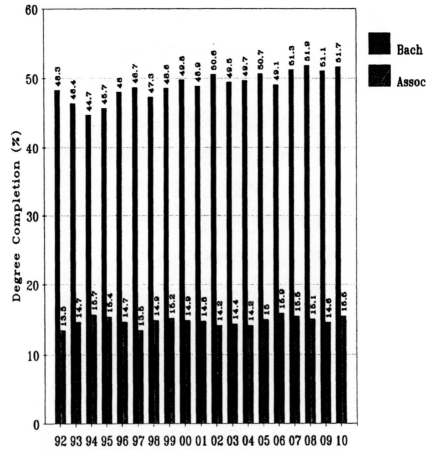

Figure 2.16. **Undergraduate Degree Completion by Age 25 to 29 for Those Who Entered College 1992–2010.** *Source:* Census Bureau

twenty-nine-year-olds. Unless noted otherwise (prior to 1992) these graduation rates are the ratio of those ages twenty-five to twenty-nine years with
bachelor's degree or more from college divided by the number of twenty-
five- to twenty-nine-year-olds with any college experience at all.

Figure 2.13 shows bachelor's degree completion rates by race/ethnicity
and gender. For all twenty-five- to twenty-nine-year-olds, 50.6 percent of
those with any college experience had completed a bachelor's degree in
2010. These rates ranged from 40.4 percent for blacks to 76.4 percent for
Asian/Pacific Islanders. Completion rates are somewhat higher for males
(55.3 percent) than for females (52.0 percent).

Figure 2.14 shows the associate's degree–only completion rates by these
same gender and racial/ethnic categories. For all twenty-five- to twenty-

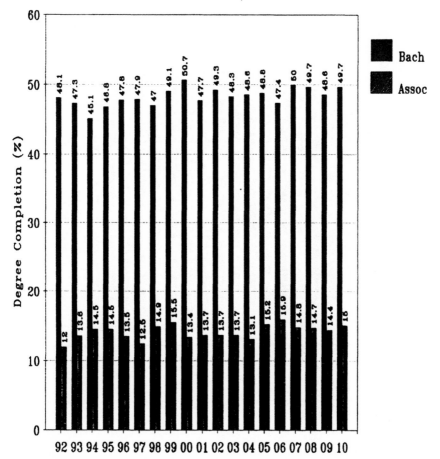

**Figure 2.17.   Undergraduate Degree Completion for Males by Age 25 to 29 for Those
Who Entered College 1992 to 2010.** *Source:* **Census Bureau**

nine-year olds in 2010, 15.5 percent of those with any college experience had an associate's degree and no more from higher education. Completion rates ranged from 9.6 percent for Asian/Pacific Islanders to 19.1 percent for Hispanics—a flip-flop of the bachelor's degree range for these groups. Women were slightly more likely than men to report having completed an associate's degree.

Bachelor's degree completion rates by age in 2010 are shown in Figure 2.15. These rates peak quickly at age twenty-five to twenty-nine years, although over time they might rise somewhat further as some adults in their thirties or later complete their bachelor's level educations. These data also suggest that about half of those who start college eventually complete a bachelor's degree.

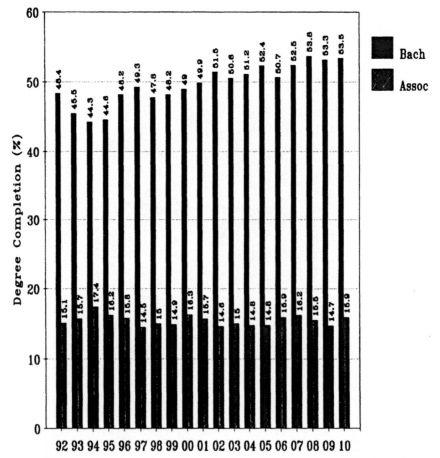

Figure 2.18.   Undergraduate Degree Completion for Females by Age 25 to 29 for Those Who Entered College 1992 to 2010. *Source:* Census Bureau

Figures 2.16 through 2.22 show bachelor's and associate's degree completion rates overall, by gender, and by racial ethnic group for the years 1992 through 2010. This spans the years of the Census Bureau's most recent definition of educational attainment: highest degree completed divided by those with any college experience. (Prior to 1992 the Census Bureau reported four years or more of college divided by those with one year or more of college.) During this relatively short time span, bachelor's degree completion rates have tended upward. The picture is more mixed for associate's degree completion rates.

Finally, the bachelor's degree completion rates may be compared across countries that are members of the Organization for Economic Cooperation and Development (OECD). Over the last two decades the OECD has

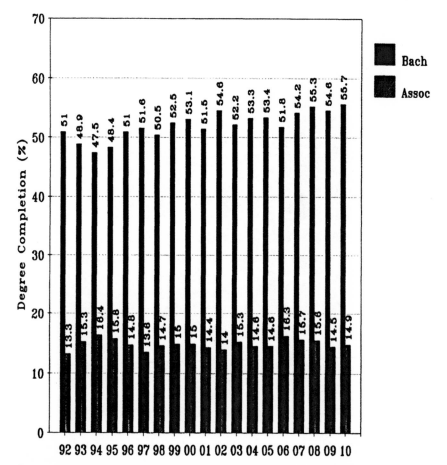

Figure 2.19.   Undergraduate Degree Completion for White non-Hispanics by Age 25 to 29 for Those Who Entered College 1992 to 2010. *Source:* Census Bureau

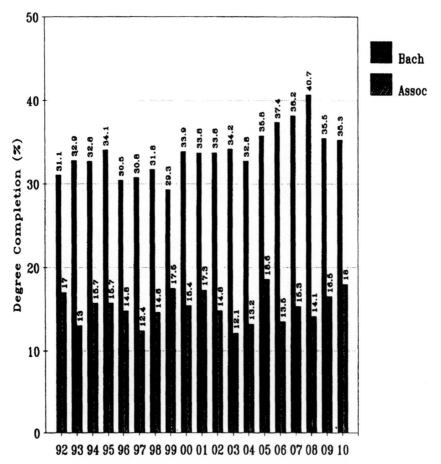

Figure 2.20.   Undergraduate Degree Completion for Black non-Hispanics by Age 25 to 29 for Those Who Entered College 1992 to 2010. *Source:* **Census Bureau**

worked to collect comparable data on the education performance and achievements of the thirty-one member countries that are described as the industrial democracies of the world. Here data comparability issues are truly formidable due to the uniqueness of each country's educational system.

Nevertheless, after twenty years of trying, data system design has evolved to the point where bachelor's degree completion rates have been compiled and reported for most of the OECD countries and a few partner countries (see Figure 2.23). (Note that OECD uses "tertiary type-A" to describe what we in the United States refer to as bachelor's degrees.) The resulting rank-

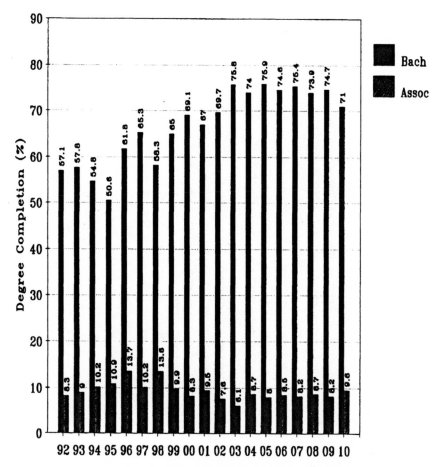

Figure 2.21. Undergraduate Degree Completion for Asian/Pacific Islanders by Age 25 to 29 for Those Who Entered College 1992 to 2010. *Source:* Census Bureau

ings are shown below. In 2008 the United States ranked twenty-fourth out of twenty-six countries in graduating the students admitted to bachelor's degree programs.

These data tell important stories about what is happening to students as they move through the education pipeline toward adulthood and independence. Definably distinct groups of students move at different rates. These data do not explain why—just that there are differences across time and between groups of students in the education pipeline.

These data must be used with caution, as illustrated twice here. Different data can correctly say that a retention or graduation rate is moving up, or

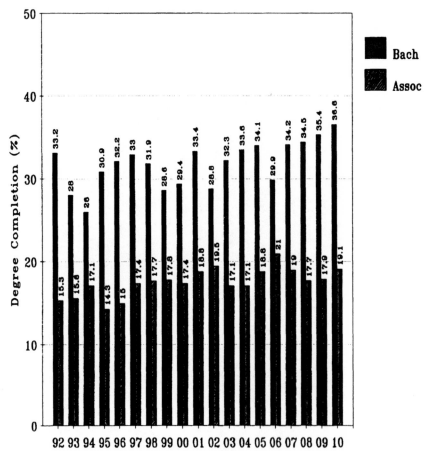

Figure 2.22. Undergraduate Degree Completion for Hispanics by Age 25 to 29 for Those Who Entered College 1992 to 2010. *Source:* **Census Bureau[1]**

down, or remains flat. Differently defined data will inevitably produce different results. Data definitions and limitations must be carefully understood before findings are reported, conclusions drawn, and recommendations made.

NOTE

1. The school enrollment statistics from the Current Population Survey are based on replies to the interviewer's inquiry of whether the person was enrolled in regular school. Interviewers were instructed to count as enrolled anyone who had been enrolled at any time during the current term or school year in any type of public, parochial, or other private school in the regular school system. Such schools include nursery schools, kindergartens, elementary schools, high schools, colleges, universi-

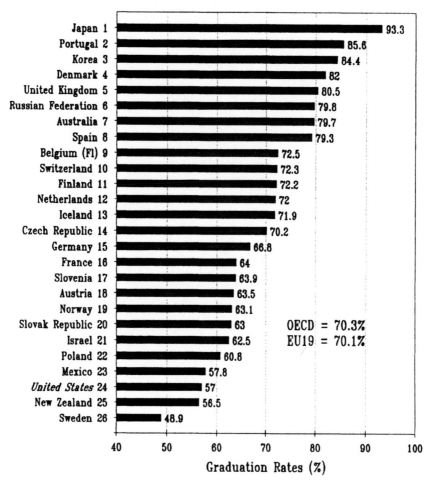

Figure 2.23. Tertiary Type-A Completion Rates in OECD and Partner Countries 2008.
Source: OECD Education at a Glance 2010, Table A4.1

ties, and professional schools. Attendance may be on either a full-time or part-time basis and during the day or night. *Regular schooling is that which may advance a person toward an elementary or high school diploma, or a college, university, or professional school degree.* Children enrolled in nursery schools and kindergarten are included in the enrollment figures for regular schools and are also shown separately. Enrollment in schools not in the regular school system, such as trade schools, business colleges, and schools for the mentally handicapped, which do not advance students to regular school degrees, is not included. People enrolled in classes that do not require physical presence in school, such as correspondence courses or other courses of independent study, and in training courses given directly on the job, are also excluded from the count of those enrolled in school, unless such courses are being counted for credit at a regular school.

3

Retention Theories, Models, and Concepts

Lonnie Morrison and Loretta Silverman

More than 1,700 college student retention references can be found at the reference link on the Center for the Study of College Student Retention website. Clearly, there has been an abundance of studies on college student retention. For those who want to be informed, the vast amount of information available in the field of college student retention can be overwhelming. This chapter is an attempt to review, summarize, and highlight the major retention theories, models, and concepts from the plethora of available references. For purposes of our review, college student retention refers to the study of students who begin a postsecondary education program but have been unsuccessful in attaining their academic or personal goals (Seidman, 2005a).

Even though colleges have been in existence since the 1600s, the majority of these retention studies were conducted in the last fifty years (Berger & Lyon, 2005). In the early years (1600s to mid-1800s), colleges were concerned with surviving, as "most did not even stay open long enough to develop a graduating class" (Berger & Lyon, 2005, p. 9). Then, from the mid-1800s to 1900s, colleges were occupied with curricular expansion and admission of a more diversified student population, from privileged white males only to a population including women and other non-privileged men. The expansion and diversification of admission continue to this day.

The first study on college student retention was conducted in the 1930s (Berger & Lyon, 2005). According to Berger and Lyon, "One of the first widespread studies to examine multiple issues related to the departure of students at multiple institutions was conducted by John McNeely and published in 1938" (p. 14). The importance of this and other retention studies was not recognized by educators, researchers, and institutions until the early 1970s, when enrollment began to appear as an issue (Berger & Lyon, 2005). During the 1980s, the anticipated decline in the number of traditional college-age students provided the impetus for much of the student retention research that was conducted at that time. This was particularly the case for many private institutions of higher education, since the literature suggested that the decline in student enrollment was likely to have its greatest impact on such institutions (Arbeiter, 1984; Centra, 1980; Dallam & Dawes, 1981; Maeroff, 1985; Shulman, 1976; Tinto, 1987; Willlingham, 1985; Willingham & Breland, 1982). Shulman (1976) observed that colleges faced a decline in the number of potential freshmen and therefore needed to retain those students already enrolled to maintain their financial stability and the breadth and strength of their academic programs. Students lost through attrition may not be readily replaced.

Although institutional fiscal stability continues to be a major concern, the notion of global competitiveness, changing demographics on college campuses, and declining state and federal support have provided new impetus for colleges and universities to be interested in student retention (Hossler, 2005). Hence, stagnant persistence and completion rates of college students matter for both the college itself and society in general. According to Seidman (2005a), students who do not accomplish their personal and academic goals "will surely become a burden to society" (p. xii). Similarly, Schuh (2005) and others (e.g., Bishaw & Semega, 2008) have argued that students who do not complete a college degree have, on average, lower earnings than those who complete a college degree. For the college, the loss in revenue is substantial when students do not persist (Schuh, 2005; Seidman, 2009). These losses have been projected to be in the millions (Schuh, 2005; Seidman, 2009). Seidman argued that there are also negative ramifications among the communities that support the local colleges when students do not persist. Local restaurants and stores, along with book publishers, also lose revenue.

Despite the availability of copious literature on college student retention, rates have remained essentially unchanged over the last two decades (American College Testing [ACT], 2009; Seidman, 2005a; Mortenson, 2005; Tinto, 2005). For example, the national freshman-to-sophomore persistence rates ranged from 65.7 percent to 68.7 percent for the years 1983–2009 (ACT, 2009). In addition, the freshman-to-sophomore persistence rates of public and private two-year institutions during 1983–2009 showed that private institutions outperform the public institutions consistently (ACT, 2009). Within the private two-year institutions during 1983–2009, the average freshman-to-sophomore persistence rates fluctuated between 55.5 percent and 72.6 percent (ACT, 2009). In comparison, the average freshman-to-sophomore persistence rates for public two-year institutions during 1983–2009 fluctuated between 51.3 percent and 53.7 percent (ACT, 2009; Mortenson, 2005).

As the cohort of traditional college-age students continues to decrease and the enrollment of nontraditional students increases, enhancing both the academic success and the persistence of enrolled students becomes an increasingly important issue, particularly among private colleges and universities (Carmody, 1988; Centra, 1980; Hartley, 1987; Hossler, 1985; Jackley & Henderson, 1979; Mayhew, 1979; Ramist, 1981; Sanford, 1982; Sedlacek, 1989; Tinto, 1982, 1987; Voorhees, 1985; Willingham, 1985).

There are many theories, models, and concepts on college student retention. Most tend to focus on four-year institutions. Since student enrollment at four-year institutions has traditionally been composed of younger, full-time, and on-campus residential students, the retention theories and models were mainly centered on the concepts of academic and social integration (Astin, 1985; Tinto, 1987).

The purpose of this chapter is to provide an overview of the following theories, models, and concepts of college student retention (in chronological order): McNeely (1937), Summerskill (1962), Astin (1966, 1985), Spady (1970), Meyers (1970), Kamens (1971), Tinto (1975, 1987, 1993), Bean (1980, 1983), Bean and Metzner (1985), and Seidman (2005a, 2005b). With a comprehensive understanding of these existing theories, models, and concepts it is hoped that researchers, faculty, and others can develop more effective policies and programs to improve the persistence of their students. Although the researchers have attempted to summarize the major theories, models, and concepts, changing demographics suggest that application of these theories, models, and concepts will have to be customized to institutional needs since results from such research may not be particularly relevant.

RETENTION THEORIES, MODELS, & CONCEPTS

John N. McNeely

One of the earliest studies of student attrition was conducted by McNeely (1937). Specifically, McNeely was interested in determining the extent to which students withdrew from college and the factors responsible for such behavior. Implemented during 1936–1937, the study was conducted under the auspices of the Project in Research in Universities of the Office of Education, financed under the Emergency Relief Appropriations Act of 1935, and based on regulations of the Works Progress Administration (WPA). The study was a WPA Depression-era work program developed by the federal government "to afford gainful and socially desirable employment to college graduates or former students in the type of work for which they were best prepared" (p. vi).

It is interesting to note that the research was being conducted in order to facilitate· reforms in higher education—discovery, accumulation, and interpretation of factual data. McNeely (1937) argued that these steps were essential in order to provide the empirical understanding of the myriad issues pertaining to institutional reorganization, one of which was student mortality. For purposes of his study, McNeely defined student mortality as failure to remain in college until graduation. He further subdivided mortality into what he described as *gross* and *net* mortality. Gross mortality was defined as students leaving during or at the end of four years without obtaining a degree, although they may return at some later date, whereas net mortality was defined as a student who leaves and fails to return at a later date.

The sample was made up of twenty-five universities, fourteen public and eleven private, one of which was Howard University, a "negro" university: 15,535 students who initially enrolled as freshmen in 1931–1932, with twice as many men as women students. Analysis was reported for the entire sample and by institution. Data analysis was further subdivided on the basis of gender, type of institutional control, geography, size of student body, and location. Even at this early phase of research on student attrition, there was an understanding that differences in student mortality could be attributed to a number of factors. McNeely (1937) used the term "causal relationship" to understand such differences, although the statistical methodology he used did not lend itself to ascertaining causal relationships.

McNeely (1937) found that public institutions had higher gross and net mortality rates than private institutions. Although there were gender differences in student mortality between public and private institutions, men were more likely to drop out. Students attending private institutions were more likely to obtain a degree than students attending public institutions. Regarding students returning, McNeely found that men were more likely to return to continue their education than were women.

Looking at student mortality on the basis of years in college, McNeely (1937) found that freshmen were more likely to leave, with a progressive decline in subsequent years; 33.8, 16.7, 7.7, and 3.9 percent, respectively; and at the junior and senior year, men were more likely to leave than women.

On the basis of geographic mortality, which was divided into four regions, McNeely (1937) found that institutions located in New England and the Middle Atlantic States had the lowest gross and net mortality rates. He attributed some differences to institutional policies, indicating that some schools encouraged students to return, while other institutional policies discouraged students from returning.

A small relationship was found between size of community and student mortality; gross mortality was found to be higher for students attending school in large communities, but the relationship was reversed for net mortality, with more students returning to institutions located in large communities (McNeely, 1937). Size of student body, however, was found not to have any correlation to gross mortality, although a higher proportion of students attending universities with fewer than two thousand students were more likely to earn degrees at the end of four years. Students enrolled in arts and sciences had the highest gross and net mortality, whereas law students had the lowest mortality rates.

Academic failure and financial difficulties were found to be factors contributing to student mortality. Other factors that were explored, such as death and sickness, being needed at home, and lack of interest, either were not found to be significant factors or there was insufficient sample size on which to base any findings.

McNeely (1937) did attempt to look at various sociological factors related to student mortality, such as age (immaturity and maturity), location of home, place of lodging, participation in extracurricular activities, and part-time employment. Age was found to be a factor, with a higher percentage of mature students dropping out than younger students. McNeely provided two explanations to account for the differences: younger students may have more intellectual ability and older students may have outside interests or obligations forcing them to withdraw.

Distance from home was found to be a factor in student mortality, with students more likely to drop out the farther they were from home. Students living at home or in a fraternity or sorority house were less likely to drop out than students living at a rooming house or college dormitory. However, extracurricular activities and part-time employment had little or no relationship to student mortality.

Regarding academic achievement, students taking a light load (twelve or fewer credits) were more likely to withdraw than students with a heavy load (nineteen or more credits). McNeely (1937) concluded that "there is little likelihood that a burdensome academic load was a responsible factor in causing the student to leave universities" (p. 85). Grade point average was found to be inversely related to student mortality: the higher the average, the less likely that the student dropped out.

In spite of a number of limitations, McNeely's (1937) research was salient because it represented an early attempt to establish an empirical relationship between a number of institutional and noninstitutional factors and student retention. Some of his findings were a product of the period during which the study was conducted and have limitations in terms of generalizability, in particular to minority students. It is interesting to note that although Howard University was one of the twenty-five institutions in the study, there is no evidence that McNeely attempted to incorporate ethnic status as a variable. Nevertheless, it is important to recognize the contribution of McNeely's research to our understanding of student attrition in higher education and its contribution to the work of Summerskill.

John Summerskill

Summerskill (1962) argued that research on college student attrition has yielded relatively little knowledge of the process of attrition and attributes this to the lack of a concerted effort to pull research together. Although he credits the federal government for their role in supporting attrition studies conducted by Iffert (1954) and McNeely (1939), he suggests that the knowledge gained had been fragmentary and results lacked significant value. It is important to note that McNeely's research was conducted from an institutional and administrative perspective, focusing on institutional effectiveness, efficiency, and economic stability. Summerskill argued that research conducted from such a perspective generally did not result in policies or strategies designed to reduce student attrition. A more important aspect of his analysis of student dropout was his criticism of the social science profession, which he argued had not taken an active interest in what he perceived to be an important area for higher education.

Summerskill (1962) realized that the reasons students withdrew from college were complex and attributable to psychological, familial, social, and economic issues and recommended that further research focus on institutional factors that may contribute to academic failure. However, it was Summerskill's recognition of motivational factors related to student attrition, grounded in psychological and sociological concepts and theories that provided the impetus for subsequent theory-based research in student retention. His suggestion that one can distinguish between motivation with respect to a college and motivation with respect to graduation from that college can be considered a rudimentary paradigm to Tinto's (1975) concept of social and academic integration. In exploring the role of motivation in student attrition, Summerskill suggested that such a concept was not immutable and that there were factors, internal and external, capable of being manipulated in ways that might have a positive impact on reducing student attrition.

Summerskill (1962) suggested that students' behavior, attitudes, and satisfaction could be influenced by external and internal factors and recommended that further research be grounded in the social sciences, in particular psychology and sociology. He argued that student attrition should no longer be evaluated in terms of neat, mutually exclusive categories, that factors that impact student attrition are "multicausal."

Summerskill's (1962) contribution was important, not for any quantitative research that he may have conducted, but for his insight in suggesting an innovative perspective that influenced our understanding of the complex nature of student attrition, and for his recommendation that psychological and sociological theories and concepts provide the empirical framework for subsequent research in this area, an approach that appears to have been embraced by Spady, Tinto, and others.

Alexander W. Astin

Even though Astin (1975, 1985) acknowledged that there were many predictive factors of student retention in college, he recognized two main predictive factors: personal and environmental. Personal factors, according to Astin (1975), included academic background, family background, educational aspirations, study habits, expectations about college, age, and marital status. Environmental factors included residence, employment, academic environment, and characteristics of the college.

In a longitudinal study, Astin (1975) revealed that personal factors were predictive of student's college academic retention. In descending order of impact were:

1. Past academic grades—those with stronger past academic grades were more likely to persist.
2. Educational aspiration—those with higher degree aspiration were more likely to persist.
3. Study habits—those who turned in homework on time and did homework at the same time every day were more likely to persist.
4. Parents' education—those with more educated parents were more likely to persist.
5. Marital status—married males and single females were more likely to persist.

With these personal factors taken into account, Astin (1975) argued that there were additional experiential factors upon entering the college that can enhance student retention. These were, in descending order of impact:

1. Grades—those with better grades were more likely to persist.
2. Marital status—women who remained single were more likely to persist.
3. Children—those without children were more likely to persist.
4. Residency—those living on campus were more likely to persist.
5. Job—those who had part-time jobs on campus were more likely to persist.

6. Extracurricular activity—those who participated in extracurricular activity such as ROTC, sports, or fraternities/sororities were more likely to persist.

Astin contended that these experiential factors supported the involvement theory; that is, the more directly involved the student was in the academic and social life of the college, the more likely that student would persist.

Student involvement, according to Astin (1985), was comprised of five basic postulates. The first postulate was physical and psychological energy. Involvement calls for the investment of both physical and psychological energy in various "objects," which range in levels from highly specific, such as studying for an exam, to very generalized, such as the first-year experience. It is important that both physical and psychological energy be present. How a student behaved was just as important, if not more important, than how that student thought or felt.

Astin's (1985) second postulate was that involvement occurs along a continuum. Levels of involvement vary from student to student and from object to object. Different students might show varying degrees of involvement on the same object. Similarly, a student might show different intensities of involvement in one object over another.

His third postulate was that involvement had both quantitative and qualitative attributes. How much the student was involved can be measured both quantitatively and qualitatively (Astin, 1985). For example, the academic involvement of preparing for a test could be determined by the amount of time a student spent studying (quantitative) and also by the activities that a student did while studying, such as daydreaming (qualitative).

The fourth postulate was that "the amount of student learning and personal development associated with any educational program was directly proportional to the quality and quantity of student involvement in that program" (Astin, 1985, p. 136). Students had a better chance of staying in college if they were more involved in their academic experience.

The fifth postulate was that "the effectiveness of any educational policy or practice was directly related to the capacity of that policy or practice to increase student involvement" (Astin, 1985, p. 136). Institutions can contribute by offering activities or programs that enhanced student involvement. For example, orientation sessions could provide students with information about "factors in their own background and in their environment which affect their dropout chances (where they live, whether they hold a job, whether they marry, and so forth)" (Astin, 1975, p. 152). Student involvement calls for responsibility from both the student and the institution.

William G. Spady

Spady (1970) argued that research demonstrating a relationship between attrition and various factors lacked theoretical and empirical coherence and that, given the advanced multivariate statistical techniques and available computer programs, further research of that nature be discontinued. Citing research conducted by Knoell (1960) and Marsh (1966), Spady suggested that retention research, viewed from a philosophical or theoretical perspective, generally fell into the following categories: census studies, autopsy studies, case studies, and descriptive and predictive studies. Census studies attempted to quantify attrition, transfer, and retention rates from an institutional or.system-wide perspective. Autopsy studies sought explanations directly from students who withdrew. Case studies were a longitudinal analysis of students initially identified as at-risk. Prediction studies sought to produce equations for measures of student success.

Spady (1970) suggested an interdisciplinary-based theoretical longitudinal approach that would provide a more thorough understanding of why students drop out from higher education, a limitation also noted by other researchers cited by Spady. He developed a sociological model highly influenced by the integration concept posited by Emile Durkheim's suicide theory. Although dropping out of school is significantly less dramatic than committing suicide, Spady argued that, as a construct, the social conditions that give rise to dropping out are similar to those that result in suicide.

Spady (1970) suggested that it is the interaction between the student and college academic and social systems that best explains the dropout process. Successful integration into the academic system can either be extrinsic (i.e., grades) or intrinsic (i.e., intellectual development). Successful integration within the social system is a function of having personality factors that are compatible with others (normative congruence) and close relationships (friendship support).

It is important to note that Spady's (1970) model was appropriate for the analysis of dropout behavior for a single institution as opposed to system-wide analysis, a point that Spady recognized as a limitation of his model. It is also interesting to note that even Spady questioned the long-term validity of these studies given what he described as the "democratization of American higher education," i.e., recognition of the changing enrollment demographics.

John W. Meyer

Meyer (1970) argued that institutions of higher education were socializing organizations and that they had the ability to influence values, personality needs, and social roles or identities, which he referred to as their charter. He described this concept of institutional socialization as diffuse socialization, the acquisition of qualities that guide agreed-upon social definitions. Although Meyer indirectly alluded to the notion of integration in describing the organizational conditions of diffuse socialization, his analysis provided the framework for the concept of social integration, for subsequent retention theories.

Meyer (1970) argued that, if students were integrated into a peer structure that reinforced the values of the school and if they were involved in high rates of interaction structured around the appropriate values and act in ways that exemplify such values, students would take on the values of the school. Retention was encouraged on the belief that graduation would bestow privileges and prestige that others were unable to obtain.

David H. Kamens

Kamens (1971) suggested that his research extended the sociological paradigm developed by Meyer (1970) and his theory of college effects by focusing on institutional structures and their effects on students, in particular the effects of college size on student retention and occupational choice.

Kamens (1971) argued that as a result of their structural linkage to occupational and economic groups, colleges had the ability to bestow a certain social status on their graduates, and that this ability had an impact on student retention and occupational choices. Hence, their charter was to function as an agency of socialization and role allocation; the more prestigious the college's perceived identity, the higher the level of economic positions and occupational roles. Kamens suggested that the more the importance of membership was enhanced, the greater the perception of value. The result was a stronger level of organizational commitment and a decline in the dropout rate.

Kamens (1971) found that dropout rates were lower at larger colleges, which he attributed to their ability to facilitate entry into professional occupations. He also concluded that students attending small colleges with similar professional aspirations were more likely to drop out. Moreover, at large schools, retention was further enhanced due to the number and diversity of specialized, high-status occupational roles that students believe they would obtain by attending these schools.

An interesting finding related to college size was the perceived impact on occupational choice. Kamens (1971) suggested that interaction with faculty was more likely to impact academic career choices that were institutionalized in the structure of the college, but had little impact on professional careers. Hence, small colleges were more effective in recruiting students to academic careers as a result of the frequency of their interaction with faculty. With regard to gender differences, Kamens suggested that women came to college with lower occupational ambition and concluded that large colleges may have had less impact on dropout behavior because occupational status allocation was less important to them, a finding that is probably not valid today.

Unfortunately, given the size of his sample, Kamens's (1971) findings regarding the relationship between size and student persistence were inconsistent and inconclusive, not unlike other studies conducted during that period (Astin, 1977; Pantages & Creedon, 1978; Ramist, 1981; Tinto, 1975). However, Kamens's research provided an important framework for understanding the importance of external environmental factors in student retention.

Vincent Tinto

In his theory of individual departure, Tinto (1987) conjectured that student departure from colleges was a result of individual student attributes, skills, commitment, intentions, and interaction with members of the college. Tinto posited that the most important factor was the student's experiences within the college, which he referred to as integration. He claimed that the more integrated a student was to the academic and social communities of the college, the more likely that the student would persevere toward their academic goals. Tinto based his theory on the works of Arnold Van Gennep, a social anthropologist who studied the process of becoming a member in a tribal society, and Emile Durkheim, a sociologist who studied suicide.

Using Gennep's theory, Tinto (1987) hypothesized that students needed to progress through three stages in order to become integrated into the college community. These three stages were (1) separation from communities of the past, (2) transition between communities, and (3) incorporation into the communities of the college. He warned that these stages were not clearly defined, nor sequentially experienced. Some students might experience each stage partially while others might experience all the stages simultaneously.

The first stage was separation from communities of the past. In this stage, students were required "to disassociate themselves, in varying degrees, from membership in the communities associated with the family, the local high school, and local areas of residence" (Tinto, 1987, p. 95). For college students who resided at home, this separation stage would not consist of physical separation but rather mental separation. According to Tinto, students who did not successfully separate themselves from family or past peers who devalue the purpose of a higher education would have more difficulty integrating and would, thus, be less likely to persist.

The second stage was transition, the period between the full integration with the new communities and the separation from the old communities.

Students who came from past communities similar to those of a college would have a shorter transition period than those who did not. Stated differently, students whose parents went to college were more likely to persist because their parents could guide them through the academic bureaucracy and advise them on the social challenges. Students could decrease the stress and period of transition if they were able to "correctly anticipate the character of transition they will have to make" (Tinto, 1987, p. 97) prior to their formal entry. Tinto warned that students were unlikely to predict accurately all the characters of transition that they would encounter during their college career and thus would most likely experience some difficulties during the transition phase.

The last stage was the incorporation into the college communities. Students at this stage were able to integrate into the college communities. Based on the work of Durkheim, Tinto (1987) posited that students needed to assimilate into both the academic and social communities of the college. The academic community, like the social community, was made up of two components, formal and informal. Formal academic integration referred to the congruence between the student's abilities and skills, and the academic demands from the college. Students who were underprepared or students who were underchallenged were more likely to leave the college. Informal academic integration referred to the congruence between the common values held by the members of the college and those held by the student. The day-to-day interactions between faculty, staff, and other students outside the formal classrooms provided the opportunities for students to align any deviant academic values that might have disconnected them from others.

Tinto (1987) suggested that contacts between members of the college and a student did not guarantee congruence, but the absence of such contacts might reinforce or leave unchecked the values that separate the students from other members of the college. Social integration was understood to be the interactions between students within the social system of the college. Formal social integration could be measured by the involvement of a student in the college's newspaper, clubs, student government, or other forms of social activities. Informal social integration was defined as peer-group interaction, such as a student's group of friends.

Tinto (1987) acknowledged that external events have an impact upon a student's departure from college. More specifically, he posited that "for the most part they [two-year colleges] are nonresidential in character and are frequently located in settings where the influence of external communities may be substantial" (p. 169). He further stated that there existed some research citing that student integration into the communities of the two-year college might not be as important for student retention as it was for four-year institutions (p. 169). However, he also stated, "Though external events may be important for some students, for most their impact upon institutional departure is seen as secondary to that of one's experiences within the college" (p. 125). Therefore, his downplay of the importance of external events and the importance of student integration probably indicated that his theory might be more applicable to four-year institutions even though he argued that "much of the preceding discussion [about social and academic integration] can also be applied to the development of retention programs in two-year colleges" (p. 168).

John P. Bean

Bean (1980) argued that there was insufficient evidence to suggest that Durkheim's theory of suicide was an appropriate theoretical basis for understanding withdrawal behavior, as explicated by Tinto. He considered the analogy to be a weak one. In reference to Spady (1970) and Tinto (1975), he writes the following:

> The main problem with these previous models of student attrition (Spady, 1970; Tinto, 1975) lies in the fact that the definition of variables used in the analysis rendered the models unsuitable for path analysis. Specifically, strict attention was not paid either to the recursiveness (directional causality) of the variables in the theoretical models, or to the discreteness of the variables. (p. 156)

Bean (1980) proposed a paradigm adapted from a model developed by Price (1977) who conducted research in the area of turnover in work organizations, arguing that student attrition was analogous to turnover in work organizations. He suggested that the reasons students withdrew from college were similar to those that cause employees to leave work organizations. Although his model evolved into one based on a psychological conceptual format, it was similar to Tinto's model in that it recognized that student retention was a complex and longitudinal process, and that an institution had an academic and social milieu in which student interaction occurs, influencing student persistence. However, it is important to note that Bean's paradigm also differed from Tinto's (1975). Bean appears to have placed greater emphasis and importance on the impact of environmental factors on student retention. His model contained four categories of environmental variables developed from a synthesis of the literature on turnover in work organizations and student attrition: (a) dropout is the dependent variable; (b) satisfaction and institutional commitment are intervening variables; (c) five background variables reflect prematriculation characteristics; and (d) twenty-one variables reflect organizational determinants.

Bean (1980) suggested that the organizational determinants influence satisfaction, which in turn influences dropout behavior. Background variables reflected the influence of a student's prematriculation characteristics on the student's interaction with the organizational determinants. College grade point average, along with institutional quality and practical value, were surrogates for pay, which Price (1977) found to be a significant indicator of turnover in work organizations.

Bean's (1980) model provided another approach to the study of student retention. However, the fact that his model failed to account for approximately 80 percent of the variance in dropout for women, and approximately 90 percent for men makes it difficult to understand why he would argue that his model would be more appropriate for understanding the process of withdrawal from college than the model proposed by Tinto (1975). In fact, studies of student retention that utilize the conceptual framework proposed by Bean are limited. This may say something about the perceived value of the theoretical framework of the model among other researchers (Walsh, 1973).

Discussing the nature of theory, Walsh writes the following:

> . . . the most significant attribute of a theory is concerned with the empirical research generated by theory. If a theory can be shown to have had a developmental effect upon relevant areas of research, we would likely have to conclude that it is an effective theory. Of course, a judgment must be made regarding the definition and meaning of relevant research. (p. 5)

John P. Bean and Barbara S. Metzner

Bean and Metzner (1985) argued that student retention theories from Spady (1970), Tinto (1975), and Pascarella (1980) focused too heavily on the social variables, which contributed very little to nontraditional student retention. Their conceptual model was developed to take into account that nontraditional students were rarely socially integrated with their institutions. Nontraditional students, according to Bean and Metzner (1985), were students who meet at least one of the following criteria: (a) older than twenty-four years; (b) commuter; or (c) enrolled part-time. They hypothesized that nontraditional student dropout decisions were based on four sets of variables: (a) academic; (b) background; (c) psychological; and (d) environmental. They emphasized that environmental variables were the most influential in dropout decisions for nontraditional students.

Academic variables, according to Bean and Metzner (1985), referred to study habits, academic advising, absenteeism, major certainty, and course availability. They conjectured that students with poor study habits were more likely to drop than those students with stronger study habits. Similarly, students with more absenteeism were also more likely to drop than those who attend class.

Background variables included age, enrollment status, residence, educational goals, high school performance, ethnicity, and gender (Bean &

Metzner, 1985). They hypothesized that students with strong high school grade point averages were more likely to persist than those with lower grade point averages. Likewise, students with greater aspiration in terms of their educational goals were also predicted to persist when compared to those with lesser academic aspirations.

Psychological variables were comprised of utility, satisfaction, goal commitment, and stress (Bean & Metzner, 1985). Bean and Metzner noted that despite high grade point averages, some students dropped out of college if they had negative psychological outcomes (low level of utility, satisfaction, or goal commitment) or had a lot of stress. For example, students who viewed getting a college degree as a necessity to getting a good job were more likely to be retained than those who did not.

Of all the variables, Bean and Metzner (1985) conjectured that environmental variables had the most effect on dropout decisions for nontraditional students. Environmental variables consisted of finances, hours of employment, outside encouragement, family responsibilities, and opportunity to transfer (Bean & Metzner). They argued that when environmental variables were bad (e.g., lack of child care or rigid and long work schedules) but academic variables were good (e.g., excellent academic advising or high grade point average), students would not stay enrolled. Thus, these students were more likely to drop than those with both positive environmental and academic variables.

Alan Seidman

Based on Tinto's (1987) retention model, Seidman (2005a) hypothesized that institutions could retain students if their retention programs were powerful enough to make substantial transformation. He postulated that if a program follows his retention formula, where retention equals early identification combined with early, intensive, and continuous intervention, increased retention would follow.

Retention, according to Seidman (2005b), is "defined as student attainment of academic and personal goals, regardless of how many terms a student [was] at the college" (p. 21). Using this definition, Seidman acknowledges that a student might reach his or her academic and/or personal goals before graduation or a student might graduate without completing the goals. Therefore, retention measurements that assess only the number of students in a course or program without aligning them to students' academic and/or personal goals might not provide a complete view.

Early identification referred to detecting a student's deficiencies as soon as possible, both academic and personal (Seidman, 2005a). This early identification could be accomplished at the time of application, whereby a college could use the student's past academic records and standardized test scores. Furthermore, a college could also require placement testing prior to enrolling in a course at the college. The college could use this information to help students reach their academic and personal goals.

Early intervention means that a college could provide support immediately to students who were identified as benefiting from such assistance (Seidman, 2005a). He argued that such support did not have to wait until the student was enrolled in a course. Colleges could offer intervention programs or services the quarter before enrollment, even during high school. Seidman goes so far as to recommend that colleges make the completion of these initial interventions a requirement prior to being accepted into college.

Intensive intervention, according to Seidman (2005a), referred to an intervention that was powerful enough to permanently change the student's academic or personal behavior toward achieving his or her goals. The intensive intervention typically required a substantive amount of time, such as two or more hours a day for all five school days per week. Intensive did not necessarily mean comprehensive, however. The intensive intervention programs or services should only target the individualized skills identified for each student. Students should not be forced to repeat courses for skills that they already have successfully completed and mastered.

Continuous intervention means that students should be provided support until the desired skills are attained (Seidman, 2005a). The artificial timelines of quarter or semester divisions of an academic year should not be a consideration for the intervention process. Students should be given adequate time to acquire the skills necessary for reaching their academic or personal goals.

Seidman (2005a) argued that his retention formula should not be implemented as a punishment to students who lack necessary skills for obtaining their academic or personal goals but rather should be used as a preventative approach. To illustrate that such retention programs or services were preventive, he recommended that colleges openly communicate the reasons behind the process. Students should "understand the process, the reason he or she was asked to participate in it, the expected outcomes, and the consequences" (p. 300). In addition, Seidman recognized that preventive approaches mean that the responsibility lay not only with students to seek help, but also with colleges to be proactive in seeking students who need their support.

CONCLUSION

An analysis of all the various theories, models, and concepts pertaining to college student retention is beyond the scope of this chapter. By focusing on McNeely (1937), Summerskill (1962), Astin (1966, 1985), Spady

(1970), Meyer (1970); Kamen (1971), Tinto (1975, 1987, 1993), Bean (1980, 1983), Bean and Metzner (1985), and Seidman (2005a, 2005b) chronologically, the authors attempted to demonstrate the evolution and interrelationship of the research conducted by the researchers. Nevertheless, we realize that there are other theories, models, and concepts utilized by researchers to explain student retention. St. John, et al. (nd) suggested the use of price-response theories that focus on the influence of institutional cost and financial aid on student persistence. Stanton-Salazar (1997) suggested the network-analytic concept of social capital and institutional support as a framework for understanding the socialization and academic experiences of minority students. Rendon, et al. (2000) suggested models of biculturalism and dual socialization. Regardless of the particular theory, model, or concept, it is Tinto's model of academic and social integration that is generally the cornerstone of the research, along with the notion of institutional fit. Institutional fit is based on congruency theory: the greater the congruence of the individual's background, values, attitudes, and interest with those of a significant cohort of individuals at the college, the more likely the individual will persist.

No single intervention strategy will adequately prevent all students from departing college. In fact, many different and varying interventions, services, or programs are needed depending on the period of a student's academic life and also on the form of departure. Therefore, it is up to the individual institution to decide which forms of dropout are deserving of institutional actions. Tinto (1987) recommended that colleges focus their attention primarily on those forms of departure that are understood by both the college and the student as educational failure. However, each college must create and implement its own program uniquely designed to meet its own available resources and institutional purposes.

REFERENCES

American College Testing [ACT]. (2009). *2009 retention/completion summary tables* (Report No. 13759). Retrieved May 1, 2010 from www.act.org/research/policy-makers/reports/graduation.html.

Arbeiter, S. (1984). Guns, butter or sheepskin: The military, business, and college competition for high school graduates in the 1980s. *College Board Review*, 137, 16+.

Astin, A. W. (1966). Trends in the characteristics of entering college students, 1961-65. (Report No. ACE-RR-VOL-1-NO-4-1966) Washington, D. C.: American Council on Eduction. (ERIC Document Reproduction Service No. ED011671).

Astin, A. W. (1975). *Preventing students from dropping out*. San Francisco: Jossey-Bass.

Astin, A. W. (1977). *Four critical years*. San Francisco: Jossey-Bass.

Astin, A. (1985). *Achieving educational excellence*. San Francisco, CA: Jossey-Bass Publishers.

Bean, J. P. (1980). Dropouts and turnovers: The synthesis and test of a causal model of student attrition. *Research in Higher Education, 12*(2), 155–187.

Bean, J. P. (1983). The application of a model of turnover in work organizations to the student attrition process. *Review of Higher Education, 6*(2), 129–148.

Bean, J. P., & Metzner, B. S. (1985). A conceptual model of nontraditional undergraduate student attrition. *Review of Educational Research, 55*(4), 485–540.

Berger, J. B., & Lyon, S. C. (2005). Past to present: A historical look at retention. In A. Seidman (Ed.), *College student retention: Formula for student success* (pp. 1–30). Westport, CT: Praeger Publishers.

Bishaw, A., & Semega, J. (2008). *Income, earnings, and poverty data from 2007 American community survey*. U.S Census Bureau report (ACS-09). Retrieved May 1, 2010 from www.census.gov/hhes/www/income/income.html.

Carmody, D. (1988). Colleges seek ways to keep black students. *New York Times*. February.

Centra, J. A. (1980). College enrollment in the 1980s: Projections and possibilities. *Journal of Higher Education, 51*(1), 18–39.

Dallam, J. W., & Dawes, B. E. (1981). What followup studies can tell about student retention. *College and University 56*(2), 151–159.

Hartley, M. P. (1987). H.E.L.P. for students: One university's action approach to increasing student retention. *College and University, 63*(1), 80–94.

Hossler, D. (1985). Managing enrollments for institutional vitality. *College Board Review, 137*, 26–29.

Hossler, D. (2005). *Managing student retention: Is the glass half-full, half-empty, or simply empty?* A white paper for AACRAO's strategic enrollment management (SEM) conference, Chicago, IL, November 13–16.

Iffert, R. E. (1954). What ought colleges and universities do about student mortality? *Association for Higher Education, Current issues in higher education*. Washington: National Education Association. 170–180.

Jackley, J. P., & Henderson, C. (1979). *Retention: Tactics for the eighties*. ACE Policy Brief. Washington, DC: American Council on Education, December.

Kamens, D. H. (1971). The college "charter" and college size: Effects on occupational choice and college attrition. *Sociology of Education*. Vol. 44 (Summer), 270–296.

Kamens, D. H. (1974). Colleges and elite formation: The case of prestigious American colleges. *Sociology of Education*. Vol. 47 (Summer), 354–378.

Knoel, D.M. (1960). Institutional research on retention and withdrawal. In H.T. Sprauge (Ed.) *Research on college students*. Boulder: Western Interstate Commission for Higher Education, 1960. 41–65.

Maeroff, G. I. (1985). Public-private college rivalry heats up. *New York Times*, August 19.

Marsh, L.M., (1966). College dropout: A review. *Personnel and Guidance Journal, 44*, 475-481

Mayhew, L. B. (1979). *Surviving the eighties*. San Francisco, CA: Jossey-Bass.

McNeeley, J. H. (1937). *College student mortality*. U.S. Departmentof Interior Bulletin, No. 11.

McNeeley, J. H. (1939). College student mortality studies. *Journal of American Association of College Registrars*, Vol. 15, 119–124.

Meyer, J. W. (1970). The charter: Conditions of diffuse socialization in schools. In W. R. Scott (Ed.), *Social process and social structures: An introduction to sociology* (pp. 564–578) New York: Henry Holt Co.

Mortenson, T. G. (2005). Measurements of persistence. In A. Seidman (Ed.), *College student retention: Formula for student success* (pp. 31–60). Westport, CT: Praeger Publishers.

Pantages, T.J. (1978). & Creedon, C.F. Studies of college attrition: 1950–1975. *Review of Educational Research, 48*(1), 49–101.

Pascarella, E.T. (1980). Student-faculty informal contact & college outcomes. *Review of Educational Research, 50*, 545–595.

Price, J. L. (1977) *The study of turnover*. Ames: Iowa State University Press.

Ramist, L. (1981). College student attrition and retention. Findings. *ETS Research Bulletin*, 6(2), Princeton, NJ: Educational Testing Service.

Rendon, L. I., Jalomo, R. E., & Nora, A. (2000). Theoretical considerations in the study of minority student retention in higher education. In J. M. Braxton (Ed.), *Reworking the student departure puzzle* (pp. 127–156). Nashville, TN: Vanderbilt University Press.

Sanford, T. R. (1982). Predicting college graduation for black and white freshman applicants. *College and University 57*(3), 265–278.

Schuh, J. H. (2005). Finances and retention. In A. Seidman (Ed.), *College student retention: Formula for student success* (pp. 277–293). Westport, CT: Praeger Publishers.

Sedlacek, W. E. (1989). Noncognitive indicators of student success. *Journal of College Admissions*, (125), 2–10.

Seidman, A. (2005a). Where we go from here: A retention formula for student success. In A. Seidman (Ed.), *College student retention: Formula for student success* (pp. 295–316). Westport, CT: Praeger Publishers.

Seidman, A. (2005b). Minority student retention: Resources for practitioners. In G. H. Gaither (Ed.), *Minority retention: What works?* (pp. 7–24). San Francisco, CA: Jossey-Bass.

Seidman, A. (2009). *Retention primer slide show* [PowerPoint presentation]. Retrieved May 1, 2010 from *www.cscsr.org/retention_slideshow.htm*.

Shulman, C. H. (1976). Recent trends in student retention. *Research Currents. American Association for Higher Education*, 3–4.

Spady, W. (1970). Dropouts from higher education: An interdisciplinary review and synthesis. *Interchange, 1*, 64–85.

Stanton-Salazar, R. D. (1997). A social capital framework for understanding the socialization of racial minority children and youths. *Harvard Educational Review 57*(1), 1–40.

St. John, E. P., Cabrera, A. E., Nora, A., & Asker, E. H. (ND). Economic influence on persistence reconsidered: How can finance research inform the reconceptualization of persistence models.

Summerskill, J. (1962). Dropouts from college. In N. Sanford (Ed.), *The American College* (pp. 627–637). New York: John Wiley and Sons.

Tinto, V. (1975). Dropout from higher education: A synthesis of recent research. *Review of Educational Research, 45*(1), 89–125.

Tinto, V. (1982). Limits of theory and practice in student attrition. *Journal of Higher Education, 53,* 687–700.

Tinto, V. (1987). *Leaving college: Rethinking the causes and cures of student attrition.* Chicago: The University of Chicago Press.

Tinto, V. (1993). *Leaving college: Rethinking the causes and cures of student attrition* (2nd ed.). Chicago, IL: University of Chicago Press.

Tinto, V. (2005). Research and practice of student retention: What next? *Journal of College Student Retention: Research, Theory, & Practice, 8*(1), 1–19.

Voorhees, R. A. (1985). Financial aid and persistence: Does the federal campus-based aid program make a difference? *Journal of Student Financial Aid, 15*(1), 21–30.

Walsh, W. W. (1973). *Theories of person-environment interaction: Implications for the college student.* Iowa City: The American College Testing Program.

Waterman, A. S. (1971). A cross-institutional study of variables relating to satisfaction with college. *Journal of Educational Research 65*(3), 132–136.

Willingham, W. W. (1985). *Success in college: The role of personal qualities and academic ability.* New York: College Entrance Examination Board.

Willingham, W. W., & Breland, H. M. (1982). *Personal qualities and college admissions.* New York: College Entrance Examination Board.

4

How to Define Retention

A New Look at an Old Problem

Linda Serra Hagedorn

In the more than six years since I pondered the question of the definition of retention in the first edition of this book, the difficulty of the assignment has neither lessened nor decreased in importance. There remains little agreement on the appropriate measure of a standard formula for the measure of college student retention, regardless of institutional type. While this chapter will focus specifically on retention, it is important to note that the problems associated with an appropriate measurement system are common to other often-researched outcomes in higher education. For example, there is no agreed-upon standard for the measure of transfer between two- and four-year institutions, student learning, or student engagement. From the perspective of higher education, the power to retain students remains the most crucial outcome if students are to be successful in life.

Since the last edition of this work, President Barack Obama has supported efforts to boost US degree production. In his third State of the Union address he specifically focused on college completion if America is to "win the future." Despite the recent attention, measuring college student retention remains complicated, confusing, and context-dependent. Higher education researchers will likely never reach consensus on the "correct" or "best" way to measure this very important outcome. However, the purpose of this chapter is to thoroughly review the associated problems; discuss the methods, juxtaposed with highlights of each; and ultimately recommend policy to reach a national consensus.

Let us begin with the most basic and noncontroversial definitions of a college persister and a non-persister. A student who enrolls in college and remains enrolled until degree completion is a persister. A student who leaves college without earning a degree and never returns is a non-persister.

While these definitions are simple and easy to understand, student paths are rarely this direct or straightforward. When looking at enrollment patterns that defy, or at least stretch, these basic definitions we find:

- Student A: Enrolls in a university, remains enrolled for two years, and stops out to return six years later.
- Student B: Enrolls in a university, remains for one year, and transfers to another university to complete the degree.
- Student C: Enrolls in two community colleges simultaneously, ultimately earning a certificate from one of them.
- Student D: Enrolls in college but does not complete any credits. The next year the student re-enrolls and remains continuously enrolled to degree completion.
- Student E: Begins in a community college and successfully transfers to a university. However, the student is not successful at the university and leaves prior to earning any credits. The next semester the student returns to the community college, taking the remaining courses necessary to earn an associate's degree.
- Student F: Enrolls for a full-time load of five courses (fifteen units of college credits), but drops all but one class (three units).
- Student G: Enrolls in two courses but drops one, keeping only a physical education course.
- Student H: Enrolls in a community college for a full load of remedial courses, re-enrolling in the same courses the next semester because he or she has not yet mastered the material.
- Student I: Enrolls in a full-time load of courses, but due to low GPA and lack of progress is academically suspended.
- Student J: Due to unlawful behavior is judiciously expelled from the university.
- Student K: Finishes one course at a community college and decides to continue his or her education in an online college.
- Student L: Enrolls in a community college in hopes to transfer to a four-year institution but ends up graduating with a certificate.

These are but a small sample of the conundrums that confront the definition of retention. But the list appropriately highlights the variability in student enrollment patterns that make it difficult to label one student a persister and another a non-persister. Clearly, the simple dichotomous student outcome measures often employed in quantitative analysis do not capture the complexity in student progress. Rather, retention requires a series of measures and perhaps even perspectives to allow researchers and administrators to measure student progress more accurately. To further illustrate the need for multiple descriptors of a particular phenomenon, I offer the example of "snow." The English language has one word for "snow" that appears sufficient to describe the precipitation that falls from the sky when the weather outside dips below freezing. However, for the Yup'ik Eskimos of Alaska, there are multiple words for snow: a word for powdered snow, another for blowing snow, another for melted snow, and so forth (Jacobson, 1984). Life in central Alaska requires and therefore recognizes the differentiation of snow types. In similar fashion, this chapter promotes the recognition and differentiation of different types of college retention and promotes a more complex, rather than simplistic, measurement system within an environment that requires more differentiation.

RETENTION AND DROPOUT

Two of the most widely used dichotomous measures in educational research and practice are retention and dropout. Typically conceptualized as two sides of the same coin, retention is staying in school until completion of a degree and dropping out is leaving school prematurely. It seems simplistic that retention and dropout are just purely opposites. However, more than four decades ago, Alexander Astin identified the dropout concept as a problem in his book *Predicting Academic Performance in College* (1971). According to Astin,

> . . . the term "dropout" is imperfectly defined: the so-called dropouts may ultimately become non-dropouts and vice versa. . . .But there seems to be no practical way out of the dilemma: A "perfect" classification of dropouts versus non-dropouts could be achieved only when all of the students had either died without ever finishing college or had finished college. (p. 15)

Astin added that defining dropout was further complicated by the prevalence of student enrollment in several different institutions throughout their educational career (Astin, 1971). According to the National Center for Education Statistics (2010), approximately 57 percent of first-time students seeking a bachelor's degree and attending a four-year institution full time in 2001–2002 completed a bachelor's degree in six years. This value does not acknowledge students who may return later to finish the degree. It is clear that retention rates can vary depending on the perspective and time frame of measurement.

The often-cited Vincent Tinto (1987) agreed that there are limits to our understanding of student departure: " . . . the label *dropout* is one of the more frequently misused terms in our lexicon of educational descriptors"

(p. 3). In fact, Tinto (1987) added that many who leave college do not see themselves as failures, but rather see their time in postsecondary instruction as a positive process of self-discovery that has resulted in individual social and intellectual maturation.

John Bean (1990), agreeing with Tinto, acknowledged that students who drop out might have already achieved their goals during their limited time in colleges. Hence, he suggested that neither the student nor the college should be considered failures. Retention, as he explained, must consider student educational goals. A dropout would then be defined in comparison to student outcome versus original intent. It is only when students leave college before achieving their goals that they should be labeled a dropout.

More Recent Retention Literature

Since the last publication of this work, the nation has plunged into a period of economic recession. During the same time period, the nation has witnessed great growth and acceptance of online education and online college degrees, often delivered through for-profit institutions (Heyman, 2010). While online education may be popular, the medium has not produced higher retention rates. In fact, according to the limited extant research, online programs generally have lower retention than traditional programs (Heyman, 2010). This lower retention is juxtaposed with more recent retention literature such as that by John Schuh (2005), who has argued that higher levels of student retention have the potential to bring both social and economic benefits. Further, it is through an educated society prepared for work that a nation can better achieve higher levels of economic prosperity.

Whereas most of the earlier retention research focused exclusively on the first year of college and generally operationalized retention as returning after the first year, Lipka (2006) documented that a number of institutions have begun to focus on second-year students retention because a significant number of students who persist through their first year of college were unable to persist after their second year. Such research to reach beyond first-year students is a testament that retention and persistence measurements are important measures throughout the educational process and not simply after the first year.

DROPOUT, GRADUATION, PERSISTENCE, RETENTION, AND ATTRITION

While a dropout could be viewed as "anyone who leaves college prior to graduation," it must be accepted that a "dropout" may eventually return and transform into a "non-dropout" any time prior to death, thereby negating any earlier designations used for studies, research, or retention rates. Former dropouts may return as full-time or part-time students, to the same institution or another institution; they remain in the same major or switch to another major.

Let me shift to a basic source of confusion: The words "persistence" and "retention" are often used interchangeably. Yet the National Center for Education Statistics (U. S. Department of Education, 2003) differentiates the terms by using "retention" as an institutional measure and "persistence" as a student measure. In other words, institutions retain and students persist. Another term commonly used (or misused) with retention is "attrition." Attrition is the diminution in numbers of students resulting from lower student retention.

Two important related terms are *graduate* and *graduation*. Starting with a commonly used definition of a graduate as a former student who has completed a prescribed course of study in a college or university, it is clear that all graduates have persisted. However, not all persisters will graduate. Furthermore, a graduate can only claim one institution regardless of prior enrollment at other colleges or universities. While the institution from whence a student graduates will count that student as a persister, previous institutions that the student attended will likely count him or her as a nonpersister or dropout. Graduation rates are clearly not the same as retention rates, while both are measures under the heading of retention. Using the example from above, the student who transferred to another institution would negatively affect the graduation rate at the initial institution.

Further adding to the complexity of the vocabulary is variation in time spans used to measure graduation rates. Typically, colleges and universities report four-year rates, while ACT publishes five-year rates and the National Collegiate Athletic Association (U.S. Department of Education, 2003) and the IPEDS (National Center for Education Statistics, 2010) report six-year rates. There is even less agreement concerning the length of time to measure the associate's degree graduation rate at community colleges. The national norms reported by Berkner, Horn, and Clune (2000) indicate that the average time between first enrollment and graduation for community college associate's degree earners was about three and a half years, suggesting that the graduation rates should be measured over at least a five-year time period. However, one study proved that a six-year period would yield a more accurate account of graduation rates for community colleges (Bailey, Crosta, & Jenkins, 2006). Additionally, President Obama has asked for all high school graduates to strive for one more year of educational training (White House, 2009). This additional year, without achieving a degree or certificate, creates another level of complexity for institutions to account for when considering retention. If a student receives an additional year of education without acquiring a degree or certificate, the benefits of the additional year of schooling may be beneficial to the student; however, the institution can count the student as neither a persister nor a graduate.

MODELS OF RETENTION

In a quest to understand retention and its supporting terminology, I turn to the literature and proposed models of retention. The most often cited model is that of Vincent Tinto (1975) who introduced the importance of student integration (both socially and academically) in the prediction of student retention (1975, 1993). This framework was based on the work of Emile Durkheim's suicide theory (1951) that pointed to one's unsuccessful integration into society as a strong precursor of suicide. In a similar manner, Tinto's Integration Model suggested that retention is related to the student's ability and actions to become an involved actor in her or his institution (Tinto, 1987). The Integration Model suggests the need for a match between the institutional environment and student commitment. A good match leads to higher student integration into the academic and social domains of college life and thus greater probability of persistence. Conversely, students are more likely to drop out or transfer to another institution when the match between the students and institution is poor.

John Bean (1990) is in full agreement with the necessity of integration as he stated, "Retention rates are related to the interaction between the students attending the college and the characteristics of the college" (p. 171). As the author of the Student Attrition Model based on the Price/Mueller model of employee turnover behavior (Bean, 1980), Bean deviates from Tinto's model and stresses that students' beliefs, which subsequently shape their attitudes, is the predictor of their persistence. Moreover, students' beliefs are affected by the interaction between the students and different components of the institution, similar to interaction between employees and corporations.

While Tinto and Bean remain the early pioneers in the retention research and model arena, the importance of the issues brought on a virtual explosion in the subsequent years. A Google Scholar search on college or university retention returns in excess of three million articles. A scholarly refereed quarterly journal dedicated solely to the subject, the *Journal of College Student Retention: Research, Theory & Practice,* is in operation, and new books and monographs are regularly being published. A contemporary retention researcher, John Braxton, edited a book in which several authors reworked and examined college student retention and recommended new views on the revered theories, ideas that may more appropriately address the needs of diverse college students (2000). Other contemporary works include the latest release of the Pascarella and Terenzini classic *How College Affects Students: A Third Decade of Research*, published in 2005. Gabriel and Falke wrote *Teaching Underprepared Students: Strategies for Promoting Success and Retention in Higher Education*, published in 2008. Braxton, Hirschy, and McClendon wrote *Understanding and Reducing College Student Departure: ASHE-Eric Higher Education Report*, which was published in 2004. In addition, the Center for the Study of College Student Retention provides an online space to discuss and learn more about retention. While the purpose of this chapter is not merely a review of the literature, it is important to establish the firm and substantial literature base that has evolved over the last quarter century as a testament of the importance of this issue. Curious, however, is that despite the plethora of articles and books on the topic, the concept of retention and its appropriate measurement tools still remain cloaked in a significant level of ambiguity.

MEASURING RETENTION

Ambiguity aside, all colleges and universities are required to submit retention figures to federal and state entities. This task is disproportionately more difficult for community colleges due to their higher turnover rates and more diverse student enrollments, including many students who attend more than one institution at a time (Hagedorn & Castro, 1999). Despite the difficulty, maintaining an appropriate account of student attendance is of the utmost importance because an institution's reputation and sometimes its funding levels depend on its ability to retain a significant number of its students as proof of academic success (Tichenor & Cosgrove, 1991; Schuh & Associates, 2009). With higher education under more scrutiny, the movement toward assessment of the public investment in higher education has centralized on graduation rates and retention.

In his review of retention studies in the 1960s, Summerskill (1962) showed that within each type of institution, institutional retention rates varied from 18 percent to 88 percent. He also alluded to the necessity of a standard formula for measuring retention so that the reported rates could be accurately compared. Five decades later, a standard formula has not yet been universally accepted. However, the United States government has established a federal definition of graduation rate as part of the Student Right-to-Know and Campus Security Act (Pub. L 101-542).

The Student Right-to-Know and Campus Security Act, signed Nov. 8, 1990, requires colleges to reveal their graduation rates to enable prospective applicants to make a more informed decision regarding the suitability of the institution. The graduation rate was defined as the percentage of full-time, first-time, degree-seeking enrolled students who graduate after 150 percent of the normal time for completion: six years for four-year colleges (eight semesters or twelve quarters excluding summer terms) and three years for two-year colleges (four semesters or six quarters excluding summer terms).

Although the law is an attempt to provide comparative information for prospective college students, this definition obviously excludes a large number of students enrolled in colleges and universities, including students who are:

a) transfers from other colleges
b) enrolled part-time
c) enrolled but not currently working toward a degree or certificate
d) entering at any other time except with the traditional fall cohort
e) undeclared in majors
f) enrolled in remedial coursework that will extend the time from first enrollment to completion

The formula is obviously *less* appropriate for community colleges, which frequently enroll a majority of students who are part-time, returning, and/ or require deep remediation.

The Practices of Measurement

It must be noted that the federal definition is a graduation rate and not a retention rate. A search of the literature, the Internet, plus numerous telephone calls and e-mails revealed the dominant retention and other completion measurement practices currently used.

There are two federal retention formulas employed by the National Center for Education Statistics for use in the Integrated Postsecondary Education Data System (or IPEDS): one for colleges described as "less than four-year," and another for "four-year" institutions. The only difference between the two formulas is that students finishing a program such as a short-term certificate are included in the retained proportion for colleges described as "less than four-year." The retention rate is based only on enrollment from the fall of the first year of enrollment to the fall of the next (students enrolling for the first time during the preceding summer are also included in the fall counts). Included in the calculation are only first-time, degree/certificate-seeking students. It is important to note that the retention rate is a short-term measure that covers only one year and thus is not adjusted for students who may leave the college after the first year but before a degree is earned. Colleges submit retention rates separately for full- and part-time students. Specifically excluded from the calculation are students who are deceased, permanently disabled, have joined armed forces or foreign aid service of the federal government, and those students on official church missions (NCES, 2003). The currently posted formulas for retention rate (RR) are:

IPEDS RR$_{\text{less than 4-year}}$ =
((Number of students re-enrolled in the following fall + Number of students who have completed)

_____

(Number of students in the fall cohort—Exclusions))*100

IPEDS RR $_{\text{4-year}}$ =
Number of students re-enrolled in the following fall

_____

(Number of students in the fall cohort—Exclusions)*100

In essence, the formulas used for IPEDS leads the field as the dominant formula used in the calculation of retention rates as it is the formula generally used to report to the federal and state governments, but there remains differentiation on calculations and reported values among some institutions and policymaking bodies. For example, the National Information Center for Higher Education Policymaking and Analysis (NCHEMS), a body that provides state policymakers and others with information used to make important decisions, calculates and provides multiple data on completion rates by state using measures such as three-year associate's degree (ADR$_3$) and six-year bachelor's degree (BDR$_6$) acquisition rates; the associate's (ADR$_{100}$) and bachelor's degrees (BDR$_{100}$) awarded per 100 undergraduates; and the number of degrees awarded per high school graduates three and six years earlier (AD$_{HS3}$ and BD$_{HS6}$) (NCHEMS, no date).

The ADR$_3$ and BDR$_6$ include only first-time, full-time degree-seeking students and thus exclude all part time and transfer students, while the ADR$_{100}$ and BDR$_{100}$ include all students (headcount). The AD$_{HS3}$ and BD$_{HS6}$ are also based on headcounts but at the high school level, and therefore include only those students who go directly to college after high school graduation (NCHEMS, no date).

Common Data Set

The Common Data Set (CDS) is a joint effort by the higher education community and publishers including the College Board, *Peterson's, U.S. News and World Report,* and others to establish and develop clear standard definitions on the data items to be used in educational research (Petersons, 1998). CDS is an important initiative to improve the comparability of data reported by colleges and to assist colleges and universities to ask survey questions in a standard way. While the CDS is not a mechanism for forwarding specific measures, its popularity among institutions supports the calculations and dissemination of specific institutional measures. The Common Data Set consists of ten areas of data:

1. general information
2. enrollment and persistence figures
3. first-time, first-year (freshman) admission
4. transfer admission
5. academic offerings and policies
6. student life
7. annual expenses
8. financial aid
9. instructional faculty and class size
10. degrees conferred.

The Common Data Set for 2010–2011 has approximately 120 definitions that cover terms from "tuition" to "Carnegie units." As the initiative develops, new items are added and some items are edited. The CDS measurement for persistence is the same as that reported for IPEDS for both four-year and less-than-four-year institutions and thus further serves to nationalize the calculations; however, other measures help define success in more diverse ways.

Community Colleges

There is more variation regarding the measure of retention among community colleges. The Research and Planning Group for California (RP Group, no date), and the Transfer and Retention of Urban Community College Students Project (TRUCCS) both support the use of the successful course completion ratio (SCCR) (Hagedorn, 2004). Simply stated, a course completion ratio is the proportion or percentage of courses that a student completes as compared to the number of courses in which the student enrolls. Mathematically, the calculation is:

$$SCCR = \frac{\text{Number of courses with the grade of A, B, C, D, CR, or P}}{\text{\# of courses of enrollment}}$$

Completion ratios can be computed for different periods of time (example: semester, academic year, or over several years) and can flex to accommodate the full- or part-time student. The SCCR is a continuous measure (from 0 to 100 percent), and compares a student's progress to her or his goals. One of the major problems associated with measuring community college student retention is that many students enter the college without the goal of continuing enrollment or of ultimate graduation. Some students have achieved their postsecondary goals by taking a course, a few courses, or transferring to another institution prior to graduation. The typical measures of retention/persistence provide misleading evidence of success and non-success. The SCCR makes a basic assumption: a student enrolling in a course is declaring the goal of completing the course. Thus, a student who enrolls in four courses and successfully completes all of them has an SCCR of 100 percent. Likewise, a student who completes only two courses would earn an SCCR of 50 percent. The SCCR makes sense as a tool of measurement in institutions where students may frequently "stopout" and return, have diverse academic goals, are not all degree-seeking, and may be enrolled in more than one institution.

TYPES OF RETENTION

The formulas and discussion presuppose that retention exists in one variety—that is, that students either remain at an institution or they do not. The truth is that retention comes in multiple varieties. There are at least four basic types of retention: institutional, system, in the major (discipline), and in a particular course.

Institutional Retention.   Institutional retention is the most basic and easy to understand and is the type measured in the formulas discussed in this chapter. In essence, institutional retention is the measure of the proportion of students who remain enrolled at the *same* institution from year to year.

System Retention.   System retention focuses on the student and disregards in which institution a student is enrolled. Using system persistence as a measure, a student who leaves one institution to attend another is considered a persister. Therefore, system persistence accommodates the frequent occurrence of transfer or re-enrollment at another campus, in another state, or in another institutional type (for example, a for-profit). Some states, such as Texas and New York, have coordinating boards that track students who have transferred to other universities within the state, thus keeping track of a limited type of system retention (i.e., system retention within the state university system). Nevertheless, those who transferred out of institutions governed by the coordinating board are generally not tracked. While the measure of system persistence is important to truly understand and measure student success, it requires tracking—a very expensive and difficult procedure. Currently, the only national tracking done is via the National Student Clearinghouse.

The National Student Clearinghouse is a nonprofit organization designed to verify degrees and standardize student loan status. Participation in the Clearinghouse, at a small per-student fee, requires that participating colleges submit a student enrollment status report. While the National Clearinghouse data are frequently used for system persistence measures, it must be stated that the data were not originally designed to be used in that manner and not all institutions participate.

Retention within a Major or Discipline.   Another type of retention takes a more limited view of the topic by viewing retention within a major area of study, discipline, or specific department. For example, a student who declares engineering as a major but then switches to biology may be retained in an institutional sense but is lost to the College of Engineering. Non-persisters in one discipline may earn a degree in another major within the institution of original entry and thus be institutionally retained but departmentally non-retained. Retention within certain majors, such as engineering, may be of special interest due to the difficulty of recruitment and the predicted shortages in the fields. Engineering has a high rate of non-retention in the major, especially among women and people of color (Daempfle, 2003; Chesler, Barabino, Bhatia, & Richards-Kortum, 2010). Retention within the major may be tracked by specific colleges or universities but is not nationally tracked and remains difficult to measure. However, some institutions have made it a priority to retain students in the College of Engineering by utilizing student affairs models developed to increase the number of students of color. For example, some HBCUs (Historically Black Colleges and Universities) have made great strides to retain students of color in the College of Engineering (Palmer, Davis, & Thompson, 2010).

Retention within the Course.   The smallest unit of analysis with respect to retention is that measured by course completion. Studying at the course level allows the specific determination of which courses are not being completed even though a student may be retained within the institution. As specific as course retention appears to be, it is still fraught with questions of measurement. The TRUCCS Project documented large variation in course completion depending on the time of measurement (Hagedorn, 2003). Course completion is much lower when using the first day of class as the marker to determine if a student attempted a course versus waiting until after the add/drop time. The add/drop period is provided to allow institutions the flexibility to close courses that have inadequate enrollments and to allow students to drop courses that may be inappropriate (too easy or too hard) and to add others that may be more suitable. Using the cessation of the add/drop period as the timing for the calculation means that an attempt is defined as a course in which a student obtained a letter grade (A, B, C, D, F, W, P, or I). While the add/drop process most certainly has a positive function from both the student and the institutional viewpoint, it must be stated that during the registration process, courses frequently close when the maximum enrollment is reached, thus barring other students who may desire to enroll in the course. When enrolled students drop the course they leave open seats that may have been better utilized by other students who were denied enrollment. Course completion is not nationally posted or compared. Community colleges more typically measure course completion as they generally have more variation in the measure.

PROBLEMS WITH THE CURRENT MEASURES

The current definitions and formulas do not include all students and as such may provide inaccurate measures of retention. Again, as an example of exclusions and confusions, the reader is directed to the initial vignettes of students provided at the beginning of the chapter—those student activities that defy the current definitions. Furthermore there may be a bit of university "sleight of hand" associated with practices that reflect on reported figures. For some time now the *U.S. News and World Report* has published its annual rankings of colleges and universities. The rankings serve as a prestige barometer and create an intense competition, especially among top research universities. To establish the highest rankings, universities can be somewhat creative in who is counted and who is not. For example, some universities will admit only those students with the very highest admission scores (SAT or ACT) in the fall cohort while extending admission to a second group of students with slightly lower scores for the spring semester or quarter. This procedure allows the universities to post their incoming freshman average SAT scores as higher than it would be if all admits (fall and spring) were included. While the reports of fall-to-fall retention are surely accurate, they include only those students who were admitted in the fall: students with the highest admissions criteria and thus are those more likely to be retained.

The current formulas for retention include those students who are more likely to persist and thus may provide an inflated figure less representative of the variation of student persistence. In short, the formulas generally exclude:

- part-time students
- returning students
- transfers
- students who prematurely leave after the second year of enrollment

On the other hand, the formulas for retention allow the inclusion of some students as retained who probably should not be, for example, the student who enrolls in fall, drops all courses, but re-enrolls the next fall (maybe to drop again). The point being made is that the retained formula does not contain all those retained and the dropout figures do not include all those who prematurely leave or are ambiguously enrolled. We have no descriptor or measurement for the student who takes courses in a haphazard manner such that while credits are accrued (retained), no degree progress is made. No descriptor or formula includes those who appear trapped in remedial courses and, although enrolled and earning credits, are not earning credits that can be counted for a college degree. The institution can claim higher retention rates and students are persisting, but the goal of achievement remains elusive.

RETENTION FROM MULTIPLE ANGLES: PROPOSED FORMULAS

Clearly, single measures of retention do not tell the whole story of student persistence. To fully understand an institution's rate of student success, multiple indicators should be calculated and reported. At a minimum, institutions should regularly report institutional persistence, transfer rates (both of the proportion of students who transfer to other institutions and the proportion that transfer in from other institutions), and course completion ratios.

It is recommended that a new measure of pure institutional retention that includes part-time students, continuing students, transfer students, advanced students, and students who begin enrollment at times other than with the fall cohort be reported, perhaps juxtaposed with the fall cohort variety that is frequently but solely used. The new proposed formula for degree-seeking students that could be calculated each year:

$$
\text{Pure institutional persistence: Performed annually} = \frac{\text{Current total FTE degree-seeking enrollment} - (\text{current year newly enrolled students})}{\text{Past year's fall FTE degree-seeking enrollment} + (\text{FTE enrollment of degree-seeking spring and summer}) - \text{FTE graduates}}
$$

A system persistence formula could be similarly calculated. Of course, while a formula can be proposed, actual tracking of all college students on a national level is currently not available.

Pure system persistence: Performed annually

$$\frac{\text{Current total national FTE degree-seeking enrollment} - (\text{current year newly enrolled students})}{\text{Past year's total national fall FTE degree-seeking enrollment} + (\text{FTE enrollment of degree-seeking spring and summer}) - \text{FTE graduates}}$$

Persistence by major may also be performed for most disciplines, thus providing a retention measure of the students declaring their initial interest areas. The calculation should be similarly cast as above but substituting the FTE students graduating within a major with those FTEs originally declaring the major.

Two final equations are suggested to complete the picture of student retention successful course completion ratios (SCCR) and graduation rates. Successful course completion ratios can be calculated globally (all courses in the college/university) and within departments to provide a final and fine-tuned measure of retention. The formula for SCCR was provided earlier in the chapter. Graduation rates provide a measure of retention along with a measure of progress. The proposed equation is similar to that currently used, except it employs FTEs and includes transfers in.

$$\text{Graduation rate}_{4 \text{ year institution}} = \frac{\text{FTE graduates throughout the academic year}}{\text{FTE students entering academic year 6 years ago (including fall, spring, summer entrants)}}$$

CONCLUSION

Why are college retention and its appropriate measurement so important? The difference in earnings between a college graduate and a high school graduate is at least $1 million over the lifetime (U.S. College Search, 2008). Lower incomes generally correlate with many social problems and lower living standards (McMahon, 2000). Physical quality of life, which includes weight (obesity rates), level of physical activity, and lower body mass index, was correlated with higher levels of income (Sallis et al., 2009). Retention not only has an impact on the individual and her or his family but also produces a ripple effect on the postsecondary institutions, the work force, and the economy.

College Effect.   Retention is one of the most common ways students, parents, and stakeholders evaluate the effectiveness of colleges. A positive reputation increases a college's ability to attract the best students and faculty. Furthermore, when a student withdraws from college the invested institutional resources were not spent wisely, forcing the college to invest additional resources to recruit new students (Ackerman & Schibrowsky, 2007–2008). Noel-Levitz (2004), acknowledging the significant institutional costs, posted their *Retention Savings Worksheet* providing a formula to calculate the amount of institutional savings when first-to-second year dropout rate is reduced. While the formula is rather complex, the two provided examples—one for a public institution and one for a private institution—show that significant savings can be accrued when the dropout rate is reduced by even a small percentage.

Workforce Effect.   Non-persisting students lack the college training and credentials to enter the professional workforce. Industries not finding sufficiently trained workers either must invest in their own training programs or relocate to areas where sufficiently trained workers are more available, sometimes even overseas. There is evidence, for example, of a decline in retention to science and engineering graduate programs having a significant workforce effect (Andrade, Stigall, Kappus, Ruddock, & Oburn, 2002). Further, the importance of diversifying the pipeline to ensure a higher quality and quantity of successful workers for the United States to participate in a global market should be analyzed more deeply.

Economic Effect.   From the economic point of view, higher education attainment leads to decreases in long-term poverty, higher personal per-capita income, a higher state tax base, and a stronger economy (McMahon, 2000; Hanushek & Woessmann, 2008). In short, a more educated citizenry leads to advantages on many levels.

The importance of the topic is obvious. The current measures are insufficient to understand the topic and thus hinder researchers from validly identifying the predictors. The inaccurate research prevents policymakers from constructing the best policy to increase student success. Issues of retention and persistence affect different groups in a wide variety of ways. More accurate measurements of retention reveal the experiences of various groups. Moreover, it is hoped that a national tracking system that includes all colleges and universities, including accredited for-profits and online education, will be constructed to track student progress. Although such a system will be very expensive, the importance of this project speaks loudly for its necessity. The old adage attributed to Derek Bok, "if you think education is expensive, try ignorance," may be apt.

REFERENCES

Ackerman, R., & Schibrowsky, J. (2007–2008). A business marketing strategy applied to student retention education initiative. *Journal of College Student Retention: Research, Theory, and Practice, 9*(3), 307–336.

Andrade, S. J., Stigall, S. Kappus, S. S., Ruddock, M., & Oburn, M. (2002). *A model retention program for science and engineering students: Contributions of the institutional research office.* Texas.

Astin, A.W. (1971). *Predicting academic performance in college: Selectivity data for 2300 American colleges.* New York: The Free Press.

Bailey, T., Crosta, P. M., & Jenkins, D. (2006). Is Student Right to Know all you should know? *Research in Higher Education, 47*(5), 491–519.

Bean, J. P. (1980). Dropouts and Turnover: The synthesis and test of a causal model of student attrition. *Research in Higher Education, 12*(2), 155–187.

Bean, J. P. (1990). Using retention research in enrollment management. In Hossler, D., Bean, J. P., & Associates (Eds.), *The strategic management of college enrollments* (pp. 170–185). San Francisco, CA: Jossey-Bass Publishers.

Berkner, L., Horn, L., & Clune, M. (2000). Descriptive summary of 1995–96 beginning postsecondary students: Three years later, NCES 2000-154. Washington, DC.

Braxton, J. M.(Ed.). (2000). *Reworking the student departure puzzle.* Nashville, TN: Vanderbilt University Press.

Chesler, N., Barabino, G., Bhatia, S., & Richards-Kortum, R. (2010). The pipeline still leaks and more than you think. *Annals of Biomedical Engineering, 38*(5), 1928–1935. Retrieved on March 15, 2011, at http://dx.doi.org/10.1007/s10439-010-9958-9. Doi: 10.1007/s10439-010-9958-9.

Daempfle, P. A. (2003). An analysis of the high attrition rates among first year college science, math, and engineering majors. *Journal of College Student Retention, 5*(1), 37–52.

Durkheim, E. (1951). *Suicide.* New York: The Free Press.

Hagedorn, L.S. (2003). *Executive reports.* Unpublished reports from TRUCCS to the Los Angeles Community College District. Los Angeles.

Hagedorn, L.S. (2004, April). *Speaking community college. A glossary of appropriate terms.* Paper presented at the meeting of Council for the Study of Community Colleges (CSCC), Minneapolis, MN.

Hagedorn, L. S, & Castro, C. R. (1999). Paradoxes: California's experience with reverse transfer students. In B. K. Townsend (Ed.), *Understanding the impact of reverse transfer students on community colleges* (pp. 15–26). San Francisco, CA: Jossey-Bass.

Hanushek, E.A., & Woessmann, L. (2008). The role of cognitive skills in economic development. *Journal of Economic Literature, 46*(3), 607–668. Retrieved on March 28, 2011 at http://www.jstor.org/stable/27647039.

Heyman, E. (2010). Overcoming student retention issues in higher education online programs. *Online Journal of Distance Learning Administration Contents XIII*(4, Winter 2010). http://www.westga.edu/~distance/ojdla/winter134/heyman134.html

Jacobson, S. (1984). *Yup'ik Eskimo dictionary.* Fairbanks, AK: University of Alaska Press.

Lipka, S. (2006). After the freshman bubble pop: More colleges try to help their sophomores thrive. *The Chronicle of Higher Education,* 53(3), A34.

McMahon, W. W. (2000). *Education and development: Measuring the social benefits.* Oxford University Press, London.

National Center for Education Statistics (2003). Instructions for enrollment. Retrieved March 1, 2011, from http://nces.ed.gov/ipeds/pdf/webbase2003/ef_inst.pdf

National Center for Education Statistics (2010). The Integrated Postsecondary Education Data System (IPEDS). Retrieved January 12, 2011, from www.nces.ed.gov/ipeds/

National Center of Higher Education Management Systems–NCHEMS (2002). Retrieved April 29, 2004, from http://www.higheredinfo.org/

Noel-Levitz (2004). Retention savings worksheet. Retrieved March 15, 2011 from www.noellevitz.com/pdfs/RetSvgsWkst.pdf

Palmer, R. T., Davis, R. J., & Thompson, T. (2010). Theory meets practice: HBCU initiatives that promote academic success among African Americans in STEM. *Journal of College Student Development* 51(4), July/August 2010.

Petersons (1998). Peterson's News about the Common Data Set. Retrieved March 15, 2011 from www.petersons.com/research/he/cds

RP Group (no date). Retrieved March 15, 2011, from http://rpgroup.org/Projects/Oper_Definitions/definitions1.htm

Sallis, J. F., Saelens, B. E., Frank, L. D., Conway, T. L., Slymen, D. J., Cain, K. L., Chapman, J. E., & Kerr, J. (2009). Neighborhood built environment and income: Examining multiple health outcomes. *Social Science & Medicine,* 68(7), April 2009, 1285–1293. Retrieved on March 15, 2011 at http://dx.doi.org/10.1016/j.socscimed.2009.01.017.

Schuh, J. H. (2005). Finances and retention: Trends and potential implications. In A. Seidman (Ed.), *College student retention: Formula for student success* (pp. 277–294). Westport, CT: Praeger.

Schuh, J. H. & Associates (2009). *Assessment methods for student affairs.* San Francisco: Jossey-Bass.

State Higher Education Executive Officers–SHEEO (2004). Retrieved March 15, 2011 from www.sheeo.org.

Student-Right-To-Know and Campus Security Act, Nov 8, 1990. Pub.L 101-542. U.S.C. 1001.

Summerskill, J. (1962). Dropouts from college. In Nevitt Standards (Ed.), *The American college.* New York: John Wiley and Sons.

Tichenor, R., & Cosgrove, J. J. (1991). Evaluating retention-driven marketing in a community college: An alternative approach. *New Directions for Institutional Research,* 18(2), 73–81.

Tinto, V. (1975). Dropout from Higher Education: A Theoretical Synthesis of Recent Research. *Review of Educational Research,* 65 (Winter): 89–125.

Tinto, V. (1987). *Leaving college: Rethinking the causes and cures of student attrition.* Chicago: The University of Chicago Press.

Tinto, V. (1993). *Leaving college: Rethinking the causes and cures of student attrition.* (2nd ed.). Chicago: The University of Chicago Press.

Trosset, C. & Weisler, S. (2010). Using longitudinal assessment data to improve retention and student experiences. *New Directions for Institutional Research, 2010,* 79–88. Doi: 10.1002/ir.374.

University of Phoenix. Retrieved on March 15, 2011 from www.phoenix.edu/students/how-it-works/degree-program-completion-time.html.

US Census Bureau (2000). Retrieved January 13, 2004 from www.census.gov.

US College Search. (2008). The difference between a college graduate and a high school graduate is $1 million. Retrieved on January 31, 2011 from www.uscollegesearch.org/blog/career-planning/the-difference-between-a-college-graduate-and-a-high-school-graduate-is-1-million.

US Department of Education, National Center for Statistics, (2003). The condition of education, NCES 2003-067, I. Washington, DC: U.S. Government Printing Office, 2003.

White House (2009). Remarks of President Barack Obama, Address to Joint Session of Congress. Retrieved on January 13, 2011 at www.whitehouse.gov/the_press_office/Remarks-of-President-Barack-Obama-Address-to-Joint-Session-of-Congress/.

5

Finances and Retention

Trends and Potential Implications

John H. Schuh and Ann Gansemer-Topf

A volume on issues related to student retention would be incomplete without a discussion of the relationship between student retention and finance. Financing higher education has become a complex, high-stakes activity for students and their institutions. Many students, in effect, are betting their economic future on their college experience. In turn, colleges, their benefactors, and various governmental authorities, especially the federal government, have made and are likely to continue to make significant commitments to students so that they can attend college. Consequently, this chapter will examine some of the salient issues related to how students finance their education, the amount of debt they incur to finance their education, and the implications for institutions of higher education when students do not persist to graduation. Admittedly, this discussion will be superficial. Many lengthy volumes have been written on this topic, and the aim of this chapter is to examine selected highlights of this set of complex topics. A list of references is provided and the reader is urged to consult with these materials for additional information about the subject matter.

CURRENT FISCAL ENVIRONMENT

Contemporary financing of higher education has involved an increasing reliance on students and their families to provide revenues for colleges and universities. Students, in turn, increasingly are relying on financial aid to finance their education. Loans are a central element in student financial aid. These conclusions will be discussed in detail in the next section of this chapter.

It is important to remember while reviewing this chapter that in spite of the costs associated with college attendance, from an employment perspective, college graduates are more likely to be employed than those who have not earned a bachelor's degree. In January 2011, the unemployment rate for those with less than a high school diploma was 14.2 percent. The rate for those workers with a high school diploma was 9.4 percent, while the rate was 8.0 percent for those with some college or an associate's degree. The unemployment rate for those with bachelor's degree or more education was 4.2 percent (Bureau of Labor Statistics, 2011, n.p.). Therefore, while the costs of a college education have increased dramatically over the past several decades, and students are incurring ever-increasing debt to finance their education, the price college graduates pay appears to result in better opportunities for employment than for those who have completed less education than a bachelor's degree.

How Institutions of Higher Education are Financed

One of the most important trends in higher education finance over the past two decades is the ever-increasing reliance that institutions of higher education have on tuition and fee revenue. This is true for publicly assisted institutions as well as private not-for-profit and for-profit institutions. For example, "Four-year public institutions received 20 percent of their revenues from tuition and fees, compared to 78 percent at private not-for-profit institutions, and 88 percent at private for-profit institutions" (Knapp, Kelly-Reid, & Ginder, 2011, p. 5) in fiscal 2009. The following data are introduced in support of this conclusion.

Public Institutions.   In reporting year 1980–1981, public degree-granting institutions received 12.9 percent of their revenue from tuition and fees (U.S. Department of Education, 2003, Table 330). This percentage grew to 16.67 percent of their income in reporting year 2006–2007. In constant dollars, two-year public institutions received $1980 on average per student in 2003–2004. This amount increased to $2133 per student in 2006–2007 (Snyder & Dillow, 2010, Table 352). At four-year institutions the amount received per student in constant dollars grew from $5883 in 2003–2004 to $6624 in 2006–2007. As will be discussed later, students who do not persist represent significant revenue loss for their institution, particularly those that have less of an emphasis on research activities and accordingly rely on tuition income as their primary source of income.

Private, Not-for-Profit Institutions.   In 1980–1981, private, not-for-profit institutions relied on tuition and fees for 35.9 percent of their income. By 1995–1996, tuition and fees accounted for 41.5 percent of their income (U.S. Department of Education, 2003, Table 332). By 2006–2007, the percentage of revenue from tuition and fees at four-year institutions had declined to 25.96 percent (Snyder & Dillow, 2010, Table 355). The amount of revenue in constant dollars from tuition and fees on a per-student basis had grown from $14,328 in 1997–1998 to $16,676 in 2006–2007 (Table 355). The decline in the percentage of revenue can be explained by the phenomenal growth in investment returns at private, not-for-profit institutions. In 1997–1998, these institutions received 23.53 percent of their income from this source ($12,184 per student in constant dollars) but by 2006–2007, the proportion had grown to 30.72 percent ($19,370 per student in constant dollars).

Of course, investment income is not necessarily a steady source of revenue, for during declining stock markets the amount of investment income can be reduced precipitously. For example, at four-year not-for-profit institutions, in 2001–2002, investment return contributed a negative return of –7.82 percent, or in constant dollars, a loss of $2984. In that year tuition accounted for 39.59 percent of institutional revenues (Snyder & Dillow, 2010). One way of thinking about the relationship of tuition income and investment income is that, as investment income increases, colleges can ease the increases they charge students for tuition and fees, but as investment income declines, tuition and fee charges increase.

Private, for-Profit Institutions.   Private, for-profit institutions are the most heavily tuition-driven colleges and universities. That is; they rely more on tuition and fee income than state-supported institutions and private, not-for-profit institutions. In some respects this can be explained by the fact that they do not receive state appropriations as do public institutions, and they receive very little income from investments when compared with private, not-for-profit institutions.

Four-year, for-profit institutions received 86.10 percent of their income from student tuition and fees in 1997–1998. By 2006–2007, this source of revenue represented 89.52 percent of their income. In constant 2007–2008 dollars, the amount grew from $12,280 per student in 1996–1997 to $13,590 in 2006–2007 (Snyder & Dillow, 2010, Table 357). These data indicate quite clearly the increasing dependence of these institutions on student tuition and fees as their primary source of income. While private institutions (for-profit or not-for-profit) are more dependent on student tuition and fee income than are state institutions, the fact is that even at state institutions, tuition and fee income has evolved into an increasingly important source of revenue.

How Students Pay for Their Education

Students use a variety of sources to pay for their postsecondary education, including savings, work, assistance from parents, and financial aid. The following discussion will identify the sources of support that students use to pay for their education. It will also look at the influence of how such factors as family income and work influence students' ability to pay for college.

Not all students attend college on a full-time basis. In fact, of the 15.6 million undergraduates enrolled in degree-granting institutions in 2007, over 9.8 million were enrolled full-time while over 5.7 million were enrolled part-time (Snyder & Dillow, 2010, Table 192). Attendance status will affect the number of types of financial aid a student can receive. Students who attend college on a part-time basis have very limited access to financial aid.

Price of Attendance.   Price or cost of attendance is defined this way: "The total price of attendance includes the tuition and fees as well as all other expenses related to enrollment: books and supplies; room and board (or housing and meal allowances for off-campus students); transportation; and other personal living expenses" (U.S. Department of Education, 2011, p. G6). The average cost of attendance for students ranges considerably, depending on the type of institution students attend. According to the U.S. Department of Education (Snyder & Dillow, 2010, Table 336), the range in the median institutional price of tuition and room and board has increased in constant dollars from 2000–2001 to 2008–2009 regardless of institution type. For public four-year institutions the increase has been from $8,468 to $13,911, and for private, not-for-profit institutions, the increase has been from $22,493 to $34,658. By 2010–2011, the published enrollment-weighted charges for in-state undergraduates were $16,140 at public, four-year colleges, and $36,933 for undergraduates at private, not-for-profit institutions (Baum & Ma, 2010, Table 1A).

However, when one reviews the price of attendance, it is important to remember that the range in what institutions charge is substantial, and that students have a wide variety of financial choices when they select their college. For example, the majority of full-time students attending four-year public institutions (64 percent) choose to attend institutions with a published tuition and fee charge of $6,000 to $11,999, according to the College Board (Baum & Ma, 2010, Figure 2). More students attended public colleges with a published cost of less than $6,000 than attended public institutions with a tuition and fee price of more than $12,000, so opportunities to attend relatively lower-cost institutions certainly are available (Baum & Ma, Figure 2).

As mentioned above, the published charges of four-year, private, not-for-profit institutions are greater than their public counterparts. Over 75 percent of students attending private, not-for-profit institutions in 2010–2011 attended institutions with a published cost of tuition of more than $21,000 (Baum & Ma, 2010, Figure 2). Of course, these charges do not include room and board and do not represent any reduction in the cost of attendance as a result of the student's receiving financial aid in the form of grants.

Financial Aid

Financial aid is a large, complex enterprise. For example, in 2009–2010, financial aid to undergraduates totaled $154.46 billion, and the largest single source of this aid took the form of federal loans, $65.8 billion or 43 percent of all undergraduate aid (Baum & Ma, 2010, Figure 2A). "During the 2008–2009 academic year, institutions reported that 79 percent of the 3.1 million full-time, first-time degree/certificate-seeking undergraduates attending Title IV institutions located in the United States received financial aid" (Knapp, Kelly-Reid, & Ginder, 2011, p. 4).

Financial aid primarily takes four forms: grants, loans, tax credits and deductions, and work-study. The next section of this chapter will provide an overview of these forms of financial aid, although work-study will be skipped since it provides just 1 percent of all financial aid. Over the 1999–2000 to 2009–2010 time period, grants and loans have been the most significant sources of financial aid. This time period began with grants being the most significant source of aid, but loans became more significant from 2004–2005 to 2008–2009. In 2009–2010 grants again became the largest course of aid, representing 50 percent of aid out of total aid from all sources plus nonfederal loans, while loans were 45 percent of the financial aid from these sources (Baum & Ma, 2010, Figure 8A).

Financial aid has increased over the time period 1994–1995 through 2009–2010. At the beginning of the time period the average grant aid per FTE was $3,278 and the average loan aid per FTE was $2,628. By the end of this time frame, the average grant aid per FTE was $6,041 and the average loan aid was $4,883 (Baum & Ma, 2010, Figure 11A). These data are reported in constant 2009 dollars.

Grants.   Grants, defined as financial aid that does not have to be repaid, are the most significant source of financial aid. Some grants are designed to assist students who demonstrate financial need, while others are awarded on the basis of merit, which could include special talents or skills possessed by the student that the institution wishes to reward in the form of a grant. In 2009–2010, grants totaled $94 billion (Baum & Ma, 2010, Figure 3). The federal government provided the largest proportion of grants (44 percent), followed by institutional grants (36 percent), private and employer grants (11 percent), and state governments (9 percent) (Baum & Ma, Figure 3). Tracking changes in the source of grant aid from 1999–2000 to 2009–2010, the primary change is the growth in the proportion of federal grants, from 29 percent in 1999–2000 to 44 percent in 2009–2010. "After adjusting for inflation, federal grant aid was more than three times greater in 2009–2010 than a decade earlier" (Baum & Payea, 2010, p. 12). As a proportion of grants, institutional grant aid fell from 44 percent in 1999–2010 to 36 percent in 2009–2010.

Looking at the time period from 1995–1996 through 2007–2008, African American students were more likely to receive grants than members of other racial and ethnic groups (U.S. Department of Education, 2011, Figure 2.1-B). In 1995–1996, 54.4 percent of African American students received grants, and by 2007–2008, 63.5 percent of African American students received grants. Asian Pacific Islander students were the least likely to receive grants: 35.9 percent in 1995–1996 and 43.8 percent in 2007–2008. However, Asian Pacific Islander students received the largest average grants, $4,200 in 1995–1996 and $6,200 in 2007–2008. The smallest average grants were received by Hispanic students in 1995–1996 ($2,400) and by Hispanic and American Indian students in 2007–2008 ($4,300). For students from all racial/ethnic groups, the percentage of students receiving grants and the average grants received grew from 1995–1996 through 2007–2008 (Figure 2.1-B). These data are reported in current dollars.

By institutional type, from 1995–1996 through 2007–2008, the largest proportion of students receiving grants attended private, not-for-profit institutions and these students received the largest average grants (U.S. Department of Education, 2011, Figure 2.1B). In 1995–1996, 61.6 percent of students attending private, not-for-profit institutions received grants, and the percentage grew to 73.6 percent by 2007–2008. The smallest percentage of students receiving grants attended public two-year colleges; these students also received the smallest amount of grant aid. In 1995–1996, 27.4 percent of these students received an average of $1,300 in grant aid, and by 2007–2008, 39.6 percent of students attending two-year public institutions received an average grant of $2,200. For all institutional types, the percentage of students receiving grants and the amount they received grew from 1995–1996 through 2007–2008 (Figure 2.1B). These data are not inflation-adjusted.

By income category, dependent students from the lowest family income group were most likely to receive grants (64.1 percent) in 1995–1996, and that was still the case by 2007–2008 (74.7 percent) (U.S. Department of Education, 2011, Figure 2.1.B). Dependent students from the highest income category were the least likely to receive grant aid, 20.6 percent in 1995–1996 and 36.8 percent in 2007–2008 (Figure 2.1.B). In 1995–1996, dependent students from the lowest family income category received the largest average grant, $3,700, but by 2007–2008 dependent students from the highest family income category received the largest average grant, $6,800. For all income categories, the percentage of dependent students receiving grant aid and the average amount they received increased from 1995–1996 through 2007–2008 (Figure 2.1B). All data are reported in current dollars.

Loans. Loans are the second most common form of financial aid. The federal government is the source of the largest proportion of loans. In 2009–

2010, for example, students borrowed $105.3 billion, 42 percent of which took the form of unsubsidized Stafford loans and 35 percent took the form of subsidized Stafford loans (Baum & Payea, 2010, Figure 4). Other loans included Parent (PLUS) loans (8 percent), graduate student PLUS loans (5 percent), Perkins and other loans (1 percent), and nonfederal loans (8 percent) (Baum & Payea, Figure 4). The biggest change in the mixture of loans is that in 1999–2000, the most common form of loans was subsidized Stafford loans (44 percent), followed by unsubsidized Stafford loans (33 percent) (Baum & Payea, Figure 4). "Subsidized loans are available only to students with documented financial need, and the government pays the interest on these loans while the student is in school. Unsubsidized Stafford Loans are available to all undergraduate and graduate students" (Baum & Payea, 2010, p. 15). "Unsubsidized Stafford loans are available to students regardless of financial need. The interest on an unsubsidized Stafford loan must be paid by the student (or added to the principal of the loan) while the student is still enrolled" (U.S. Department of Education, 2010, n.p.).

According to a College Board report (Baum & Payea, 2010, p. 15), 35 percent of undergraduate students received some form of a federal loan in 2009–2010, on average borrowing $6,550. This profile of borrowing compares with 23 percent of all undergraduates who received a federal loan in 1999–2000, who borrowed an average of $5,670 (in 2009 dollars). In 2004–2005, 28 percent of undergraduates received a federal loan and they borrowed an average of $5,560 in 2009 dollars.

Which students borrow money to pay for college and the amount they borrow appear to be related to family income. In 2008 42.1 percent of dependent students from the lowest income quartile (less than $36,149) on average borrowed $6,200 to pay their college expenses (U.S. Department of Education, 2011, Table 2.1C). About a third (33.1 percent) of students from the highest income quartile ($104,587 or more) borrowed on average $7,800 to pay their college expenses. These patterns of borrowing also were true for 1999–2000 and 2003–2004, i.e., a larger proportion of students from the most modest income group borrowed to pay for their college education, but they also borrowed the smallest amount of money. Conversely, the smallest proportion of students from families from the highest income group borrowed to pay for their college education, but those who received loans borrowed more than did those who borrowed from other income groups. It is worthy of note that the amount borrowed by those from the lowest income group grew from $4,200 to $6,200, but from the highest income group, the amount grew from $5,800 to $8,000 (U.S. Department of Education, 2011, Table 2.1C). These data are not adjusted for inflation.

From 1995–1996 through 2007–2008, African American students were more likely to borrow than were members of other racial or ethnic groups (U.S. Department of Education, 2011, Table 2.1C). In 1995–1996, the percentage of African American students who borrowed was 32.2 percent. The percentage grew to 49.5 percent in 2007–2008. The largest amount borrowed in 1995–1996 was $3,900 by white students and students who identified two or more races. African American and Hispanic students borrowed the least, on average $3,600. By 2007–2008, the largest amount borrowed was $7,200 by white students and students who identified two or more races. American Indians borrowed the least in 2007–2008, $5,800. Students who identified their race as Asian Pacific Islander were the least likely to borrow, 21.6 percent in 1995–1996 and 26.2 percent in 2007–2008 (Table 2.1C). Across all races the percentage of students grew, as did the amount borrowed. These data are reported in current dollars.

The Project on Student Debt (2010) added that not only has the percentage of graduates with loans increased, the amount of their debt has increased. For example, in 2004, students graduating with debt on average had borrowed $18,650; by 2008 the amount was $23,200. By institutional type, average debt for students at private, for-profit institutions was the greatest, increasing from $26,850 in 2004 to $33,050 in 2008. At public institutions the increase was from $16,850 to $20,200, and at private, not-for-profit institutions the increase was from $21,500 in 2004 to $27,650 in 2008.

Institutional Type and Financial Aid.   The type of institution in which students enroll has a relationship to the type of aid that students receive. For example, students enrolled in public two-year colleges in 2008 received a larger proportion of Pell grants than students enrolled in other types of institutions (Baum & Payea, 2010, Figure 7). The largest proportion of campus-based grants went to students enrolled in private, not-for-profit colleges. While students enrolled in for-profit institutions comprised 11 percent of undergraduate full-time equivalent enrollment, they received 25 percent of all Stafford subsidized loans and 28 percent of all unsubsidized Stafford loans (Baum & Payea, Figure 7).

Borrowing patterns across institutional types was consistent from 1995–1996 through 2007–2008 (U.S. Department of Education, 2011, Table 2.1-C). In 1995–1996, students who attended for-profit private institutions.were the most likely to borrow (61.3 percent) and in 2007–2008, 91.6 percent of these students borrowed. Students who attended private, not-for-profit institutions borrowed the most money: In 1995–1996, those who borrowed took out an average of $4,300 and by 2007–2008 an average of $9,100 (Table 2.1-C). Students who enrolled in two-year public colleges were the least likely to borrow and those who borrowed received the least amount of loan support. Over this time period (1995–1996 through 2007–2008), regardless of institutional type, a larger percentage of students borrowed, and those who borrowed received increasingly larger loans (Table 2.1-C). These data are not adjusted for inflation.

Education Tax Credits and Tuition Deductions.   Ninety percent of education tax credits go to taxpayers with an Adjusted Gross Income (AGI) of between $25,000 and $100,000. The amount of the tax credit ranged from $455 for those with an AGI of $25,000 or less to $858 for those with AGIs of $100,000 to $160,000. The total amount of this form of financial aid was $5.3 billion in 2008 (Baum & Payea, 2010, Figure 12A). Tuition Tax Deductions, however, are used more commonly by higher income earners. In 2008, 67 percent of these deductions were used by those with AGIs of $100,000 to $160,000. For those earning less than $25,000 the deduction was $226, while for those with an AGI of $100,000 to $160,000, the deduction was $606. The total amount of this form of aid was $1.4 billion (Figure 12A).

Out-of-Pocket Price.   Out-of-pocket price is defined as representing "the estimated 'out-of-pocket' expense to students remaining after all financial aid, including loans, is received. For students who did not receive any financial aid, this amount is the same as the price of attendance" (U.S. Department of Education, 2011, p. G5). For full-time, full-year students this amount has increased from $7,600 in 1994–1995 to $12,000 in 2007–2008 (U.S. Department of Education, 2011, Table 3.2). By institutional type, students with the lowest out-of-pocket price attended two-year public colleges, paying $9,100 in 2007–2008, compared with $5,600 in 1995–1996. Private, not-for-profit four-year colleges had the highest out-of-pocket price. In 1995–1996, the out-of-pocket price was $10,600 and by 2007–2008 it grew to $16,600 in current dollars.

Average Net Price.   One last measure of the price of attendance to consider is the average net price paid by students. Average net price is defined as "the net price of attendance after all grants" (U.S. Department of Education, 2011, p. G5). For full-time, full-year undergraduates, the average net price has grown from $10,100 in 1994–1995 to $17,600 in 2007–2008 (U.S. Department of Education, 2011, Figure 3.1). Two-year public colleges were the least expensive, where the average net price was $6,200 in 1994–1995 and $10,600 in 2007–2008. Four-year private, not-for-profit institutions were the most expensive, with an average net price of $12,800 in 1994–1995. Private, for-profit institutions were the most expensive in terms of average net price at $25,800 in 2007–2008 (U.S. Department of Education, 2011, Figure 3.1) in current dollars.

Influence of Price Increases on Student Attendance.   The financial environment described to this point does not report what happens to certain groups of students when the price of attendance changes. When the price of attendance increases, students from various income groups are affected in different ways. Heller (1997) observed that students from lower-income families are more sensitive to changes in tuition and financial aid than students who come from middle-income or upper-income families.

African American students are more sensitive to price changes than Caucasian students. Heller also reported that the evidence is more mixed for Hispanic students. He observed that as the federal government has shifted its financial aid policy from grants to loans, the higher education community increasingly has been concerned about the impact of this change on access.

Paulsen and St. John (2002) found similar results in their study of social class and college choice. They concluded the following: "low-income and lower-middle-income students are far more responsive to prices than students from upper-middle and upper-income families" (p. 228). They added, "The high-tuition, high-loan environment is clearly problematic for poor and working-class students. For such students, the cost of tuition, net of available aid, is clearly not affordable" (p. 230). In some cases, such students are particularly at risk in terms of defaulting on their loans.

Current data support these conclusions. For example, according to The Project on Student Debt (2010), "In 2008, 67 percent of students graduating from four-year colleges and universities had student loan debt. That represents 1.4 million students graduating with debt, up 27 percent from 1.1 million students in 2004. In 2008: 62 percent of graduates from *public* universities had student loans; 72 percent of graduates from *private nonprofit* universities had student loans; and 96 percent of graduates from *private for-profit* universities had student loans (a major increase from 2004, when 85 percent of these graduates had student loans)" (n.p.).

The risk of defaulting appears to be especially high for students who attend private, for-profit colleges. The Project on Student Debt observed the following about loan default:

> New data released late today by the U.S. Department of Education show 13.8 percent of student loan borrowers defaulting on their loans within three years of entering repayment. The cohort default rate (CDR) at for-profit colleges was highest at 25.0 percent, nearly double the national average. At private non-profit schools the rate was 7.6 percent, and at public schools it was 10.8 percent. The new "three-year CDR" data reveal that about 467,000 students who entered repayment in 2008 had defaulted by 2010. Nearly half (48 percent) of defaulters attended for-profit colleges, which enroll about one in 10 students and receive one in four federal student aid dollars. (2011, n.p.)

Factors that Contribute to Loan Default. Flint (1997) examined a number of variables to determine their influence on the repayment of student loans. He found that the potential for default was increased by three characteristics: being male, being black, and each year of age beyond twenty-one. Higher grade point averages were associated with avoiding default. Finally, two characteristics after college were associated with default: lower disposable income and greater incongruence between undergraduate major and current employment.

Volkwein, Szelest, Cabrera, and Napierski-Pranci (1998) also examined factors related to loan default. Their analysis resulted in several conclusions. First, they found that default rates are based more on the nature of borrowers and their achievements than the types of institutions they attended. Second, such factors as having a parent who attended college, completing a degree, being married, and not having dependent children are factors associated with reduced default rates for all those included in their study, and these factors were even more powerful on the African-Americans included in the study. Third, regardless of racial or ethnic group, Volkwein et al. concluded that borrowers who have similar earned degrees, marital status, and family income exhibit almost identical records of earned income and loan repayment.

Students Who Work. The financial category of financial support for students in this discussion is student work, be it on campus or off campus, while they are enrolled in college. The percentage of full-time students who worked while attending college grew from 34 percent in 1970 to 52 percent in 2000 and has leveled off to about 45 percent in 2008 (Aud, Hussar, Planty, Snyder, Bianco, Fox, Frohlich, Kemp, & Drake, 2010, Indicator 45). Most commonly, students worked 20–34 hours per week. Those enrolled in public, two-year colleges were the most likely to work (52.9 percent in 2008) while those attending private, four-year institutions were less likely to work (38 percent in 2008), virtually the same percentage for students attending private four-year institutions in 1990, when 38.1 percent of such students worked. Part-time students most commonly worked (79.4 percent in 2008), most often thirty-five or more hours per week (44.4 percent). Often these persons are considered workers who study as opposed to students who work.

Undergraduate female students were more likely to work than undergraduate men (48.7 percent compared with 41.6 percent). White undergraduate students (49.1 percent) were more likely to work than members of other racial or ethnic groups. Asian Pacific Islanders were the least likely to work (28.9 percent) in 2008 (Aud, Hussar, Planty, Snyder, Bianco, Fox, Frohlich, Kemp, & Drake, 2010, Indicator 45).

Another U S. Department of Education Report (1998) examined some of the effects of working on students. Thirty percent of the students included in this study reported that working limited their number of classes, 40 percent indicated that working limited their class schedule, 26 percent reported that working limited their access to the library, and 36 percent indicated that working reduced their class choices (p. 8). The greater the number of hours students worked, the more restricted their schedules and choices were. Did working affect academic performance negatively? Thirty-seven percent reported that it did, while 15 percent indicated that working had a positive effect on their performance. The balance (48 percent) reported that working had no effect on their performance (p. 9).

Summary

The first section of this chapter has tracked important, selected trends in financing higher education related to students. The data clearly demonstrate that institutions increasingly are relying on tuition and fee income as sources of financial support. In turn, an increasing percentage of students are relying on financial aid to finance their education. Financial aid, to a great extent, takes the form of loans to students. Longitudinal data illustrate that a greater percentage of students are participating in loan programs, and those who are participating in such programs are borrowing an increasingly greater amount, leaving them with increasingly larger debt upon graduation.

INSTITUTIONAL COSTS OF NON-PERSISTENCE

To this point, this chapter has examined the increasing cost of attendance for students. These costs can be substantial, ranging from the expenses associated with attending college but not graduating, to an inability to repay college debt and a potential lifetime of lower income for those who do not complete a baccalaureate degree. There are also negative financial implications for institutions when students do not persist to graduation. The balance of this chapter will present a conceptual framework that illustrates institutional costs associated with students not persisting to graduation. This framework has three elements:

- Immediate direct institutional costs;
- Immediate indirect institutional costs; and
- Long-term institutional costs after students leave their institution.

Each of these will be discussed in detail in this chapter.

Immediate Direct Costs

Institutions have a number of direct costs when students fail to graduate. Four of these are identified in this section of this chapter and they reflect the investment that is made in students who do not persist as well as income that is not realized when students leave their college before graduating.
Student Recruitment. Institutions spend substantial resources to recruit students, whether they are highly selective or have an open admissions policy. In a poll conducted by Noel-Levitz (2009), the median cost of recruiting a student at a four-year private college was $2,143 and the median cost of a recruiting a student at a four-year public college was $461. Using these figures, if students attending Private College X persist to graduation

and, on average, finish in four years, the recruitment cost per student per year is reduced to approximately $500 per year; for a student at Public University Y, the cost per student per year is reduced to less than $120 per year. To replace each student who drops out, Private College X must spend an additional $2,000, and Public University Y must spend an additional $460.

Suppose that the persistence rate at both institutions is 80 percent. If the entering first-year class at Private College X consists of four hundred students, an 80 percent persistence rate means that eighty students will leave after the first year. If the entering first-year class at Public University Y is four thousand, an 80 percent persistence rate means that eight hundred students will leave. In gross terms, Private College X will have spent $160,000 on the recruitment of these eighty students and Public University Y will have spent $320,000 on recruitment, but each institution will have received only one year's worth of income from them. The net revenue loss is substantial.

Granted, there are colleges and universities that must limit their enrollment and may have lists of students waiting for the chance to enroll when a student withdraws. These institutions may not need to expend additional resources to recruit students. However, the majority of institutions must expend additional dollars to recruit additional students. So, in purely economic terms, institutions are far better served when their students persist to graduation.

Financial Aid.   The costs to institutions are far more than just the costs associated with recruitment. Institutions also invest money into financial aid programs to assist in recruiting and retaining students. Whether this is a discount on the amount of tuition students pay or actual dollars given to students to help them defray their costs, this money is given to students and does not need to be repaid.

Although financial aid increases the likelihood that a student will persist, it does not provide a guarantee that the student will persist. Let's return to our example. If half of the students at Private College X receive some form of college-based aid, and the average award is $5,000, then an investment of $200,000 has been lost if forty students do not persist to their sophomore year. If half of the students receive some form of college-based aid at Public University Y and the average award is $1,000, then an investment of $400,000 has been lost if four hundred students do not persist.

This college-based aid could have been invested in other students who attended the college, offered to students who were leaving because of financial difficulty, or used to provide an incentive to other students who were recruited by the college but did not attend because financial aid was not available to them (because it was awarded to students who did not persist). The point is that institutionally based aid that is invested in students who do not persist is an investment lost. It can be used in succeeding years to attract and retain students, but the aid invested in students who leave the institution cannot be recovered.

Lost Tuition Income.   One of the obvious financial implications of students not persisting is that after students drop out, they will not pay tuition and fees. The average cost of tuition and fees is approximately $27,000, whereas the average cost of tuition and fees for an in-state student at a public institution is approximately $7,600 (Baum & Ma, 2010). If eighty out of the four hundred (using an 80 percent retention rate) drop out of Private University X, then the gross amount of tuition lost for the second year is $2,160,000 less any institutionally provided merit aid. We estimated that $200,000 of institutional merit aid was invested in the students who did not return for their second year, so the net tuition loss was $1,960,000. If eight hundred out of the four thousand students drop out of Public University Y, the gross amount of tuition lost is $6,080,000 minus $400,000 in institutional aid, resulting in a net tuition loss of $5,680,000. Unless the college can replace the students who leave with transfer students, this income stream is lost. Add in the junior and senior years, and the total income lost at Private College X is $5,880,000 and $17,040,000 at Public University Y. So it certainly is in the institutions' interest to retain as many students as possible.

Other Lost Income.   Tuition is not the only loss of income to an institution. Let's assume that housing and dining costs at both Private College X and Public University Y is roughly $8,000. Private College X is a residential institution, where more than 95 percent of the student body lives on campus for all four years of their education. So when students leave, payments to the institution for other services also cease. If Private College X charges $8,000 per year for room and board and 95 percent of the eighty students who left lived in campus housing, the amount of gross revenue lost in one year is $608,000. Multiply the $608,000 in lost income by the three years that the students would have lived in the residence halls, had they attended until graduation, and gross revenues lost to the residence system, unadjusted for cost increases, would be $1,824,000. A similar cost can be calculated for Public University Y by factoring in the percentage of first-year students who typically live in residence halls and the number of years they stay.

In addition to tuition, housing, and dining, students pay for a variety of other services such as bookstore purchases, entertainment, special services such as tutoring, and/or money spent by family and friends who come to campus. Those who drop out do not purchase these goods and services, and consequently the institution does not realize additional income.

Admittedly, these measures are crude and are only rough approximations of the costs to an institution if students leave and are not replaced. This example does, however, underscore how dramatic the costs can be if students leave their institution. Some institutions have higher persistence rates than 80 percent, but many more have lower persistence rates. As persistence rates fluctuate, the financial implications are more or less dramatic, depending how much revenue is foregone. In any event, each student who leaves can represent substantial income lost to an institution of higher education.

It is unreasonable to expect that an institution will have a 100 percent retention rate, and many institutions would be challenged to attain a 90 percent retention rate. Nevertheless, even a 2 percent increase in retention can have dramatic financial benefits. An 82 percent (versus 80 percent) increase at Private College X means that eight fewer students have left the institution, which is an additional $750,000 if students persist to graduation. Increasing retention by 2 percent at Public University Y results in eighty more students being retained which—even using conservative estimates—could generate more than $2.5 million if students persist to graduation. Although the number of students may not seem significant, applying the tuition and room and board fees generated by these additional students over three years is substantial.

Immediate Indirect Institutional Costs

In addition to the direct costs to institutions of students not persisting, there are some indirect institutional costs, particularly if one considers the value of the time that faculty and staff devote to students.

Faculty and Staff Salaries.   One of the largest outlays of expenditures in higher education is personnel. Institutions hire faculty and staff based upon the anticipated needs of the institution. Individuals are given a salary based upon their qualifications and experience—their salary does not fluctuate based on the number of individuals served. If a faculty member is hired to teach three sections of twenty students each and only forty students enroll, the faculty member receives the same compensation. Staff salaries are set at least a year in advance and, except in extreme circumstances, are not adjusted if students leave mid-year. Academic advisors, counselors, and career placement staff are all hired to assist students in developing and meeting their academic goals. Their salaries are set at least a year in advance and require a commitment of funds from the university. Except in extreme cases, salaries are not adjusted, even if students leave during the year. We are not advocating this practice, but simply pointing out that it can be costly and highly inefficient when personnel are not fully utilized.

Facilities.   The maintenance and upkeep of campus facilities also are costly. As mentioned earlier, some items such as water use and trash collection may decrease slightly if fewer students are on campus, but many expenditures do not. The library, health center, and recreation facilities will remain open roughly the same hours even if retention drops 20 percent.

Heating and cooling costs for a classroom building are about the same if the classroom is being utilized for five classes of one hundred students or two classes of twenty students. Similar to staff salary expenditures, institutions are inefficient when facilities are being underutilized.

Long-Term Potential Institutional Costs

One other category of institutional costs is worthy of note. This has to do with a set of outcomes that are difficult to predict or quantify, but certainly have the potential to be harmful to institutions when students do not persist. While one may be able to point to some anomalies, typically institutional benefactors do not emerge from those who do not achieve their educational goals. There may be some notable exceptions, but in the main, graduates are more likely to serve as benefactors of their institutions than those who drop out. Those who do not persist are unlikely to donate time or money to their former institution in the future.

Those who do not persist also may be less inclined to recommend to others that they should attend their former institutions. Siblings, children, friends, or others may be the recipients of such advice. Whether it is persuasive or not is beside the point. Non-persisters are less likely to be "friends" of their institution than those who graduate. In short, if the old adage "you can never have too many friends" has any validity, then those who do not persist represent individuals who have less potential for being a friend to their institution than those who graduate.

CONCLUSION

This chapter has examined such issues as how students finance their education, the financial implications faced by students who do not persist, and the costs to institutions when students do not persist. The point is that in addition to the losses of talent development and human capital that arise from students who do not persist, the financial implications of students who do not persist are noteworthy. The effect is negative for both the students and their former colleges.

REFERENCES

Aud, S., Hussar, W., Planty, M., Snyder, T., Bianco, K., Fox, M., Frohlich, L., Kemp, J., Drake, L. (2010). The Condition of Education 2010 (NCES 2010-028). National Center for Education Statistics, Institute of Education Sciences, U.S. Department of Education. Washington, DC.

Baum, S., & Ma, J. (2010). *Trends in college pricing 2010*. Washington, DC: The College Board.

Baum, S., & Payea, K. (2010). *Trends in student aid*. Washington, DC: The College Board.

Bureau of Labor Statistics. (2011, February 4). Table A-4. Employment status of the civilian population 25 years and over by educational attainment. Washington, DC: Author.

Flint, T. A. (1997). Predicting student loan defaults. *Journal of Higher Education, 68*, 322–354.

Heller, D. E. (1997). Student price response in higher education. *Journal of Higher Education, 68*, 624–660.

Knapp L. G., Kelly-Reid, J. E., & Ginder, S. A. (2011). *Enrollment in postsecondary institutions, fall 2009; graduation rates, 2003 & 2006 cohorts; and financial statistics, fiscal year 2009*. (NCES 2011-230). U.S. Department of Education. Washington, DC: National Center for Education Statistics.

Noel-Levitz. (2009). 2009 Cost of recruiting report: Comparative benchmarks for two-year and four-year institutions. Retrieved April 21, 2011 from www.noellevitz.com/documents/shared/Papers_and_Research/2009/CostofRecruiting Report09.pdf.

Paulsen, M. B., & St. John, E. P. (2002). Social class and college costs. *Journal of Higher Education, 73*, 189–236.

Snyder, T. D., & Dillow, S. A. (2010). *Digest of education statistics 2009* (NCES 2010-013). National Center for Education Statistics, Institute of Education Sciences, U.S. Department of Education. Washington, DC.

The Project on Student Debt. (2010, January). *Quick facts about student debt*. Oakland, CA: The Institute for College Access & Success.

The Project on Student Debt. (2011, February). *For-profit college student loan default rates soar*. Oakland, CA: The Institute for College Access & Success.

U.S. Department of Education. (1998). *Undergraduates who work*. NCES 98-137. Washington, DC: National Center for Education Statistics.

U.S. Department of Education. (2003). *Digest of education statistics, 2002*. NCES 2003-060. Washington, DC: National Center for Education Statistics.

U.S. Department of Education. (2010). *Trends in Undergraduate Stafford Loan borrowing*. NCES 2010-183. Washington, DC: Author.

U.S. Department of Education. (2011). *Trends in financing of undergraduate education: Selected years: 1995-1996–2007-2008*. (NCES 2011-218). Washington, DC: Author.

Volkwein, J. F., Szelest, B. P., Cabrera, A. F., & Napierski-Prancl, M. R. (1998). Factors associated with student loan default among different racial and ethnic groups. *Journal of Higher Education, 69*, 206–238.

6

Pre-College and Institutional Influences on Degree Attainment

Alexander W. Astin and Leticia Oseguera

Degree completion is one of the few student outcomes in higher education in which virtually all constituencies have a stake. Most students and parents, for example, view attainment of the degree as an essential step in realizing the student's career aspirations. Parents, in addition, have an economic stake in the student's ability to complete the degree in a timely fashion. Institutional faculty and staff view the retention and graduation of each student as a sign that their efforts have been successful, while legislators and policymakers are inclined to see an institution's degree completion rate as an indicator of its "performance."

From any of these perspectives, empirical studies of college student retention have at least two very practical applications: *prediction* and *control*. When we speak of predicting a dichotomous outcome such as degree completion (versus non-completion), what we really have in mind is our capacity to *estimate* the student's chances of completing a degree within a specified period of time: "What are the odds that this student will complete a bachelor's degree within six years after entering?" Such information is obviously of potential value to college officials who are responsible either for admitting students or for designing special programs for "high-risk" students. The issue of "control" refers to our capacity to *enhance* students' chances of completing a degree: "What types of college, or what particular conditions of attendance, offer this student the best chances of completing the degree?" Such information is of obvious value not only to prospective students, but also to college officials or policymakers who wish to improve degree completion rates.

The principal purpose of this chapter is to assess what recent empirical studies of degree completion can tell us about the prediction and control of undergraduate degree completion. We shall focus on three types of information that can be useful in estimating any student's chances of completing college: (1) pre-college characteristics of the student; (2) the characteristics of the college that the student attends; and (3) environmental "contingencies" of attendance (e.g., whether the student lives at home or on campus, financial aid, work status, and so on). To insure that our conclusions have wide generality, we shall rely primarily on multi-campus studies involving diverse samples of baccalaureate-granting institutions rather than studies conducted at single institutions. And while the bulk of the chapter will focus on findings from a recent large-scale national longitudinal study (Astin & Oseguera, 2005), we shall first present a brief overview of other recent studies of degree completion.

PREVIOUS RESEARCH

A substantial portion of the empirical research on undergraduate degree completion during the past thirty years has focused on the development and testing of theoretical models for explaining degree attainment (Braxton, Sullivan, & Johnson, 1997). These range from status attainment models (Sewell, Haller, & Ohlendorf, 1970), in which researchers examine the role of ascribed status in the degree attainment process, to holistic models (Tinto, 1987), whereby researchers examine pre-college attributes and within-college experiences that might explain degree attainment, to comprehensive models integrating multiple theoretical frameworks for explaining variations in success among different groups (Cabrera, Castaneda, Nora, & Hengstler, 1992; Cabrera, Nora & Castaneda, 1993). Given our emphasis on prediction and control, this brief review will necessarily be circumscribed to focus on the three categories of predictors noted above: (1) individual characteristics (including prior experiences) of the entering college student; (2) institutional characteristics; and (3) environmental contingencies (place of residence, etc.).

Pre-College Characteristics

Researchers have repeatedly found that students' chances of degree attainment are to a substantial degree a function of their own individual backgrounds (Astin, 1991, 1993a, 1996; Carter, 2001; Pascarella & Terenzini, 1991, 2005; Tinto, 1993). These variables include school grades, gender, ethnicity, parental income and education, standardized test scores, and age. Although the predictive power of traditional admissions criteria varies somewhat from study to study, standardized test scores and high school grades have consistently been shown to be among the strongest predictors of degree attainment among undergraduates (Adelman, 2006; Astin, 1993b; Astin, Tsui, & Avalos, 1996; Astin & Oseguera, 2003, 2005; Attewell, Heil, & Reisel, 2011; Pascarella, Smart, & Ethington, 1986; Stoecker, Pascarella, & Wolfe, 1988). There is some evidence to suggest, however, that standardized test scores may not be as predictive of degree completion as originally posited, especially for students of color (Fleming, 2002). Fleming and Garcia (1998) reviewed twelve studies of predictive validity and showed that test scores and grades differed in their ability to predict retention among non-white students. Over the last thirteen years, Fleming and Garcia have concluded that SAT scores and high school grades are consistent predictors of degree completion for white students but that their predictive power for black students is inconsistent.

Both parental education and parental income have been shown to affect college completion directly and indirectly (Astin, 1993b; Astin & Oseguera, 2005; Attewell, Heil, & Reisel, 2011; Mow & Nettles, 1990; Oseguera, 2006). The student's initial aspirations and goals have also been shown to be significant predictors of college completion (Astin, 1975; Bean, 1982; Pascarella, Smart, Ethington, & Nettles, 1987). Generally, the higher the level of one's educational or occupational aspirations, the greater the likelihood of college completion.

Studies also provide some support to suggest that social integration is useful in examining degree completion. Allen and Nelson's (1989) and Cabrera, Nora, and Castaneda's (1992) single-institution studies both reported that a student's level of social integration is significantly and positively related to eventual degree completion. This finding was also confirmed in multi-institutional studies which defined social integration in terms of measures such as peer relations, participation in extracurricular activities and student clubs, participation in student government, and satisfaction with social life (Astin, 1993b; Braxton, Vesper, & Hossler, 1995; House, 1996; Munro, 1981). With respect to gender differences, Stage (1988) found that social integration, as measured by peer group relations, residency, and hours spent engaged in social activities and intercollegiate athletics, was more influential in degree completion among men than among women.

In separate, national studies of degree completion using Cooperative Institutional Research Program (CIRP) data, degree completion was found to be enhanced by expecting to join a fraternity/sorority, participating in volunteer/community service, being elected to student office, maintaining a social activist agenda (i.e., desire to be a community leader, desire to influence social values) and participating in student groups. However, the student's chances of persisting toward a degree were negatively affected by engaging in hedonistic activities (i.e., smoking cigarettes, drinking beer, partying) and socializing with friends (Astin, 1984; Dey & Astin, 1989; Astin & Oseguera, 2005).

In a national study of college students using CIRP data, Dey and Astin (1989) found that commitment to goals such as raising a family and influencing social values were positive predictors of degree completion. Wanting to write original works, expecting to develop a meaningful philosophy of life, and wanting to get involved in programs to clean up the environment were negative predictors. In another multi-campus study of college freshmen, Astin and Oseguera (2005) found that self-ratings of academic ability, drive to achieve, and intellectual self-confidence are positively predictive of degree completion.

Institutional Characteristics

This literature is necessarily limited to multi-institutional studies. Several researchers have found that institutional control, size, costs, and selectivity affect a variety of educational outcomes, including degree attainment (Astin, 1993b; McClelland, 1990; Smith, 1990). The available research on institutional control (public vs. private) is not entirely consistent, but it does suggest that attending a private rather than a public college or university has a net positive influence on bachelor's degree attainment, even after controlling for pre-college characteristics (Anderson, 1984; Astin, 1977; McCormick & Horn, 1996). In a national longitudinal study of undergraduates, Astin and Oseguera (2005) and Oseguera (2006) confirmed an earlier national study by Astin, Tsui, and Avalos (1996) that found that small institutional size, private control, and selectivity all have positive effects on degree completion. Positive effects of selectivity have also been reported by Adelman (2006).

In a later study Astin (1993b) found that degree completion was positively affected by the percentage of resources invested in student services, the percentage of graduate students in the student body, the percentage of Catholics in the student body, and the percentage of students majoring in physical sciences, and negatively affected by institutional size. Also, as reported in earlier studies (Astin, 1977, 1982), the percentage of men enrolled in the student body had a negative effect on degree attainment. All of these institutional effects are net of entering student characteristics.

Using multi-institutional data from the CIRP's annual survey of entering freshmen, the Higher Education Research Institute's (HERI) Faculty Surveys, campus registrars' offices, and Integrated Postsecondary Education Data System (IPEDS) data, Oseguera and Rhee (2009) evaluated the extent to which peer institutional retention climates and faculty-perceived campus climates influenced individual six-year retention rates and found that institutional retention climate, as defined by a student body's aggregated report of withdrawal intentions, did independently determine whether a student would persist or not. Other recent studies have shown that diverse dimensions of institutional context such as campus racial climates, peer cultures, and faculty normative environments may also be involved in students' departure decisions (Berger 2000, 2001–2002; Titus, 2004, 2006a,b).

Attending institutions with a large percentage of student commuters negatively influences both four- and six-year degree completion (Astin, 1993b; Oseguera, 2006). In all likelihood, having a lot of commuting students detracts from the institution's ability to create a climate that encourages student engagement with campus resources, facilities, and personnel.

Student retention is also enhanced in institutions that have relatively large expenditures on instruction and academic support services and a lower student faculty ratio and thus more faculty involvement (Oseguera, 2006; Pascarella, 1980; Titus, 2006a).

Environmental "Contingencies"

The environmental contingency that has been most consistently related to undergraduate degree completion is the student's place of residence (Astin, 1975, 1977, 1993b; Astin & Henson, 1977; Chickering, 1974; Pascarella & Terenzini, 1991, 2005; Schudde, 2011). Specifically, living in a campus residence hall, when compared to living at home, has been shown to enhance students' prospects of completing a degree program. Living off campus in an apartment or private home has been associated with mixed results.

Evidence on the effect of the entering student's preferred academic major tends to be mixed because, according to Hearn (1987), the study of academic majors is "complex and multidimensional." Nevertheless, college major has been shown to influence degree completion (Hartnett & Centra, 1977; Astin & Oseguera, 2005; Oseguera, 2006). Specifically, students in engineering and the hard sciences are less likely to attain a baccalaureate degree within four years (Astin, 1975, 1993b; Oseguera, 2006), while students in the social sciences have the highest rates of degree completion (Mow & Nettles, 1990; Pascarella, Ethington, & Smart, 1988).

Financial concerns are commonly cited in the research literature as important reasons students give for their departure from college. In a meta-analysis of thirty-one studies of the effect of financial aid on college persistence, Murdock (1987) showed that family influences play a small, yet significant influence on college persistence. Murdock reported that students from lower socioeconomic groups consistently report that financial burdens influence the decision to withdraw from college. Additionally, among the non-completers, Murdock reported that concerns about financing college was often cited as a greater influence by students who dropped out early in their degree programs compared to students who dropped out at the later stages of their degree programs. These findings were later confirmed by Cabrera, Stampen, and Hansen (1990). Some research, however, suggests that there are trivial or no significant effects of financing college on eventual degree completion (Stampen & Cabrera, 1986).

Working full time clearly appears to impede persistence among traditional age students (Astin, 1975; Anderson, 1981). Part-time work, however, does not appear to produce similarly negative effects, and employment on campus can positively influence degree completion (Anderson, 1981; Astin & Oseguera, 2003, 2005; Oseguera, 2006). Related factors that have been posited to influence degree completion are students' commitments that are external to the institution (Tinto, 1993). Having responsibilities off-campus and having outside family commitments, for example, have been shown to negatively influence degree attainment of undergraduates (Tinto, 1993; Astin & Oseguera, 2005).

There is another class of environmental contingencies that we might call "post-entry" contingencies that cannot be used in computing pre-college estimates of the student's chances of completing the degree because there is no way to assess them at the time the student first enters college. However, since these post-entry contingencies are often included in retention models and have been shown to have substantial relationships with degree completion, we shall briefly review some of the recent research that utilizes them.

Past research has demonstrated, for example, that academic achievement during college powerfully influences degree attainment (Astin, 1975, 1993; Carter, 2001; Tinto, 1987, 1993b; Titus, 2004). (In the current study, pre-college *expectations* for academic success can be viewed as a kind of "proxy" for actual college achievement.) Other post-entry contingencies that positively affect degree completion include involvement and interactions with faculty and peers (Gurin & Epps, 1975; Stoecker, Pascarella, & Wolfe, 1988; Astin, 1993) as well as involvement in extracurricular activities (Pascarella & Chapman, 1983; Waldo, 1986). Involvement in either the academic and social aspects of college has also been shown to positively influence degree attainment of undergraduates (Grosset, 1991; Tinto, 1993). In sum, the past twenty years of research on undergraduates suggests that the most potent forms of positive involvement are with academics, faculty, and peers, and that degree completion, in particular, is negatively affected by noninvolvement (Astin, 1977, 1984, 1993b; Pascarella & Terenzini, 1991, 2005; Tinto, 1993).

METHOD

The data for this study were drawn from a national sample of baccalaureate-granting institutions that participated in the Cooperative Institutional

Research Program's annual survey of entering freshmen in the fall of 1994 (Astin, Korn, Sax, & Mahoney, 1994). Four-year and six-year degree attainment data were obtained in the summer of 2000 by sending to the registrar at each institution rosters containing names of randomly selected entering freshmen who had completed the 1994 survey. A total of 90,619 students (average of about 210 per institution) were selected at random from each of 424 institutions in the original national sample. In order to obtain more reliable results by race, all Mexican American/Chicana/o, Puerto Rican, Asian American, and American Indian students, as well as 50 percent of all African American students who had participated in the original 1994 survey, were included.

Degree attainment data were eventually received on 56,818 cases at 262 institutions. Since data were obtained on virtually 100 percent of the students at each of the institutions that responded to our request, any "non-response" bias would be entirely attributable to institutions (rather than students) that did not comply with the request for data. However, a careful comparison of curricular, financial, and other institutional data between responding (N= 262) and non-responding (N= 162) institutions within stratification cells failed to reveal any institutional self-selection bias within stratification cells (as already noted, the CIRP sample is stratified by type, control, race, and selectivity level; see below as well as Astin, Korn, Sax, & Mahoney, 1994).

The data for this study have been weighted. The CIRP weighting scheme is designed to allow us to approximate the results that would have been obtained if all students from all baccalaureate-granting institutions had participated in both the 1994 entering freshman and 2000 registrars' follow-up surveys. This weighting scheme initially inflates the number of respondents within each institution to the total first-time, full-time freshman enrollment by gender, then compensates for differential sampling of institutions within stratification cells. The CIRP stratification scheme compensates for any institutional sampling bias associated with institutional type (four-year vs. university), control (public, private-nonsectarian, Roman Catholic, Other Christian), race (historically black versus nonblack), and selectivity level (institutions are stratified by selectivity separately within type and control; see Astin, Korn, Sax, & Mahoney, 1994). Differential weights were also used to compensate for the oversampling of certain minority groups (see above). All data reported here are weighted to approximate the national norms for all first-time, full-time entering freshmen in the fall of 1994.

The Higher Education Research Institute collects extensive pre-college data on the characteristics of full-time, first-time entering freshmen, including demographic and biographical information, high school grade point averages, standardized test scores, degree and career aspirations, self-concept, attitudes, values, and expectations for college. Characteristics of the student's institution that are also collected include size, control, selectivity, region, and type of institution. Environmental contingency data from the CIRP entering freshman survey include the student's place of residence (campus residence hall, private room, with parents), choice of major, and type and amount of financial aid.

For the current analyses we included measures of all pre-college characteristics, institutional characteristics, and environmental contingencies that the persistence literature has identified as potentially having an effect on the baccalaureate degree completion of college students. For a complete list of the variables included in the analyses, see Appendix A.

DATA ANALYSIS

A series of weighted descriptive analyses were run to examine degree attainment differences by institutional type, gender, and academic achievement. To more thoroughly explore the potential value of each variable in estimating the student's chances of completing the baccalaureate degree, we employed a series of stepwise linear regression analyses. The dichotomous dependent variables used in the analyses were either a) degree completion within four years, or b) degree completion within six years. Our dependent variables were selected based on earlier research (Astin, Tsui, & Avalos, 1996) suggesting that time-to-degree is prolonged among certain student subgroups and at certain institutional types. Thus, it is important to identify factors that contribute to degree completion within the traditional four-year time frame, as well as factors that contribute to this "delayed" degree completion.

Although logistic regression analysis is often recommended over OLS regression in the study of dichotomous outcomes, extensive empirical comparisons of the two methods using CIRP data show that they yield essentially identical results (Dey & Astin, 1993; Oseguera & Vogelgesang, 2003). Accordingly, we chose to use OLS regression because the SPSS program includes important options (e.g. "Beta in" for variables not in the equation) not available in the Stata logistic regression program.

In each regression analysis the independent variables were organized into three blocks according to their presumed temporal order of occurrence: (1) pre-college entering student characteristics; (2) environmental contingencies; and (3) institutional characteristics. Within each block, variables were entered in forward stepwise fashion until no additional variable within that block was capable of producing a reduction in the residual sum of squares exceeding $p = 0.0001$. Given the large number of independent variables, the p value was set at this extreme level to minimize Type I errors. And, given the large N available for each regression (56,818), Type II errors were also minimized.

A final set of regressions was run to provide a means of comparing variables that predicted degree completion within four and six years. The procedure was as follows. Separate regressions were first run for each of the two dependent variables, as described above. Then, the two regressions were rerun with the following modification: all independent variables that entered *either* of the first set of regressions were force entered into both regressions. In this way, both regressions contained exactly the same set of independent variables.

RESULTS

The results are presented in four sections. First, we examine the descriptive results, which show weighted differences in degree attainment by institutional type, gender, and secondary school achievement. In the next three sections we review factors that entered the regression analyses as the strongest predictors of degree attainment within four and six years of college entry.

Degree Attainment by Institutional Type, Gender, and High School Grades

Table 6.1 shows the overall degree attainment rates using two different time periods. Only about one in three students (36 percent) was able to complete a bachelor's degree within four years of entering college. However, this number rises by a remarkable 22 percent (to 58 percent) if we allow six years for degree completion.[1] These four-year results reinforce the popular conception that four-year degree completion rates in American

Table 6.1. Four-year and six-year degree attainment rates, by institutional type

| | Unweighted N | | Weighted percent completing bachelor's degree within | |
Institutional Type	Students	Institutions	4 years	6 years
Public university	6,650	20	28	58
Private university	4,931	18	67	80
Public college	7,457	27	24	47
Nonsectarian college	17,610	75	56	66
Catholic college	5,436	38	46	60
Other Christian college	14,734	84	51	61
All institutions	56,818	262	36	58

Note: Weighted to approximate national norms for 1994 freshmen.

higher education have been declining. Looking at both time periods makes it clear that students today may also be taking longer to graduate.

Today, degree attainment rates vary substantially by type of institution. The highest six-year rate is in the private university (80 percent), with the lowest rate in the public college (47 percent). These differences by institutional type are no doubt partially attributable to the varying preparation levels of the students entering different types of institutions. For example, nearly 70 percent of the students entering private universities, compared to only about 30 percent of those entering public four-year colleges, have an "A" grade average from high school (Sax, Astin, Korn, & Mahoney, 2000). Similarly, while each of the three types of private four-year colleges enrolls freshmen who are better prepared than those entering the four-year public colleges (39–42 percent versus only 30 percent have an "A" grade average from high school), four-year college freshmen in general are substantially less well prepared than are freshmen entering private universities (where 70 percent have an "A" grade average from high school). The public university is the only type of institution that does not follow this pattern: while their entering freshmen are better prepared (50 percent have an "A" average from high school) than freshmen at all other types of institutions except private universities, their four-year degree attainment rates continue to be much lower than the rates at all three types of private colleges, and even their six-year rates remain slightly lower. Apparently, the relatively low degree completion rate shown by students attending public universities cannot be attributed to the students' level of academic preparation at the time of college entry. Multivariate analyses (below) will shed more light on these issues.

The data in Table 6.1 also suggest that certain types of institutions are especially likely to prolong the time students spend in obtaining a bachelor's degree. For example, the absolute differences in four-year and six-year degree attainment rates are 30 and 23 percent, respectively, for public universities and public colleges, compared to only 10 percent for nonsectarian and Christian (non-Catholic) colleges. Why the students at public institutions should be taking so long to complete their degrees is not clear, but, given the rapidly declining state support for public institutions, this would certainly appear to be an important topic for future research. In other words, if public institutions could find ways to help more students complete their degrees in four years, they could substantially increase their "throughput" of students without significant additional resources.

Table 6.2 shows the four- and six-year degree attainment rates for men and women. Women are more likely than men are to attain the bachelor's degree, regardless of the time period or category. This finding confirms and extends earlier national studies (Astin, 1971, 1975, 1982, 1993b; Astin, Tsui, & Avalos, 1996), which have consistently shown that women,

Table 6.2.   Four-year and six-year degree attainment rates, by gender

	Weighted percent completing bachelor's degree		
	Men	Women	Total
4 years	33	40	36
6 years	55	60	58

Note: Weighted to approximate national norms for 1994 freshmen.

as compared to men, are more likely to complete their bachelor's degrees. These data show that such gender differences decrease slightly with time. Nevertheless, a 5-percent gender gap remains six years after college entry.

Table 6.3 shows the effect of high school grades on each degree attainment measure. School grades are indeed a major determinant of the student's chances of completing college, regardless of whether degree completion is set at four or six years. Thus, if we look at degree completion within six years, we find that students who enter college with "A" grade averages are four times more likely to finish college than are students with "C" grade averages or less. When it comes to completion within four years, the ratio is more than seven to one. Despite the relatively crude nature of our seven-letter grade categories, differences between categories are quite similar, ranging from a low of about 7 percent to a high around 12 percent for those completing within six years. This would suggest that the relationship comes reasonably close to being linear (especially for six-year completion), despite the arbitrary nature of letter grades.

Table 6.3.   Four-year and six-year degree attainment rates, by average high school grade (HSG)

Average High School Grade	Unweighted N	Percent of students who receive bachelor's degrees within	
		4 years	6 years
A, A+	12,112	58	78
A-	12,261	47	68
B+	12,090	35	59
B	11,434	25	48
B-	4,527	19	40
C+	2,582	15	33
C or less	1,212	8	20

Note: Weighted to approximate national norms for 1994 freshmen.

Pre-college Characteristics Influencing Degree Attainment

The results of the second set of regressions are summarized in Table 6.4. Clearly, the pre-college characteristic that carries the most weight in estimating the student's chances of completing college is the high school grade average. Its unique predictive power (i.e., after taking into account all other pre-college characteristics) is almost identical for both four- and six-year degree completion: Betas of 0.15 and 0.16, respectively. This contrasts with the results for admissions test scores (SAT or ACT Composite), which produced Betas (after all other pre-college characteristics were controlled) of 0.12 and 0.08. Further, while the Betas for high school grades do not change when institutional and contingency variables are controlled, controlling these additional variables further shrinks the Betas for test scores to only 0.05 and 0.03. These contrasts are all the more interesting in light of the fact that the *simple* correlations of GPA and test scores with degree completion are quite similar: 0.30 versus 0.29, respectively (four-year completion), and 0.27 versus 0.24 for six-year completion. An inspection of the step-by-step results indicates that, in addition to high school grades, the other entering variables that attenuate the relationship between test scores and degree completion are father's educational level, years of foreign language study in high school, living in a residence hall, and institutional selectivity. In other words, *the main reasons why admissions test scores are related to college degree completion is that students with high test scores also tend to get good grades and take more years of foreign language in high school, have well-educated parents, attend selective colleges, and live in campus residence halls during their freshman year.* Once these other factors are taken into account, admissions test scores are only weakly related to degree completion.

After high school grades, the two pre-college variables showing the strongest unique effects on degree completion are smoking cigarettes (final Betas of –0.06 and –0.07, respectively, for four- and six-year completion) and years of foreign language study in high school (Betas of 0.06 and 0.05).[2] In other words, even after other pre-college and institutional characteristics are controlled, the data show that nonsmokers and students who take a lot of foreign language courses have higher-than-average rates of college completion.

Other pre-college factors that contribute to our ability to estimate a student's chances of completing a bachelor's degree can be briefly summarized as follows:

Positive Factors (final Betas for four- and six-year degree completion):

- Father's educational level (0.04, 0.04)
- Mother's educational level (0.02, 0.03)
- Parents alive and living with each other (0.02, 0.03)
- Parental income (0.02, 0.01*)
- Gender: female (0.04, 0.01*)
- Religion: Roman Catholic (0.03, 0.03)

Table 6.4. Summary of four- and six-year regressions (N=48,277)

	Simple r		Beta after Inputs		Final Beta	
	4 Year	6 Year	4 Year	6 Year	4 Year	6 Year
Entering Characteristics						
Gender: Female	.09	.05	.04	<u>.01</u>	.04	<u>.01</u>
High school grades	.30	.27	.15	.16	.15	.16
Standardized test scores	.29	.24	.12	.08	.05	.03
Race: American Indian	−.06	−.06	−.02	−.03	−.01	−.02
Religion: Catholic	.01	.02	.02	.03	.03	.03
Religion: Jewish	.07	.05	.03	.03	.02	.02
Years Study: Foreign language	.23	.18	.10	.08	.06	.06
Activity: Smoked cigarettes	−.10	−.12	−.06	−.07	−.06	−.07
Activity: Overslept and missed class	−.09	−.09	−.04	−.04	−.05	−.04
Self-rating: Artistic ability	−.01	.00	−.03	<u>−.01</u>	−.02	−.01
Self-rating: Creativity	−.01	−.01	−.02	−.02	−.02	−.02
Self-rating: Emotional health	.07	.07	.04	.04	.05	.04
Self-rating: Understanding of others	.01	.00	−.03	−.02	−.03	−.02
Parental income	.14	.12	.02	.02	.02	<u>.01</u>
Father's educational level	.19	.16	.05	.05	.04	.04
Mother's educational level	.16	.14	.03	.04	.02	.03
Hours per week: Studying/homework	.18	.15	.05	.04	.03	.03
Hours per week: Participating in student clubs	.13	.10	.04	.02	.02	.02
Hours per week: Reading for pleasure	.02	−.01	−.03	−.04	−.03	−.04
Future Activity: Work full-time	−.12	−.10	−.04	−.04	−.02	−.02
Future Activity: Play intercollegiate athletics	.00	−.01	.03	<u>.01</u>	−.01	−.02
Future Activity: Need extra time for degree	−.12	−.06	−.06	<u>−.01</u>	−.03	<u>.00</u>
Future Activity: Participate in volunteer/community service work	.15	.12	.04	.03	.02	.02
Parents alive and living together	.08	.09	.02	.03	.02	.03
Environmental "Contingency"						
Major: Engineering	−.06	.00	−.07	−.02	−.07	−.03
Major: Health professions	−.03	−.02	−.04	−.03	−.04	−.03
Major: Fine arts	−.03	−.02	−.01	<u>−.01</u>	−.03	**−.01**
Aid: Parents or family	.14	.11	.05	.04	**.01**	.02
Aid: Summer savings	.06	.06	.03	.04	.02	.03
Aid: Other savings	.07	.07	.03	.03	.02	.02
Aid: Part-time work off campus	−.12	−.10	−.05	−.05	−.03	−.03
Aid: Full-time work while in college	−.06	−.06	**−.01**	−.02	<u>.00</u>	−.02
Live Plan: Residence hall	.18	.14	.10	.07	.04	.04
Institutional Characteristics						
Type: Public university	−.18	−.07	−.13	−.04	−.15	−.04
Type: Private university	.10	.09	.02	.02	−.02	<u>−.01</u>
Type: Public four-year college	−.19	−.12	−.12	−.06	−.11	−.04
Selectivity	.32	.26	.16	.12	.16	.11

Note: all variables significant at p<.0001 unless otherwise noted. Bold coefficients: .01>p>.0001. Underline coefficients: p>.01.

- Religion: Jewish (0.02, 0.02)
- Self-rated emotional health (0.05, 0.04)
- Plan to participate in community service (0.02, 0.02)
- Time spent in student clubs and groups (0.02, 0.02)

$p < 0.0001$, *$p > 0.0001$
Negative Factors:

- Race: American Indian (–0.01, –0.02)
- Will need extra time to get degree (–0.03, 0.00*)
- Plan to work full time (–0.02, –0.02)
- Overslept and missed a class or appointment (–0.05, –0.04)
- Hours spent reading for pleasure (–0.03, –0.04)
- Self-rated understanding of others (–0.03, –0.02)
- Self-rated artistic ability (–0.02, –0.01*)
- Self-rated creativity (–0.02, –0.02)

$p < 0.0001$, *$p > 0.0001$
Two patterns stand out from these lists. First, it seems clear that coming from an intact and socioeconomically "advantaged" family facilitates degree completion, even when prior achievement, test scores, and various motivational factors are taken in account. Second, students who are prone to become "involved" (community service, student clubs/groups) enjoy a greater likelihood of degree completion, whereas indicators of noninvolvement in college (full-time work, missing classes) are negatively related to degree completion. The fact that the student's self-rated emotional health at the time of entry is also positively related to degree completion suggests that student counseling and health services might well be able to play an important role in helping to enhance degree completion rates. Finally, it should be noted that several of the findings that might seem counterintuitive—the negative effects of reading for pleasure and self-rated artistic ability, creativity, and understanding of others—have been reported in previous studies (Astin, 1975, 1977, 1993b).

Environmental Contingencies Affecting Degree Attainment

The contingency showing the strongest positive effect on degree completion is living in a residence hall during the freshman year. Although the final Beta was 0.04 for both four- and six-year retention, these coefficients were substantially larger—0.10 (four-year) and 0.07 (six-year)—before other environmental and institutional variables were controlled. The shrinkage in these coefficients occurred primarily because students who live in residence halls tend to attend selective institutions and to finance college primarily through personal savings and parental support. Other contingency variables showing significant positive effects on degree completion all had to do with financing college: the amount of support provided by savings from summer work (final Betas of 0.02 and 0.03, respectively, for four- and six-year degree completion), other savings (0.02 and 0.02), and parents (0.01 and 0.02). While this next-to-last coefficient (i.e., four-year degree completion) is not significant at the extreme level we have set $(0.0001 < p < 0.01)$, it is highly significant (Beta = 0.05) prior to the entry of institutional characteristics. Some of these findings have since been confirmed by Hossler and colleagues (2008).

Environmental contingencies showing negative effects on degree completion included one financial variable—off-campus employment (Betas = −0.03 for both four- and six-year degree completion)—and three fields of study: engineering (−0.07, −0.03), health professions (−0.04, −0.03), and fine arts (−0.03 and −0.01) (this last coefficient is not significant $(0.0001 < p < 0.01)$. Given that the six-year coefficients tend to be much smaller than the four-year coefficients, these results suggest that engineering and fine arts students are more likely than other students to take more than four years to complete their baccalaureate degrees.

In sum, these findings once again underscore the importance of student involvement: students are more likely to finish college if they are able to live in a campus residence hall during their freshman year and if they do not have to work off campus. Both findings, incidentally, have been replicated in numerous earlier studies (e.g., Astin, 1975, 1977, 1993b; Chickering, 1974; Pascarella & Terenzini, 1991) as well as in a more recent national study (Schudde, 2011).

Institutional Characteristics that Affect Degree Completion

The institutional characteristic showing the strongest effect on degree completion is selectivity: final Betas = 0.16 and 0.11, respectively, for four- and six-year completion. For four-year completion, the unique effect of selectivity (final Beta = 0.16) is as strong as the unique effect of high school grades (final Beta = 0.15). (Indeed, the simple correlations of high school grades and institutional selectivity with four-year degree completion—0.30 and 0.32, respectively—slightly favor selectivity.) Highly selective institutions, of course, tend to have more resources than do less selective institutions, but their most important asset is more likely to be the student peer group, which tends to be better prepared academically, more highly motivated, and from higher socioeconomic levels than are the peer groups at less selective institutions. For any student who might be contemplating dropping out, the presence of such peers might well cause that student to reconsider. Again, this is a finding that has been reported in many earlier studies (e.g., Astin, 1982, 1993b).

Two other institutional characteristics also showed substantial effects on degree completion, but in this instance the effects were both negative: public university (final Betas = -0.15 and -0.04 for four- and six-year retention, respectively) and public four-year college (-0.11 and -0.04). Once again, this negative effect of attending a public institution replicates earlier studies (Astin, 1975, 1977, 1982, 1993b). Note, however, the sharp decline in the size of the coefficients when we switch from four- to six-year degree attainment, a finding which suggests that many students will take longer to complete their degrees if they attend a public rather than private college or university. Although there are many possible reasons for this effect, the large size and impersonal atmosphere of many public institutions no doubt play a significant role (Astin, 1993b).

CONCLUSION

The national longitudinal study discussed in this chapter is concerned with the prediction and control of baccalaureate degree completion. The four- and six-year degree attainment data used in this study, which involves more than 50,000 undergraduates attending 262 colleges and universities, suggest that fewer and fewer students today are graduating from institutions of higher education within four years of college entry. Even if some of these students manage to complete their degrees within six or more years, these trends should be a cause for concern to higher education personnel and policymakers, given that colleges and universities throughout the country are becoming increasingly overcrowded and underfunded. With the swell of enrollment that is expected in the years to come, especially in the public institutions (where retention is declining and time-to-degree is increasing), it is especially important to identify the reasons why so many students are either not being retained or are taking longer and longer to graduate.

Multivariate analyses indicate that degree completion is a complex phenomenon that can be affected by a variety of student pre-college characteristics, environmental contingencies, and institutional characteristics. Although the secondary school grade average continues to be the strongest pre-college predictor of the student's chances of completing a bachelor's degree within four or six years after starting college, a number of other demographic and personal characteristics contribute significantly to our ability to estimate the student's chances of completing college. Those with the best chances of finishing college thus tend to have good grades in high school, to come from intact families that are affluent and well educated, and to show a propensity to become highly involved or engaged in the social and academic life of the institution. Of particular interest is the finding that, once these factors are taken into account, scores on standardized admissions tests add little to our ability to estimate the student's degree completion chances.

The student's chances of completing college can also be affected by a number of environmental "contingencies." Degree completion chances can be enhanced if the student lives in a residence hall during the freshman year and is able to finance a good proportion of college expenses through parental support or personal savings. Chances are reduced if the student has to work off campus or starts college with plans to major in engineering, fine arts, or allied health professions. Majoring in such fields also tends to prolong the time to a degree. Among other things, these findings suggest that degree completion rates can be enhanced if (a) more students are provided with opportunities to live on campus, and (b) more opportunities are created for part-time employment on campus.

The institutional characteristic that has the strongest effect on the student's chances of completing the bachelor's degree is the selectivity of the college or university attended: the more selective the institution, the better the student's chances of finishing. Attending a public college or university, on the other hand, reduces the student's chances of finishing and prolongs the time to the degree. These findings present a special challenge for public institutions to find more effective ways to help students complete their undergraduate studies in four years.

NOTES

1. These figures compare favorably with a five-year rate of 47 percent (with an additional 9 percent still enrolled) derived from the Beginning Postsecondary Student (BPS) Longitudinal Study, which followed up 1989–1990 entering freshmen in 1994 (Choy, 2002).

2. These latter two coefficients would be significantly larger—0.08 and 0.10, respectively—if it weren't for the fact that students who take a lot of foreign language study in high school tend to be concentrated in selective institutions.

REFERENCES

Adelman, C. (2006). *The toolbox revisited: Paths to degree completion from high school through college*. Washington, DC: U.S. Department of Education.

Anderson, J. (1984). *Institutional differences in college effects*. Florida: Florida Atlantic University Press.

Anderson, K.L. (1981). Post high school experiences and college attrition. *Sociology of Education*, 54, 1–15.

Allen, D. F. & Nelson, J. M. (1989). Tinto's model of college withdrawal applied to women at two institutions. *Journal of Research and Development in Education*, 22(3), 1–11.

Astin, A. W. (1971). *Predicting academic performance in college*. New York: The Free Press.

Astin, A. W. (1975). *Preventing students from dropping out*. San Francisco: Jossey-Bass.

Astin, A. W. (1977). *Four critical years.* San Francisco: Jossey-Bass.

Astin, A. W. (1982). *Minorities in American higher education.* San Francisco: Jossey-Bass.

Astin, A. W. (1984). Student involvement: A developmental theory for higher education. *Journal of College Student Personnel,* vol. 25, 297–308.

Astin, A. W. (1991). *Assessment for excellence: the philosophy and practice of assessment and evaluation in higher education.* New York: Macmillan/Oryx.

Astin, A. W. (1993a). College retention rates are often misleading. *The Chronicle of Higher Education,* (22 September), A48.

Astin, A. W. (1993b). *What matters in college: four critical years revisited.* San Francisco: Jossey-Bass.

Astin, A. W. (1996). How "good" is your institution's retention rate? *Research in Higher Education,* 38 (6) 647–658.

Astin, A. W. & Henson, J. W. (1977). New measures of college selectivity. *Research in Higher Education,* (6) 1–9.

Astin, A. W., Korn, W. S., Sax, L. J., & Mahoney, K. M. (1994). *The American freshman: national norms for fall 1994.* Los Angeles: Higher Education Research Institute, UCLA.

Astin, A. W. & Oseguera, L. (2003). *Degree attainment among Latino undergraduates: Rethinking time-to-degree.* Berkeley: California Policy Research Institute. UC Latino Policy Institute.

Astin, A. W. & Oseguera, L. (2005). *Degree attainment rates at American colleges and universities. Revised edition.* Los Angeles: Higher Education Research Institute, UCLA.

Astin, A. W., Tsui, L., & Avalos, J. (1996). *Degree attainment rates at American colleges and universities: Effects of race, gender, and institutional type.* Los Angeles. Higher Education Research Institute, UCLA.

Attewell, P., Heil. S. & Reisel, S. (2011) Competing explanations of undergraduate noncompletion. *American Educational Research Journal,* 48(3), 536–559.

Bean, J. P. (1982). Student attrition, intentions, and confidence. *Research in Higher Education,* 12, 155–187.

Berger, J. B. (2000). Organizational behavior at colleges and student outcomes: A new perspective on college impact. *Review of Higher Education,* 23(2), 177–198.

Berger, J. B. (2001–2002). Understanding the organizational nature of student persistence: Empirically based recommendations for practice. *Journal of College Student Retention,* 3(1), 3–21.

Braxton, J., Sullivan, A. S., & Johnson, R. (1997) Appraising Tinto's theory of college student departure. In *Higher Education: Handbook of Theory of Research.* (Ed.) J. Smart. Vol.12. New York: Agathon Press.

Braxton, J. M., Vesper, N., & Hossler, D. (1995). Expectations for college and student persistence. *Research in Higher Education,* 36(5), 595–612.

Cabrera, A. F., Nora, A., & Castaneda, M. B. (1992). The role of finances in the persistence process: A structural model. *Research in Higher Education,* 33, 571–593.

Cabrera, A. F., Nora, A., & Castaneda, M. B. (1993). College persistence: structural equation modeling of an integrated model of student retention. *Journal of Higher Education,* 64(2), 123–139.

Cabrera, A. F., Castaneda, M. B., Nora, A., & Hengstler, D. (1992).The convergence between two theories of college persistence. *Journal of Higher Education,* 63, 143–164.

Cabrera, A. F., Stampen, J. O., & Hansen, W. L. (1990). Exploring the effects of ability to pay on college persistence. *The Review of Higher Education,* 13, 303–336.

Carter, D. F. (2001). *A Dream deferred?: Examining the degree aspirations of African American and White college students.* New York: RoutledgeFalmer Press.

Chickering, A. W. (1974). *Commuting versus resident students: overcoming educational inequalities of living off campus.* San Francisco: Jossey-Bass.

Choy, S. P. (2002). *Access and persistence: Findings from 10 years of longitudinal research on students.* Washington, DC: American Council on Education.

Dey, E. L. & Astin, A. W. (1989). *Predicting college student retention: Comparative national data from the 1982 freshman class.* Los Angeles: Higher Education Research Institute. UCLA.

Dey, E .L. & Astin, A. W. (1993). Statistical alternatives for studying college student retention: A comparative analyses of Logit, Probit, and Linear Regression. *Research in Higher Education,* 34 (5) 569–581.

Fleming, J. & Garcia, N. (1998). Are standardized tests fair to African Americans? *Journal of Higher Education,* 69, 471–495.

Fleming, J. (2002). Who will succeed in college? When the SAT predicts Black students' performance. *The Review of Higher Education,* vol. 25 (3), 281–296.

Grosset, J. M. (1991). Patterns of integration, commitment, and student characteristics and retention among younger and older students. *Research in Higher Education,* 32(2), 159–178.

Gurin, P. & Epps, E. (1975). *Black consciousness, identity, and achievement: a study of students in Black colleges.* Wiley Press: New York.

Hartnett, R. T. & Centra, J. (1977). The effects of academic departments on learning. *Journal of Higher Education,* 48, 491–507.

Hearn, J. C. (1987). Impacts of undergraduate experiences on aspirations and plans for graduate and professional education. *Research in Higher Education,* 27 (2), 119–141.

Hossler, D., Ziskin, M., Kim, S., Cekic, O., & Gross, J. (2008). Student aid and its role in encouraging persistence. In S. Baum, M. McPherson, & P. Steele (Eds.). *The effectiveness of student aid policies: What the research tells us* (pp. 101–115). New York: The College Board.

House, D. J. (1996). College persistence and grade outcomes: Non-cognitive variables as predictors for African American, Asian American, Hispanic, Native American, and White students. Paper presented at the Annual meeting of the Association for Institutional Research, Albuquerque, New Mexico.

McClelland, K. (1990). Cumulative disadvantage among the highly ambitious. *Sociology of Education,* 63, 102–121.

McCormick, A. & Horn, L. (1996). *A descriptive summary of 1992–93 bachelor's degree recipients 1 year later, with an essay on time to degree* (Statistical Analyses Report No. NCES 96-158). Washington, D.C.: U.S. Departement of Education, Office of Educatinal Research and Improvement, National Center for Education Statistics.

Mow, S. L. & Nettles, M. T. (1990). Minority student access to, and persistence in, college: A review of the trends and research literature. In J. C. Smart (Ed.), *Higher education: Handbook of theory and research* (Vol. 6, pp. 35–105). New York: Agathon Press.

Munro, B. H. (1981). Dropouts from higher education: Path analysis of a national sample. *American Educational Research Association,* 18(2), 133–141.

Murdock, T. A. (1987). It isn't just about money. The effects of financial aid on persistence. *The Review of Higher Education.* 11, 75–101.

Oseguera, L. (2006). Four and six-year baccalaureate degree completion by institutional characteristics and racial/ethnic groups. *The Journal of College Student Retention,* 7(1-2), 19–59.

Oseguera, L. & Rhee, B. (2009). The influence of institutional retention climates on student persistence to degree completion: a multilevel approach. *Research in Higher Education,* 50, 546–569.

Oseguera, L. & Vogelgesang, L. (2003) Statistical alternatives for studying college student retention: Logistic versus linear regression—An update. Unpublished manuscript, UCLA.

Pascarella, E. T. (1980). Student faculty informal contact and college outcomes. *Review of Educational Research,* 50, 545–595.

Pascarella, E. T. & Chapman, D. W. (1983). Validation of a theoretical model of college withdrawal. *Research in Higher Education,* 19(1), 25–48.

Pascarella, E. T., & Ethington, C., & Smart, J. (1988). The influence of college on humanitarian/civic involvement values. *Journal of Higher Education,* 59, 412–437.

Pascarella, E. T., Smart, J., & Ethington, J. (1986). Long term persistence of two-year college students. *Research in Higher Education,* 24, 47–71.

Pascarella, E. T., Smart, J., Ethington, J., & Nettles, M. (1987). The Influence of college on self-concept. *American Educational Research Journal,* 24, 49–77.

Pascarella, E. T., Smart, J., & Stoecker, J. (1989). College race and the early status attainment of black students. *Journal of Higher Education,* 60, 82–107.

Pascarella, E. T., & Terenzini, P. (1991). *How college affects students: Findings and insights from twenty years of research.* San Francisco: Jossey-Bass Publishers.

Pascarella, E. T., & Terenzini, P. (2005). *How college affects students: A third decade of research (Vol. 2).* San Francisco: Jossey-Bass Publishers.

Sax, L. J., Astin, A. W., Korn, W. S., & Mahoney, K. M. (2000). *The American freshman: national norms for fall 2000.* Los Angeles: Higher Education Research Institute, UCLA.

Schudde, L. T. (2011). The causal effect of campus residency on college student retention. *Review of Higher Education,* 34(4), 581–610.

Sewell, W., Haller, A. O., & Ohlendorf, G. W. (1970). The educational and early occupational attainment process: replication and revision. *American Sociological Review.* December (35), 1014–1027.

Smith, D. G. (1990). Women's colleges and coed colleges: Is there a difference? *Journal of Higher Education,* 61(2), 181–195.

Stage, F. K. (1988). University attrition: LISREL with logistic regression for the persistence criterion. *Research in Higher Education,* 29(4), 343–357.

Stampen, J. O. & Cabrera, A. F. (1986). Exploring the effects of student aid on attrition. *The Journal of Student Financial Aid,* 16, 28–40.

Stoecker, J., Pascarella, E., & Wolfe, L. (1988). Persistence in higher education. A nine year test of a theoretical model. *Journal of College Student Development,* 29, 196–209.

Tinto, V. (1987). *Leaving college: Rethinking the causes and cures of student attrition.* Chicago: The University of Chicago Press.

Tinto, V. (1993). *Leaving college: Rethinking the causes and cures of student attrition.* Second Edition. Chicago: The University of Chicago Press.

Titus, M. A. (2004). An examination of the influence of institutional context on student persistence at four-year colleges and universities: A multilevel approach. *Research in Higher Education*, 45(7), 673–699.

Titus, M. A. (2006a). Understanding the influence of the financial context of institutions on student persistence at four-year colleges and universities. *Journal of Higher Education*, 77(2), 353–375.

Titus, M. A. (2006b). Understanding college degree completion of students with low socioeconomic status: The influence of the institutional financial context. *Research in Higher Education*, 47(4), 371–398.

Waldo, M. (1986). Academic achievement and retention as related to students' personal and social adjustment in residence halls. *Journal of College and University Student Housing*, 16, 19–23.

APPENDIX A: VARIABLES USED IN FULL REGRESSIONS

I. Entering Characteristics

Background

- Father's Education
- Mother's Education
- Parent's Income
- Student's Gender: Female
- Parent's Status
  - *Both Alive—Living Together
  - *Both Alive—Divorced or Separated
  - *One or Both Deceased
- Student's Age
- Student Native English Speaker
- Student's Religion
  - *Catholic
  - *Protestant
  - *Jewish
  - *Other Religion
  - *No Religion
- Student's Race
  - *African American
  - *American Indian
  - *Asian American
  - *Mexican American/Chicano
  - *Puerto Rican American
  - *Caucasian
- Citizenship Status
  - *US Citizen
  - *US Resident

Academic

- High School GPA
- SAT Composite
- Degree Aspirations

Activities in Past Year

- Attended a Religious Service
- Was Bored in Class
- Participated in Organized Demonstrations
- Studied with Other Students
- Was a Guest in a Professor's Home
- Smoked Cigarettes
- Drank Beer or Wine or Liquor
- Performed Volunteer Work
- Came Late to Class
- Played a Musical Instrument
- Overslept and Missed Class or Appointment
- Discussed Politics
- Discussed Religion

Self-Ratings

- Academic Ability
- Artistic Ability
- Competitiveness
- Cooperativeness
- Creativity
- Drive to Achieve
- Emotional Health
- Leadership Ability
- Mathematical Ability
- Physical Health
- Popularity
- Public Speaking Ability
- Self-Confidence (Intellectual)
- Self-Confidence (Social)
- Understanding of Others
- Writing Ability

Reasons for Attending College

- Parents Wanted Me to Go
- Could Not Find a Job
- Wanted to Get Away from Home

- Get a Better Job
- Gain a General Education
- Improve Reading and Study Skills
- Nothing Better to Do
- Become a More Cultured Person
- Make More Money
- Learn More About the Things that Interest Me
- Prepare for Graduate or Professional School
- Role Model/ Mentor Encouraged Me

Student Opinions

- Too Much Concern for the Rights of Criminals
- Abortion Should be Legal
- Abolish Death Penalty
- Activities of Married Women Best at Home
- Marijuana Should be Legalized
- Prohibit Homosexual Relations
- Employers Can Require Drug Testing
- Federal Government Should Do More to Control Handguns
- College Should Prohibit Racist/Sexist Speech
- Wealthy People Should Pay More Taxes

Hours Per Week in Last Year Spent:

- Studying or Doing Homework
- Socializing with Friends
- Talking with a Teacher Outside of Class
- Exercising or Sports
- Partying
- Working for Pay
- Volunteer Work
- Student Clubs or Groups
- Watching TV
- Household or Childcare Duties
- Reading for Pleasure

Goals and Values

- Become Accomplished in Performing Arts
- Become Authority in Own Field
- Obtain Recognition from Colleagues
- Influence the Political Structure
- Influence Social Values
- Raise a Family

- Have Administrative Responsibility
- Be Very Well Off Financially
- Help Others in Difficulty
- Make Theoretical Contribution to Science
- Write Original Works
- Create Artistic Work
- Be Successful in Own Business
- Develop Meaningful Philosophy of Life
- Participate in Community Action Program
- Promote Racial Understanding
- Keep Up to Date with Political Affairs
- Be a Community Leader

Possible Future Activities

- Change Major Field
- Change Career Choice
- Get Job to Help Pay Expenses
- Graduate with Honors
- Work Full-Time While Attending College
- Play Varsity or Intercollegiate Athletics
- Make at Least a "B" Average
- Need Extra Time for Degree
- Get a Bachelor's Degree
- Participate in Student Protests
- Drop out Temporarily
- Drop out Permanently
- Participate in Volunteer or Community Service Work

II. Environmental "Contingency" Variables

Sources of Financial Aid

- Parental or Family Aid
- Savings from Summer Work
- Part-Time Job On Campus
- Part-Time Job Off Campus
- Full-Time Job While in College
- Pell Grant
- State Scholarship or Grant
- College Work-Study Grant
- Other College Grant
- Other Private Grant
- Federal Guaranteed Student Loan
- National Direct Student Loan
- Other College Loan

Undergraduate Student Majors

- Agriculture
- Biological Sciences
- Business
- Education
- Engineering
- English
- Health Professional
- History or Political Science
- Humanities
- Fine Arts
- Mathematics or Statistics
- Physical Science
- Social Science
- Other Technical
- Other Non-Technical
- Undecided

First Year Living Arrangements

- Plan to Live: Home
- Plan to Live: College Dormitory/Residence Hall
- Plan to Live: Other On Campus, not Dorm
- Plan to Live: Off Campus, not at home

III. Institutional Characteristics

Institutional Size

Institutional Selectivity

Type/Control

- Public University
- Private University
- Public Four-Year College
- Nonsectarian Four-Year
- Catholic Four-Year
- Other Christian Four-Year
- Historically Black College
- Hispanic Serving Institution
- Women's College

IV. Dependent Measures

- Retention within Four Years
- Retention within Six Years

Appendix B: Complete variable list of four- and six-year regressions

	Four-Year Regression				Six-Year Regression			
	Simple r	Beta after Inputs	Beta after Contingency	Final Beta	Simple r	Beta after Inputs	Beta after Contingency	Final Beta
Entering Characteristics								
Gender: Female	.0876	.0437	.0322	.0359	.0506	.0090	.0067	.0083
High school grades	.3025	.1545	.1556	.1537	.2745	.1633	.1641	.1565
Standardized test scores	.2914	.1236	.1099	.0513	.2368	.0840	.0732	.0288
Race: White	.0713	.0262	**.0110**	.0020	.0457	.0046	−.0067	.0020
Race: American Indian	−.0626	−.0243	−.0248	−.0145	−.0582	−.0290	−.0292	−.0224
Religion: Catholic	.0093	.0243	.0266	.0275	.0192	.0311	.0313	.0294
Religion: Jewish	.0652	.0318	.0335	.0227	.0497	.0258	.0268	.0173
Years Study: Foreign language	.2261	.0951	.0829	.0565	.1820	.0779	.0698	.0550
Activity: Smoked cigarettes	−.1048	−.0579	−.0571	−.0604	−.1182	−.0724	−.0716	−.0738
Activity: Overslept and missed class	−.0949	−.0409	−.0417	−.0454	−.0945	−.0430	−.0425	−.0442
Self-rating: Artistic ability	−.0076	−.0286	−.0204	−.0197	−.0022	−.0123	−.0082	−.0088
Self-rating: Creativity	−.0087	−.0167	−.0184	−.0183	−.0138	−.0217	−.0233	−.0235
Self-rating: Emotional health	.0697	.0419	.0445	.0451	.0683	.0412	.0422	.0414
Self-rating: Intellectual self-confidence	.0728	−.0287	−.0284	−.0144	.0607	−.0287	−.0261	−.0190
Self-rating: Understanding of others	.0056	−.0269	−.0272	−.0281	.0005	−.0214	−.0205	−.0209
Parental income	.1439	.0244	.0224	.0155	.1217	.0223	**.0168**	.0119
Father's educational level	.1878	.0528	.0451	.0356	.1612	.0513	.0447	.0391
Mother's educational level	.1641	.0337	.0264	.0207	.1401	.0353	.0291	.0258
Reason for college: Become more cultured	.0874	.0266	.0204	**.0132**	.0653	.0166	**.0131**	.0090
Reason for college: Gain general education	.0887	.0237	.0184	.0100	.0708	.0209	.0174	**.0128**
Hours per week: Studying/homework	.1750	.0513	.0501	.0302	.1491	.0437	.0418	.0295
Hours per week: Student clubs	.1258	.0367	.0243	.0220	.0968	.0239	.0160	.0157
Hours per week: Housework/childcare	−.0376	−.0324	−.0258	−.0155	−.0344	−.0232	−.0191	**−.0132**
Hours per week: Reading for pleasure	.0214	−.0259	−.0288	−.0300	−.0078	−.0413	−.0421	−.0424

Goal: Make theoretical contribution to science	-.0191	-.0286	-.0086	-.0103	-.0022	-.0142	-.0037	-.0072
Future activity: Change career choice	.0801	.0326	.0168	.0085	.0716	.0294	.0192	.0121
Future activity: Work full-time	-.1229	-.0422	-.0251	-.0201	-.1048	-.0392	-.0253	-.0234
Future activity: Play intercollegiate athletics	-.0030	.0267	.0114	-.0147	-.0078	.0050	-.0045	-.0156
Future activity: Need extra time for degree	-.1234	-.0609	-.0532	-.0293	-.0630	-.0098	-.0072	.0040
Future activity: Participate in volunteer/community service work	.1495	.0391	.0268	.0172	.1171	.0281	.0216	.0193
Parents alive and living together	.0822	.0184	.0164	.0218	.0865	.0280	.0255	.0297
Environmental "Contingency"								
Major: Engineering	-.0619	-.0736	-.0772	-.0705	-.0016	-.0199	-.0226	-.0268
Major: Health professions	-.0319	-.0395	-.0505	-.0395	-.0213	-.0307	-.0343	-.0289
Major: Fine Arts	-.0347	-.0148	-.0259	-.0265	-.0217	-.0052	-.0111	-.0119
Major: Other technical	-.0316	-.0126	-.0198	-.0157	-.0255	-.0128	-.0152	-.0138
Aid: Parents or family	.1400	.0533	.0363	.0143	.1134	.0404	.0276	.0176
Aid: Summer savings	.0622	.0341	.0227	.0220	.0626	.0382	.0307	.0284
Aid: Other savings	.0720	.0304	.0236	.0223	.0673	.0323	.0256	.0248
Aid: Part-time work off campus	-.1193	-.0525	-.0377	-.0285	-.1024	-.0462	-.0389	-.0343
Aid: Full-time work while in college	-.0557	-.0135	-.0052	-.0021	-.0568	-.0216	-.0166	-.0160
Aid: College grant	.1511	.0651	.0538	.0137	.1035	.0274	.0195	.0135
Live Plan: Residence hall	.1847	.0988	.0775	.0446	.1350	.0672	.0493	.0351
Institutional Characteristics								
Type: Public university	-.1847	-.1330	-.1175	-.1455	-.0743	-.0354	-.0281	-.0353
Type: Private university	.1004	.0232	.0283	-.0237	.0920	.0214	.0209	-.0055
Type: Public four-year college	-.1917	-.1159	-.0877	-.1079	-.1211	-.0586	-.0395	-.0352
Selectivity	.3223	.1634	.1643	.1570	.2581	.1210	.1144	.1080
Percent of Asian students at institution	.1107	.0058	.0213	-.0313	.1136	.0252	.0325	-.0006

Note: All variables significant at p<.0001 unless otherwise noted; Bold coefficients: p<.01; Underlined coefficients: not significant.

7

The Community College

Retention Trends and Issues

Gloria Crisp and Liliana Mina

The community college is lauded by many scholars as one of the most significant developments in United States postsecondary education (Brint & Karabel, 1991; Cohen & Brawer, 2008; Deiener, 1986). As a distinct type of postsecondary institution accredited to award the associate's of arts or science as its highest degree (Cohen & Brawer, 2008), the community college serves nearly 40 percent of all college students in the country (McIntosh & Rouse, 2009). The community college serves a multiplicity of educational programs to an increasingly diverse student population (Bragg, 2001), including minority and low-income students who have been historically underserved in postsecondary education (Cohen & Brawer, 2008).

Student retention has been a long-standing struggle for the community college, as the past several decades of research have consistently shown attrition rates to be substantially higher when compared to students attending four-year institutions (Schuetz, 2005; Summers, 2003). Only about half of first-time community college students persist to the second year, compared with nearly three-quarters of students who begin college at a four-year institution (McIntosh & Rouse, 2009). Moreover, retention rates and other success measures have been shown to be even lower for minority and low-income students (Bailey, Jenkins, & Leinbach, 2005).

As the largest and most important portal to postsecondary education, improving retention rates and other measures of success (e.g., degree attainment, transfer) among community college students is critical to the welfare, both economic and educational, of the United States (Wells, 2008). Although a good amount of attention has been given to improving retention at all levels of postsecondary education, relatively little attention has been devoted to understanding the unique issues in retaining community college students. Thus, the intent of the current chapter is to highlight the retention issues facing today's community colleges. We begin with an introduction of the community college context followed by a description of the characteristics and functions of community colleges and the typologies of students. Recent national data comparing community college and two-year retention rates are then provided in preface to a brief explanation of the discrepancies in success outcomes and a discussion of what we feel are the major issues facing community colleges with regard to retention. We conclude with an acknowledgment of the limitations in measuring retention among community college students.

HISTORICAL DEVELOPMENT AND FUNCTIONS OF THE COMMUNITY COLLEGE

The American community college dates back to the early twentieth century with the establishment of Joliet Junior College in 1901. The development of the community college was driven by several societal forces, including (but not limited to) the industrial revolution, a lengthened period of adolescence, and the drive for social equality (Cohen & Brawer, 2003). Innovators of the junior college, such as University of Michigan president Henry Tappan, envisioned an American college that would prepare students rigorously for university studies (Gleazer, 1968). As such, the early community colleges were termed *junior colleges*, focused on providing the first two years of coursework to students seeking to transfer to a four-year institution (Bragg, 2001).

The United States in the late nineteenth century was rapidly changing. Concomitantly, educational access for women and minorities was rising. As the industrial revolution took hold, America became more urban and industrialized. Scientific developments and a wave of European immigration converged to create a society that needed to be educated. Eaton (1994) points out that the early junior college up to 1940 had four major purposes: transfer and preparatory; preprofessional; terminal general education; and terminal occupational purpose. For example: "The preprofessional purpose provided preparation for occupational focused baccalaureate education. It implicitly acknowledged that transfer preparation could extend beyond the disciplines and that universities housed an occupational function" (p. 14). As early as the 1930s, the American Association of Junior Colleges started to promote vocational curricula, thereby increasing the importance of the vocational function (Deiener, 1986).

Up until the 1940s, a college education was open to few members of the American society (i.e., whites, males, traditionally aged students) (Bragg, 2001). However, it was not until after World War II, the enactment of the

G. I. Bill of Rights of 1944 and the President's Commission on Higher Education for American Democracy (also known as the Truman Commission), that America saw a firmly established spread and growth of community colleges as "a new system of colleges was needed in order to expand access beyond that afforded by the land-grant colleges" (Mellow & Heelan, 2008, p. 6). The map had been drawn. The manifesto called for at least half of the United States population to be educated in some manner beyond high school. Almost anyone who wanted an education beyond high school could get one.

In turn, community colleges grew at a very rapid pace during the 1950s, 1960s, and 1970s. The Civil Rights Movement, the Women's Movement of the 1970s, and the baby boom, among other societal factors, also influenced the growth and diversity of community college enrollment (Bragg, 2001; Mellow & Heelan, 2008). In many instances, these new students were not prepared to do college-level coursework. In response, the American community college created developmental programs to meet their needs (O'Banion, 1997). There is no doubt that community colleges have changed the nature of postsecondary education profoundly in the United States. For example: "Between 1950 and 2006, more than 900 community colleges were established" (Mellow & Heelan, 2008, p. 6). At present there are approximately 993 public community colleges, enrolling 40 percent of first-time undergraduates.

THE ROLE OF THE COMMUNITY COLLEGE IN TODAY'S SOCIETY

The role of the community college in today's society is multidimensional in form and process. With the broad mission of extending educational opportunity under an "open-door" admissions policy, the American community college has established itself to be the vehicle for redirecting the careers of seasoned workers, for offering general education to all types of students, and for providing workforce development and training by establishing alliances with the business sector and of course developmental education (Cohen & Brawer, 2008).

The biggest challenge community colleges face today is serving traditionally underserved populations and students who would not otherwise have the opportunity to attend college. More often than not, these students need assistance developmentally, academically, and socially. Several postsecondary education scholars contend that people who have been previously excluded from postsecondary education (i.e., minorities, underprepared, underserved) and who enroll at their local community colleges are just victims of a perpetuating class structure. These scholars maintain that community colleges are not vehicles for economic mobility because of the low retention rates and dismal successful transfers to four-year institutions. For instance, some scholars assert that, since many of these students come from lower socioeconomic backgrounds, community colleges are not playing the great democratizing role (Brint & Karabel, 1991; Pincus, 1980; Zwerling, 1986). To a certain extent, these students naturally fall into lower-level occupations because they come from populations with the highest dropout rates. Moreover, these critics maintain that community colleges in general are viewed by our own citizens with outright disdain or simply viewed as educational institutions where the mediocre or ill-prepared go because no one else will admit them. "Other commentators have also contended that the career programs divert students from lower-class backgrounds away from baccalaureate studies" (Cohen & Brawer, 2003, p. 378).

Today's community colleges offer unparalleled accessibility by not excluding students. Community colleges today place postsecondary education within the reach of marginalized students as well as students from traditional college-bound backgrounds. The United States cannot afford a decline in postsecondary education rates for minority and low-income students. Community colleges today are addressing the educational disparities among whites, African-American, and Hispanic students (Hart, 2009). These colleges assist in closing the performance gap among underrepresented populations (Berger & Lyon, 2005). Not all community college students who are academically weak remain that way. For many students, successful transfers are possible, as is good employment after graduation. These institutions are vehicles for social mobility because they provide educational services that can improve cognitive skills and study habits and provide a solid foundation for the successful completion of postsecondary education (Price, 2004).

On the one hand, today's community colleges offer enrichment courses for gifted high school students. These dual enrollment courses and programs afford students enrollment in courses that are not offered in their high school. In certain instances, students can participate in year-round programs that allow them to earn both a high school diploma and college credit at the same time (Mellow & Heelan, 2008). On the other hand, community colleges today are serving students who are first-generation learners. Since they are the first in their families to attempt a college education, they often do not have the study skills, discipline, cultural capital, and previous educational experiences that can position them for success (Levinson, 2005). Community colleges today face an interesting dilemma, namely, how to maintain the rigors of postsecondary education while providing access for those who want it and yet are academically unprepared to succeed, and having all of this occur in an era of decreased funding and increased governmental accountability.

THE ROLE OF THE FEDERAL AND STATE GOVERNMENTS

The community college is vital in developing a skilled workforce. Not only are community colleges essential for training and retraining the United States workforce, but they are essential to changing the current economic climate. "Collectively, these colleges have played an increasingly important role in higher education and have therefore become a key resource for economic growth in the communities they serve" (Felix & Pope, 2010, p. 70). Because of the current economic slump, community college attendance has risen sharply, yet funding at the state and local levels has decreased. As a result, community colleges are in a situation of having to educate more students with less funding. In an effort to help community colleges meet budgetary challenges, on July 14, 2009, President Barack Obama announced a landmark initiative designed to provide more federal support to the nation's community colleges. The American Graduation Initiative (AGI) was a $12 billion plan to reform community colleges which called for five million community college graduates by 2020. This number included recipients of certificates, associate's degrees as well as students who continued on and graduated from four-year programs (American Association of Community Colleges, 2011). Additionally, community colleges could compete for grants designed to support innovative and successful proven reforms that could be adopted nationwide.

Although the $12 billion did not fully materialize (only $2 billion was allocated) some community colleges were able to receive federal funding from Obama's AGI. The grant stipulates that practices that are successful and that demonstrate employment outcomes will receive continued federal support. It is important to note that federal involvement in workforce development has existed since the Smith-Hughes Act of 1917. The Smith-Hughes Act set aside federal dollars to provide vocational education to high school students. "After World War II, the legislation's focus was extended to the postsecondary education sector. Similarly, the law initially aimed to benefit only poor children, but shifted over time to serve a broader constituency as part of a federal economic development policy" (Jacobs, 2008, p. 1).

The Office of Vocational and Adult Education (OVAE) administers the Carl Perkins Career and Technical Education Act (CTEA). Enacted in 1984 and reauthorized in 1998 and 2006, these federal funds are earmarked for states to provide vocational and technical education to youth as well as to adults. Types of projects funded by the Perkins Act include monies for instructor training, improvement of laboratories, supplies, equipment, and even tutoring services for students. Preferences are given to proposals that are designed to increase skills in technology-type industries. Under the Perkins Act, states can receive funding for Tech Prep Education, a program of study that combines at least two years of high school with two years of postsecondary education. Tech Prep:

> . . . is designed to help students gain academic knowledge and technical skills, and often earn college credit for their secondary coursework. Programs are intended to lead to an associate's degree or a certificate in a specific career field, and ultimately, to high wage, high skill employment or advanced postsecondary training. (Tech Prep Education, 2007, para. 1)

Students who are enrolled at their local community college and meet [low] income eligibility can also use the Federal Pell Grant to subsidize their associates degree or certificate. Community college students who go on to four-year institutions can still receive the Pell Grant. This type of grant does not have to be paid back. Pell Grant monies are sent directly to the educational institution. If there is any leftover money after tuition and fees, the student receives it to pay for books and living expenses.

COMMUNITY COLLEGE STUDENTS

An understanding of community college students, in terms of background and educational goals, is needed to appreciate the retention issues facing community colleges. Community colleges are challenged by the variety of programs and services they offer to serve an increasingly diverse group of students who enroll at the college for a myriad of reasons (Bragg, 2001; Cohen & Brawer, 2008). The following paragraphs compare students who attend two- and four-year institutions and detail the major typologies of students served in an attempt to frame the major challenges faced by the community college in retaining students.

Differences between Community College and Four-Year Students

Community college students can be understood in relation to students who attend four-year institutions. To illustrate some of the important differences between these two groups, we descriptively compared the student characteristics and high school and college experiences of four-year and community college students using the most recent follow-up of the Beginning Postsecondary Students Longitudinal Study (BPS: 04/09), which includes a national sample of students who entered postsecondary education in the 2003–2004 academic year. We limited our analysis to students aspiring to earn a bachelor's degree or higher in order to control for differences in student goals. As shown in Table 7.1, findings demonstrated that, on the whole, community college students are very different from students who attend four-year institutions. When compared to four-year students,

Table 7.1. Descriptive comparison of four-year and community college students

	Four-year (n = 8,360[a])	Community college (n = 5,850)
Gender		
Male	40.9%	43.8%
Ethnicity		
White	70.6%	55.8%
African American	9.8%	17.6%
Hispanic	9.2%	16.8%
Asian American	5.6%	4.1%
American Indian	.4%	.9%
Hawaiian or Pacific Islander	.2%	.5%
Other	1.4%	1.4%
More than one race	2.7%	2.9%
Dependency Status		
Dependent	93.0%	67.3%
First Generation Status		
First generation student	42.5%	71.7%
High School Grade Point Average (GPA)		
Less than 3.0	9.6%	20.7%
Highest Mathematics Course Taken		
Algebra II	19.7%	51.5%
Trigonometry and Algebra II	20.0%	23.0%
Pre-calculus	29.2%	18.0%
Calculus	31.1%	7.5%
Average Number of Hours Worked		
Did not work	52.1%	28.7%
Less than 20 hours per week	23.4%	14.3%
21 or more hours per week	24.6%	57.0%
Highest Degree Expected		
Bachelor's degree	25.6%	49.0%
Master's degree	46.5%	36.9%
Doctoral or professional degree	27.9%	14.2%
Enrollment Intensity		
Part-time	1.3%	9.2%
Mixed (part and full-time)	29.7%	46.5%
Full-time	69.0%	44.3%
Mean years delayed enrollment in college	.76 years	3.3 years
Mean amount of financial aid received	$9,640	$3,673
First year GPA	2.95	2.91

[a] Data are rounded to the nearest 10 per IES guidelines.
Notes: Data source: U.S. Department of Education, National Center for Education Statistics, 2003–2004 Beginning Postsecondary Students Longitudinal Study, Second Follow-up (BPS:04/09).
Percentages exclude missing data.

community college students were more likely to be: African American or Hispanic; financially independent; first-generation college students; less academically prepared; working part- or full-time during college; having lower degree aspirations; attending college part-time; delaying enrollment into college following high school; receiving less financial aid; and earning a lower GPA during the first year of college.

It is notable that 34 percent of students who attended a community college were African American or Hispanic, compared to only 19 percent of students who attended a four-year university. Also, the majority of students were the first in their families to attend college (72 percent), worked more than 20 hours per week (57 percent), and did not exclusively attend college full-time (56 percent). Additionally, 21 percent of community college students earned less than a 3.0 grade point average in college and 52 percent of the sample of community college students did not complete a mathematics course higher than Algebra II during high school. Also, the average community college student delayed enrolling in college more than three years following high school and received an average of $5,967 less in financial aid support when compared to four-year students.

Community College Typologies

Community college students can also be described by explaining the variety of student types served by the institution. These student typologies largely correspond to the major curricular functions provided by the community college (Bragg, 2001). As discussed in the following paragraphs, community college students may be grouped into one or more of the following typologies: (1) transfer; (2) vocational; (3) developmental; (4) community education; (5) dual-enrollment; and (6) English as a Second Language (ESL).

Transfer Students. Preparing students to transfer to a four-year institution has always been, and remains, a central mission of the community college (Brint & Karabel, 1991; Cohen & Brawer, 2008). The majority of transfer students attend community college to complete the first two years of coursework before transferring to a four-year institution to earn a bachelor's degree. However, the transfer function may also be used by four-year students who enroll at the community college for one, or just a few, courses. Moreover, growing numbers of students are classified as *reverse transfers*; this includes students who transfer to a community college after attending or earning a degree from a four-year institution (Townsend & Dever, 1999). In certain instances, students who have been academically suspended or dismissed from their four-year institutions are advised to take classes at their community colleges as repeat equivalents to increase or change their grade point averages or to demonstrate that they are ready for college work. Moreover, it is becoming increasingly common for community college students to use multiple institutional attendance patterns (Townsend & Dever, 1999). For instance, a phenomenon labeled *swirling* describes the growing percentage of students who simultaneously earn credits at two or more four-year institutions and/or community colleges (de los Santos & Wright, 1990).

Vocational Students.   Although the number of transfer students exceeds the number of students enrolled in vocational programs, the majority of community college degrees are awarded to students in vocational fields (Townsend, 2001). Vocational students attend community colleges for a variety of reasons, including career access and mobility, retraining, or professional development. Vocational students may also include reverse transfer students who enroll in vocational classes in order to gain access to a technical career (Grubb, 2001). Programmatic offerings are largely dependent on the needs of the local community, but typically include degrees and certificates in fields such as health care, law enforcement, real estate, and retail trade (Cohen & Brawer, 2003).

Developmental Students.   The majority of community college students are either advised or required to enroll in at least one developmental (also known as remedial) class. Placement is based on student performance on the entrance exams taken upon admission to the college (Bailey, Jeong, & Cho, 2010). It has been estimated that nearly 60 percent of community college students enroll in developmental or remedial courses (Bailey, Jenkins, & Leinbach, 2005). Developmental courses typically center on teaching skills (reading, writing, and mathematics), but may also focus on study, coping, or time management skills (Cohen & Brawer, 2003).

Community Education Students.   Several terms are used in defining the community college function, including adult education, continuing education, lifelong learning, community services, community-based education, and contract training. Community education students are typically older and have varying degrees of prior academic experience and achievement, ranging from holding advanced degrees to never having completed high school (Cohen & Brawer, 2003). These lifelong learners may take classes in gardening, photography, nutrition, and auto repair, for personal enrichment or to upgrade their skills.

Dual Enrollment Students.   An increasing number of students are being served by the community colleges through the development of dual enrollment programs. Dual enrollment students are typically juniors and seniors in high school who enroll in community college courses in order to earn credit toward a high school diploma, college, and in certain instances workforce courses for a particular profession. Although once limited to high-achieving high school students, dual enrollment programs are increasingly seen as a way to support the academic preparation of average-achieving students. Unlike Advanced Placement and International Baccalaureate programs, students enrolled in dual credit courses take college courses with a college faculty member, syllabus, and curriculum, often on a community college campus (Karp, Calcagno, Hughes, Jeong, & Bailey, 2007).

English as Second Language Students. The community college also serves a number of English as a Second Language (ESL) students through Intensive English Programs (IEP) or Learning English Electronically (LEE) programs. International students or domestic students needing proficiency enroll in courses in listening, grammar, composition, pronunciation, reading, and vocabulary development in conjunction with ESL classes. ESL students are very diverse. Some students have advanced degrees while others are not literate in their own languages or have very limited educations. Others are Generation 1.5 students, who complete a significant part of their schooling in the United States and likely have a US high school diploma, yet their English proficiency is not advanced enough for regular course work (Crandall & Sheppard, 2004).

COMMUNITY COLLEGE RETENTION

The past four decades of research have repeatedly demonstrated sizable differences between the retention/persistence, degree completion, and transfer rates of community college and four-year students. For instance, data from the BPS: 04/09 reveal that community college students aspiring to earn a bachelor's degree or higher were much less likely to persist anywhere in college or earn a degree when compared to four-year students (see Table 7.2). Differences were seen as early as the end of the first academic year, as nearly all (98 percent) of four-year students were still enrolled, compared to only 92 percent of students who began college at a two-year college. Larger disparities were seen at the end of the second year of college, with 91 percent of four-year students persisting compared with only 71 percent of community college students. These differences continued through the third, fourth, and fifth years of college, with only 55 percent of community college students persisting or earning a degree or certificate by the end of the fifth year as compared with 80 percent of four-year students.

Reasons for Differences in Retention Rates

The Community College Student. Differences in the retention rates of community college and four-year students can, in part, be explained by differences in the student populations at both institutional types. For instance, research findings indicate that being older, African American, or Hispanic, a first-generation college student, a single parent or having children at home,

Table 7.2.   Retention data for four-year and community college students intending to earn a bachelor's degree or higher

	Four-year students (n = 8,360[a])		Community college students (n = 5,850)	
	Not retained and did not earn degree/certificate	Persisted in college or earned degree/certificate	Not retained and did not earn degree/certificate	Persisted in college or earned degree/certificate
Year 1	2.3%	97.7%	8.5%	91.5%
Year 2	9.3%	90.7%	28.6%	71.4%
Year 3	15.0%	85.0%	39.6%	60.4%
Year 4	18.2%	81.8%	43.2%	56.8%
Year 5	20.7%	79.3%	45.5%	54.5%

[a] Data are rounded to the nearest 10 per IES guidelines.
*Data source: U.S. Department of Education, National Center for Education Statistics, 2003–2004 Beginning Postsecondary Students Longitudinal Study, Second Follow-up (BPS:04/09).

and lacking in social and cultural capital are all characteristics associated with students' decisions to withdraw from college (Crisp & Nora, 2010; Feldman, 1993; Fike & Fike, 2008; Schmid & Abell, 2003; Wells, 2008). Although students may enroll at a community college with varying goals and intentions, early work identified students' commitment toward the institution and to earning a college degree/certificate to be related to community college students' decisions to remain enrolled in college (Bers & Smith, 1991; Napoli & Wortman, 1998; Pascarella, Smart, & Ethington, 1986).

Community college students are also much less likely than four-year students to be academically prepared for college. Academic challenges such as not earning a high school diploma, delaying entry into higher education following high school, and high school academic preparation as measured by high school grade point average (GPA) or mathematics courses taken during high school, have all been found to be related to community college retention (Conway, 2009; Crisp & Nora, 2010; Feldman, 1993; Hoachlander, Sikora, & Horn, 2003; Schmid & Abell, 2003). Additionally, many community college students are financially independent and/or face financial challenges associated with college attrition, such as relying on financial aid in the form of grants or loans (Dowd & Coury, 2006; Fike & Fike, 2008; Mendoza, Mendez, & Malcolm, 2009).

The Community College Experience.   Community college students have been found to be 10 to 18 percent more likely to drop out of postsecondary education than four-year students, even after controlling for precollege ability, background characteristics, high school grades, and degree aspirations (Dougherty, 1992). These findings suggest that discrepancies in student retention also might be explained by differences in the college experience of four-year and community college students. Unlike at four-year institutions, the majority of the community college experience occurs inside the classroom, as students typically are only on campus immediately before, during, and after class (Barnett, 2010). In turn, community college students typically do not become involved and/or integrate themselves socially and academically on campus, or at least do so differently from four-year students. Although research findings have been mixed (likely due to differences in how the constructs are measured), many researchers have found social and academic integration to play at least an indirect role in retaining community college students (Bers & Smith, 1991; Hoachlander, Sikora, & Horn, 2003; Karp, Hughes, & O'Gara, 2010–2011; Napoli & Wortman, 1998; Pascarella, Smart, & Ethington, 1986).

A literature review by Summers (2003) identified numerous college experiences related to students' decisions to remain enrolled in college, including working full-time, family responsibilities, student intentions and commitment, involvement in on-campus activities, academic and social integration, registering for classes early, and not making changes to students' schedules. Many, if not all, of these experiences reflect core differences between the college experiences of community college and four-year students. Equally common college experiences, such as enrolling part-time, working off-campus, and dropping courses, also have been found to be negatively related to retention (Crisp & Nora, 2010; Hoachlander et al., 2003; Feldman, 1993; Fike & Fike, 2008; Schmid & Abell, 2003; Windham, 1994). In addition, although the findings are somewhat mixed, enrolling in developmental coursework and the intensity of remediation needed also appear to be related to community college students' decisions to remain enrolled in college (Bettinger & Long, 2005; Crews & Aragon, 2004; Crisp & Nora, 2010; Fike & Fike, 2008; Hoyt, 1999; Jepsen, 2006).

The Community College Context.   Work by Alfonso (2006) found that, compared to four-year institutions, community colleges significantly reduce students' probability of successfully earning a bachelor's degree after controlling for educational expectations, nontraditional enrollment pathways, and college choice considerations. Therefore, although little is known about how institutional-level characteristics are related to community college student retention (Schuetz, 2005), it is fair to assume that the community college context may help explain differences in the retention rates of community college and four-year students. Similarly, although we know little about the effects of institutional practice on community college student retention (Bailey et al., 2004), we assume institutional practice to be related to differences in the retention rates of two- and four-year students. For instance, research has shown that roughly two-thirds of faculty at community colleges are part-time employees who are not typically on campus before or after class, providing students with little opportunity to engage with faculty (Schuetz, 2005).

RETENTION ISSUES FACING THE COMMUNITY COLLEGE

The following paragraphs describe major retention issues facing the American community college, beginning with the challenge of serving a diversity of students. As open-access institutions, it is typically not possible for community colleges to increase their retention or graduation rates by raising admission standards. Moreover, several states mandate that students needing remediation must enroll at a community college, thereby increasing the responsibility of the community colleges to serve academically underprepared students (Bailey et al., 2005). As such, the prevalence of developmental education is considered a critical issue, affecting community colleges (Bailey, 2009), and, more specifically, student retention.

Many student service programs, such as advising, learning communities, and supplemental instruction, have been shown to positively affect retention of developmental and non-developmental students (McArthur, 2005; Richburg-Hayes, Visher, & Bloom, 2008; Scrivener, Bloom, LeBlanc, Paxson, & Sommo, 2008; Tinto & Love, 1995; Zaritsky & Toce, 2006). However, unlike traditional four-year institutions that enroll full-time students who typically live on campus or have ample time outside of class to study with other students, participate in activities, or speak with faculty, the community college has substantially fewer opportunities to engage students. Moreover, there are many barriers to success that are common among community college students and that cannot be controlled or overcome by institution support, such as students' work and family commitments.

Another important retention issue facing community colleges is the diversity of student goals or reasons for attending. As discussed in the preceding section, students enroll at community college for a multitude of reasons, which confounds efforts to understand the relationship between student and institutional factors and student outcomes (Porchea, Allen, Robbins, & Phelps, 2010). For instance, while some transfer students may enroll at a community college intending to remain enrolled for two or more years before transferring to a four-year institution, other transfer students may only intend to take a class or two during the summer. Furthermore, many vocational programs only require a semester or year of coursework before earning a certificate or technical degree.

An absence of institutional resources is yet another significant barrier to retention. Community colleges are currently challenged by increasing enrollments, unreliable funding, and increasing responsibility (Schuetz, 2005). In terms of instructional expenditures, community colleges spend substantially less on average than do four-year institutions (Bailey et al., 2005). Moreover, funding at even the highest level is inadequate, thereby contributing to the weakness in the relationship between spending and student outcomes (Goldrick-Rab, 2010). There is also a lack of resources for faculty development. For instance, at many community colleges the most prevalent form of faculty development is one-time workshops, which have been shown to be largely ineffective (Goldrick-Rab, 2010). Additionally, support for professional development is not commonly provided to adjunct faculty, who in many cases make up the majority of faculty at the community college (Cohen & Brawer, 2003).

A lack of methodologically sound research being conducted at community colleges may also be an important issue affecting retention. On the whole, community colleges do not have adequate resources to properly assess the retention issues on their campus (Bailey et al., 2004). Unlike four-year institutions, many community colleges employ institutional researchers who lack the knowledge to conduct research to properly measure the factors influencing student retention. Also, most states do not have data warehouses that are able to track student enrollment across different postsecondary institutions within or outside of the state (Goldrick-Rab, 2010).

Although retention research and theory is well established, there is relatively little research or theory specific to community college student retention that can inform institutional policy and practice (Wild & Ebbers, 2002). Rather, the large majority of community college research is unpublished, not widely disseminated, and/or not peer-reviewed (Bailey et al., 2004). To our knowledge, there are not many scholars conducting research on community college students who attended two-year colleges as students and/or who worked in a community college setting, thereby limiting scholars' ability to interpret or make sense of findings. At the same time, it can also be difficult for community college scholars to gain access to community college campuses in order to conduct research. In addition, large-scale national datasets are limited in terms of detail provided about specific institutional characteristics and practices to allow for the evaluation of community college characteristics, policies, and practices related to student success (Bailey et al., 2004).

Traditional persistence theories, such as Tinto's Theory of Student Departure (1975, 1993), are largely based on research involving traditional-age students attending residential four-year institutions (Wild & Ebbers, 2002); such research is often assumed to be applicable to community college students (Karp et al., 2010–2011) but has been applied to community college students with mixed findings (Deil-Amen, 2011; Schuetz, 2005). Persistence theory to date has not been able to fully address the diversity of students (Karp, 2011), the community college experience, or the community college context. For example, foundational student retention theory explains that students' withdrawal decisions can be explained largely by social and academic integration (Tinto, 1975, 1993) and student involvement on campus (Astin, 1977, 1993), which, as previously mentioned, may not accurately describe the experiences of the majority of community college students.

CONCLUDING REMARKS

On a final note, although this chapter is written in a book centered on student retention and has focused on retention issues, it is important to reiterate the difficulties and limitations in measuring retention among community college students. Understanding community college retention issues requires one to identify the retention and success goals of an institution as well as the definitions and criteria (Wild & Ebbers, 2002); in doing so, defining and measuring "retention" as the single measure of success may be found to be problematic for most, if not all, community colleges (Moore & Shulock, 2009; Wild & Ebbers, 2002). The diversity of student intentions and goals have caused practitioners, policy makers, accreditation agencies, and university scholars to debate about how appropriately to measure retention or other success outcomes for community college students (Bragg, 2001), as the failure of a student to persist does not necessarily mean that students did not achieve their personal or academic goals (Bailey et al., 2005). The value of a community college education is most commonly judged through the lens of four-year universities, using conventional outcome measures such as retention and graduation rates (Bragg, 2001). However, it may be more appropriate for interested parties to consider alternative measures of student success, such as completion of developmental coursework, the percentage of credits earned versus attempted, degree attainment, or simultaneous enrollment at or transfer to another community college or four-year institution.

REFERENCES

Alfonso, M. (2006). The impact of community college attendance on baccalaureate attainment. *Research in Higher Education, 47*(8), 873–903.

American Association of Community Colleges. (2011). *American graduation initiative: Obama pledges new federal support to community colleges.* American Association of Community Colleges. Retrieved at: www.aacc.nche.edu/Advocacy/aginitiative/Pages/default.aspx

Astin, A. W. (1977). *Four critical years: Effects of college beliefs, attitudes, and knowledge.* San Francisco: Jossey-Bass.

Astin, A. W. (1993). *What matters in college? Four critical years revisited.* San Francisco: Jossey-Bass.

Bailey, T. (2009). Challenge and opportunity: Rethinking the role and function of developmental education in community college. *New Directions for Community Colleges, 145,* 11–30.

Bailey, T., Alfonso, M., Calcagno, J. C., Jenkins, D., Kienzl, G., & Leinbach, T. (2004). *Improving student attainment in community colleges: Institutional characteristics and policies.* New York: Columbia University, Teachers College, Community College Research Center.

Bailey, T. D., Jenkins, D., Leinbach, T., (2005). *Community college low-income and minority student completion study: Descriptive statistics from the 1992 high school cohort.* New York: Columbia University, Teachers College, Community College Research Center.

Bailey, T., Jenkins, D., & Leinbach, T. Barnett, E. A. (2010). Validation experiences and persistence among community college students. *The Review of Higher Education, 34*(2), 193–230.

Bailey, T., Jeong, D. W., & Cho, S.-W. (2010). Referral, enrollment, and completion in developmental education sequences in community colleges. *Economics of Education Review, 29*(2), 255–270.

Bailey, T. D., Leinbach, T., & Jenkins, D. (2005). *Graduation rates, student goals, and measuring community college effectiveness* (Issue Brief No. 28). New York: Columbia University, Teachers College, Community College Research Center.

Barnett, E. A. (2010). Validation experiences and persistence among community college students. *The Review of Higher Education, 34*(2), 193–230.

Berger, J. B. & Lyons S. C. (2005). Past to present: A historical look at retention. In A. Seidman (Ed.), *College student retention: Formula for student success* (pp. 1–27). Westport, CT: American Council on Education and Praeger Publishers.

Bers, T. H. & Smith, K. E. (1991). Persistence of community college students: The influence of student intent and academic and social integration. *Research in Higher Education, 32*(5), 539–556.

Bettinger, E. & Long, B. T. (2005). Remediation at the community college: Student participation and outcomes. *New Directions for Community Colleges, 129*, 17–26.

Bragg, D. D. (2001). Community college access, mission, and outcomes: Considering intriguing intersections and challenges. *Peabody Journal of Education, 76*(1), 93–116.

Brint, S. & Karabel, J. (1991). *The diverted dream: Community colleges and the promise of educational opportunity in America, 1900–1985.* New York: Oxford University Press.

Cohen, A. M. & Brawer, F. B. (2003). *The American community college.* 4th Edition. San Francisco: Jossey-Bass.

Cohen, A. M. & Brawer, F. B. (2008). *The American community college.* San Francisco: Jossey-Bass.

Conley, D. T. (2007). *Redefining college readiness.* Eugene, OR: Educational Policy Improvement Center.

Conway, K. M. (2009). Exploring persistence of immigrant and native students in an urban community college. *The Review of Higher Education, 32*(3), 321–352.

Crandall, J. & Sheppard, K. (2004, December). Adult ESL and the community college. *Council for Advancement of Adult Literacy,* Working Paper 7. CAAL Community College Series, New York, NY. Retrieved from www.caalusa.org/eslreport.pdf.

Crews, D. M., & Aragon, S. R. (2004). Influence of a community college developmental education writing course on academic performance. *Community College Review, 32*(2), 1–18.

Crisp, G. & Nora, A. (2010). Hispanic student success: Factors influencing the persistence and transfer decisions of Latino community college students enrolled in developmental education. *Research in Higher Education, 51*(2), 175–194. doi: 10.1007/s11162-009-9151-x.

Deil-Amen, R. (2011). Socio-academic integrative moments: Rethinking academic and social integration among two-year college students in career-related programs. *Journal of Higher Education, 82*(1), 54–91.

Deiener, T. (1986). *Growth of an American invention: A documentary history of the junior and community college movement.* New York: Greenwood Press.

de los Santos, A., & Wright, I. (1990). Maricopa's swirling students: Earning one-third of Arizona State's bachelor's degrees. *Community, Technical, and Junior College Journal, 60*(6), 32–34.

Dougherty, K. J. (1992). Community colleges and baccalaureate attainment. *Journal of Higher Education 63*(2), 188–214.

Dougherty, K. J. & Bakia, M. (2000). Community colleges and contract training: Content, origins and impact. *Teachers College Record* 102:197–243.

Dowd, A. & Coury, T. (2006). The effect of loans on the persistence and attainment of community college students. *Research in Higher Education, 47*(1), 33–62.

Eaton, J. S. (1994). *Strengthening collegiate education in community colleges.* San Francisco: Jossey-Bass.

Feldman, M. J. (1993). Factors associated with one-year retention in a community college. *Research in Higher Education, 34*(4), 503–512.

Felix, A. & Pope, A. (2010). The importance of community colleges to the tenth district economy. *Economic Review, Third Quarter.*

Fike, D. S. & Fike, R. (2008). Predictors of first-year student retention in the community college. *Community College Review, 36*(2), 68–88.

Floyd, D. L., Skolnik, M. L., & Walker, K. P., eds. (2005). *The community college baccalaureate: Emerging trends and policy issues.* Sterling, VA: Stylus Publishing.

Frye, J. H. (1992). *The vision of the public junior college, 1900–1940.* Westport, CT: Greenwood Press.

Gleazer, E. (1968). *This is the community college.* Boston, MA: Houghton Mifflin.

Goldrick-Rab, S. (2010). Challenges and opportunities for improving community college student success. *Review of Educational Research, 80*(3), 437–469.

Grubb, N. (2001). The decline of community college transfer rates: Evidence from national longitudinal surveys. *The Journal of Higher Education, 62*(2), 194–222.

Hart, R. (2009). Twenty community colleges in seven states join national student success initiative. Achieving the dream. Retrieved from: www.achievingthedream .org/Portal/Modules/f62bff99-dbc8-47ef-9633-7be78ade27bf.asset.

Hoachlander, G., Sikora, A. C., & Horn, L. (2003). Community college students: Goals, academic preparation, and outcomes. *Education Statistics Quarterly, (5)*2 121–128.

Hoyt, J. E. (1999). Remedial education and student attrition. *Community College Review, 27,* 51–73.

Jacobs, J. (2008). *From compliance to capacity building: Community colleges and federal workforce education policy.* Community College Research Center. U. S. Department of Education/ Office of Vocational and Adult Education.

Jepsen, C. (2006, April). *Basic skills in California's community colleges: Evidence from staff and self referrals.* Paper presented at the meeting of American Education Research Association (AERA), San Francisco.

Karp, M. M. (2011). *Toward a new understanding of non-academic student support: Four mechanisms encouraging positive student outcomes in the community college* (Working Paper No. 28). New York: Columbia University, Teachers College, Community College Research Center.

Karp, M. M., Calcagno, J. C., Hughes, K. L., Jeong, D. W., & Bailey, T. R. (2007). *The postsecondary achievement of participants in dual enrollment: An analysis of student outcomes in two states.* New York: Columbia University, Teachers College, Community College Research Center.

Karp, M. M., Hughes, K. L., & O'Gara, L. (2010-2011). An exploration of Tinto's integration framework for community college students. *Journal of College Student Retention: Research, Theory & Practice, 12*(1), 69-86.

Kleiner, B. and Lewis, L. (2005). *Dual Enrollment of High School Students at Postsecondary Institutions: 2002-03.* Washington, DC: U.S. Department of Education, National Center for Education Statistics. Retrieved from: http://nces.ed.gov/pubsearch/pubsinfo.asp?pubid=2005008

Levinson, D. L. (2005). *Community college: A reference handbook.* Santa Barbara: ABC CLIO.

McArthur, R. C. (2005). Faculty-based advising: An important factor in community college retention. *Community College Review, 32*(4), 1-18.

McIntosh, M. F. & Rouse, C. E. (2009). The other college: Retention and completion rates among two-year college students. *Center for American Progress.* Retrieved from: www.americanprogress.org/issues/2009/02/pdf/two_year_colleges.pdf.

Mellow, G. O. & Heelan, C. (2008). *Minding the dream: The process and practice of the American community college.* Lanham, MD: Rowman & Littlefield Publishers, Inc.

Mendoza, P., Mendez, J. P., & Malcolm, Z. (2009). Financial aid and persistence in community colleges: Assessing the effectiveness of federal and state financial aid programs in Oklahoma. *Community College Review, 37*(2), 112-135.

Moore, C. & Shulock, N. (2009). *Student progress toward degree completion: Lessons from the research literature.* Sacramento, CA: Institute for Higher Education Leadership and Policy.

Napoli, A. R. & Wortman, P. M. (1998). Psychosocial factors related to retention and early departure of two-year community college students. *Research in Higher Education, 39*(4), 419-455.

O'Banion, T. (1989). *Innovation in the Community College.* New York: American Council on Education and Macmillan Publishing Company.

O'Banion, T. (1997). *A learning college for the 21st century.* A joint publication of ACE and AACC. Phoenix, AZ: Onyx Press.

Pascarella, E. T., Smart, J. C., & Ethington, C. A. (1986). Long-term persistence of two-year college students. *Research in Higher Education, 24*(1), 47-71.

Pincus, F. L. (1980). The false promise of community colleges: Class conflict and vocational education. *Harvard Educational Review, 50*(3), 332-361.

Porchea, S. F., Allen, J., Robbins, S., & Phelps, R. P. (2010). Predictors of long-term enrollment and degree outcomes for community college students: Integrating academic, psychosocial, socio-demographic and situational factors. *The Journal of Higher Education, 81*(6), 750-778.

Price, D. (2004). Defining the gaps: Access and success at America's community colleges. In K. Boswell & C. D. Wilson (Eds.) *Keeping America's promise* (pp. 35–37). Denver: Education Commission of the State.

Richburg-Hayes, L., Visher, M. G., & Bloom, D. (2008). Do learning communities effect academic outcomes? Evidence from an experiment in a community college. *Journal of Research on Educational Effectiveness, 1*(1), 33–65.

Schmid, C. & Abell, P. (2003). Demographic risk factors, study patterns, and campus involvement as related to student success among Guilford Technical Community College students. *Community College Review, 31*(1), 1–16.

Schuetz, P. (2005). UCLA community college review: Campus environment: A missing link in studies of community college attrition. *Community College Review, 32*(4), 60–82.

Scrivener, S., Bloom, D., LeBlanc, A., Paxson, C. E., & Sommo, C. (2008). A good start: Two-year effects of a freshmen learning community program at Kingsborough Community College. MDRC publication.

Summers, M. D. (2003). ERIC Review: Attrition research at community colleges. *Community College Review, 30*(4), 64–84.

Tinto, V. (1975). Dropout from higher education: A theoretical synthesis of recent research. *Review of Educational Research, 45*, 89–125.

Tinto, V. (1993). *Leaving college: Rethinking the causes and cures of student attrition.* Chicago: University of Chicago Press.

Tinto, V. & Love, A. G. (1995). *A longitudinal study of learning communities at LaGuardia Community College.* University Park, PA: National Center on Postsecondary Teaching, Learning, and Assessment. (ERIC Document Reproduction Service No. ED380178)

Townsend, B. K. (2001). Blurring the lines: Transforming terminal education to transfer education. In D. D. Bragg (Ed.), The new vocationalism in community colleges. *New Directions for Community Colleges, 115* (pp. 63–71). San Francisco: Jossey-Bass.

Townsend, B. K. & Dever, J. T. (1999). What do we know about reverse transfer students? *New Directions for Community Colleges, 106*, 5–13.

Vaughn, G. B. (2000). *The community college story.* Community College Press. ISBN 0-87117323-9.

Wells, R. (2008). The effects of social and cultural capital on student persistence: Are community colleges more meritocratic? *Community College Review, 36*(1), 25–46.

Wild, L. & Ebbers, L. (2002). Rethinking student retention in community colleges. *Community College Journal of Research and Practice, 26*(6), 503–519.

Windham, P. (1994, August). *The relative importance of selected factors to attrition at public community colleges.* Paper presented at the 23rd Annual Conference of the Southeastern Association for Community Colleges, Savannah, GA.

Zaritsky, J. S. & Toce, A. (2006). Supplemental instruction at a community college: The four pillars. *New Directions for Teaching and Learning, 106*, 23–31.

Zwerling, S. L. (1986). The community college and its critics. *New Directions for Community Colleges*, n 54 (June 1986). San Francisco: Jossey-Bass.

8

Pathways to a Four-Year Degree

Determinants of Degree Completion among Socioeconomically Disadvantaged Students

Alberto F. Cabrera, Kurt R. Burkum, Steven M. La Nasa, and Erin W. Bibo

A bachelor's degree is no longer considered a *potential* stepping-stone to a better life. Rather, it is now fully acknowledged as the *gatekeeper* to myriad social and individual benefits, ranging from income, employment stability, and occupational prestige, to engagement in civic and political activities (Baum, Ma, & Payea, 2010; Bowen & Bok, 1998; Hossler, Braxton, & Coopersmith, 1989; Leslie & Brinkam, 1986; Murnane & Levy, 1996; Pascarella & Terenzini, 2005; U.S. Department of Education, 2008). Concerningly, however, the degree attainment rates of socioeconomically disadvantaged students significantly lag behind those of their peers of greater means (Horn & Carroll, 2006; Terenzini, Cabrera, & Bernal, 2001).

The challenges disadvantaged students face at both home and school can greatly impede their chances of completing a four-year degree. The parents of low-socioeconomic (SES) students tend to be less involved in their children's education and school activities (Cabrera & La Nasa, 2001; Gutman & Eccles, 1999). These parents are also less likely to possess knowledge about what steps they need to take to effectively plan for, and prepare their children for, college (Cabrera & La Nasa, 2001; Flint, 1992, 1993; Ikenberry & Hartle, 1998; Lareau, 1987; Lohfink & Paulsen, 2005; McDonough, 1997; Plank & Jordan, 2001; Useem, 1992). Lacking such critical tools can be disempowering; when parents have access to accurate information about college and the college choice process, their child's college-going outcomes are often enhanced (King, 1996; Wimberly & Noeth, 2005). As such, even though a vast majority of parents have high aspirations for their children to attend college, those with lower socioeconomic status levels are less likely to take any action to increase their child's chances of college-going (Cabrera & La Nasa, 2000; Catsambis & Garland, 1997; Cunningham, Erisman, &

Looney, 2007; Hossler, Schmit, & Vesper, 1999; Hossler & Vesper, 1993; Rowan-Kenyon, Bell, & Perna, 2008).

The schools low-SES students attend also compound the problem by lacking funds for support programs and services, highly qualified teachers, adequate career counseling resources, and academically rigorous course offerings (Darling-Hammond, 2004; Lankford, Loeb, & Wykoff, 2002; MacPhail-Wilcox & King, 1986; Venezia, Kirst, & Antonio, 2003). Low-SES students are also more likely than are their wealthier peers to be placed in less rigorous, non-college preparatory academic tracks (Lee & Eckstrom, 1987; Oakes, 1985; Useem, 1992).

By the end of their senior year, low-SES students are less likely to have planned for, and be academically prepared for, college (Adelman, 1999, 2006; Cabrera & La Nasa, 2000; Cabrera & LaNasa, 2001; McPherson & Schapiro, 1998; Terenzini, Cabrera, & Bernal, 2001). Moreover, if low-SES students enroll in college, their degree completion rates lag substantially behind their more affluent peers (Bowen, Chingos, & McPherson, 2009; Carroll, 1989; Paulsen & St. John, 2002; Terenzini, Cabrera, & Bernal, 2001).

Student assistance programs like Title I of the No Child Left Behind Act, TRIO, and GEAR-UP aim to address the barriers to success low-SES students face by enhancing their access to academic preparation opportunities, college information, and assistance in completing the college application process (Cabrera, Deil-Amen, Prabhu, Terenzini, Lee, & Franklin, 2006; Perna, 2002; Tierney, Corwin & Colyar, 2005). Other efforts, such as federal and state financial aid programs, recognize that the high cost of college tuition deters low-income students from pursuing, persisting in, and completing a degree (Hahn & Price, 2008; Heller, 2002; McDonough & Calderone, 2010). The growth of such financial assistance programs supports the value our society places on making a college degree an affordable and viable option for students from economically disadvantaged backgrounds. Since the 1980s, the federal government's investment in such aid programs has grown from approximately $20 billion annually (Lewis, 1989) to $113 billion in 2010 (College Board, 2010). As important as these need-based programs have been in facilitating access to and success in college, low-income students' economic need does not exclusively influence their decisions to enroll in college (Hossler, Schmit, & Vesper, 1999) or to persist (Adelman, 1999; Braxton, 2000; Cabrera, Nora, & Castañeda, 1992; Choy, 2002; Gladieux & Swail, 2000; Swail, 1995; Terenzini, Cabrera, & Bernal, 2001).

Because many studies, with few notable exceptions (e.g., Bowen, Chingos, & McPherson, 2009; Paulsen & St. John, 2002; Rowan-Kenyon, Bell, & Perna, 2008; St. John et al., 1996; Terenzini, Cabrera, & Bernal, 2001; Walpole, 2003), apply SES as a controlling factor, *we still do not know what specific factors lead some low-SES students to succeed on their path to a college degree despite overwhelming odds.* As such, there is a critical need within re-search to explicitly highlight differences in degree enrollment, persistence, and completion behaviors between low-SES students and their more ad-vantaged peers (Paulsen & St. John, 2002; Walpole, 2003). This chapter seeks to further our understanding of why postsecondary attendance and degree completion patterns differ markedly between socioeconomically disadvantaged students and their wealthier peers. In doing so, we examine the enrollment, persistence, and completion behaviors of the High School Sophomore Cohort of 1980 (HSS-1980 cohort). This chapter also ad-dresses three major shortcomings within extant literature on disadvantaged students' path to a four-year degree. First, it studies how determinants of degree completion vary across socioeconomic levels. Second, it adheres to a more comprehensive definition of persistence by focusing on degree completion rather than persistence at the end of the freshman year. Third, it examines the effect of financial aid *in addition to* other important determi-nants of degree completion. The methodology guiding the results reported in this chapter is reported in the appendix.

PATHWAYS TO A FOUR-YEAR DEGREE

In examining the HSS-1980 cohort, Adelman (1999) concluded that students' academic resources for college,[1] developed during their high school years, was the most important determinant of their four-year degree completion rates. The three major components of the academic resources measure—high school rank and GPA, curricular intensity of high school courses, and aptitude test scores—have also been found in separate lit-erature to be highly predictive of college preparedness and enrollment (Berkner & Chavez, 1997; Geiser & Santelices, 2007; NACAC, 2008; Will-ingham, Pollack, & Lewis, 2000). In fact, college admissions counselors consistently report relying heavily on each of such factors when making their enrollment choices (NACAC, 2008). More importantly, however, separate studies by Adelman (2006) and Swail, Cabrera, Lee, and Williams (2005) found the academic resources measure to be the best pre-college predictor of bachelor's degree attainment among high school graduates.

Additionally, Velez (1985) and Carroll (1989) found that the first type of postsecondary institution a student attends is also highly predictive of his or her eventual degree attainment outcomes. Their findings suggest that high school students are more likely to obtain a bachelor's degree if their port of entry to postsecondary education was a four-year institution. Considering that high school students' academic resources for college range from low to medium to high, and that students may opt to initially attend a four-year, two-year, or less-than-two-year postsecondary institution, we determined that the HSS-1980 cohort could follow nine unique pathways to a college degree (see figure 8.1). Figures 8.2 and 8.3 illustrate these pathways exclusively among the lowest and highest SES students within the cohort.

Academic Resources and SES

Students' academic resources for college varied substantially according to their socioeconomic background. While 25 percent of all lowest-SES students secured high levels of academic resources during high school, 59 percent of students from the highest-SES backgrounds obtained similarly high academic resources for college (see figures 8.2 and 8.3). Given that securing academic resources in high school seems to be a determinant of success in postsecondary education (Adelman 1999, 2006; Swail, Cabrera, Lee, & Williams, 2005), it thus appears that the vast majority of the cohort's lowest-SES students were ending their high school careers without the academic tools they needed to succeed in college.

First Type of Institution Attended and SES

As shown in table 8.1, a small but significant association existed between socioeconomic status and the initial postsecondary destinations of the study's cohort (X^2=206; 703; 6, p<0.001, r=0.290). Compared to the average high school sophomore, whose chance of enrolling at a four-year institution was almost 50 percent, the average low-SES sophomore's chance of enrolling at a four-year institution is only 30 percent. When comparing the enrollment rates at four-year institutions between the lowest- and highest-SES students, a huge disparity is evident. Highest-SES students are 37 percent more likely to enroll in a four-year institution than lowest-SES students. Moreover, only 30 percent of lowest-SES students first enrolled at a four-year institution regardless of their academic resources (see figure 8.2). In contrast, 58 percent of all highest-SES students first entered a four-year institution regardless of their academic resources (see figure 8.3).

First Type of Institution Attended and Academic Resources for College

Only half of all students who attended a postsecondary institution were academically qualified for college. That said, students' academic resources for college correlated strongly with the type of institution at which they first enrolled (r=0.412, p <0.001). While 70 percent of students with high levels of academic resources for college first enrolled in four-year institutions, only 16 percent of students with low levels of academic resources initially attended four-year institutions. In fact, for academically deficient

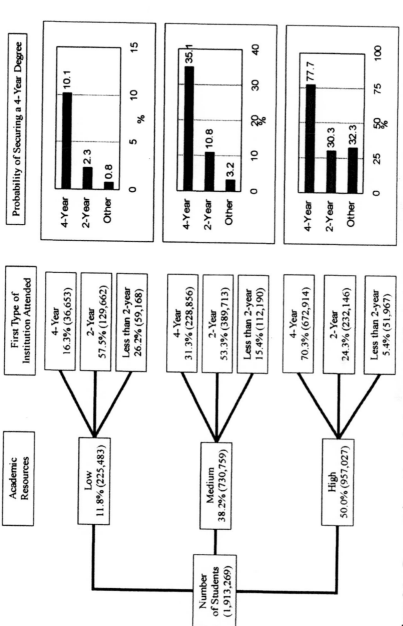

Figure 8.1. Degree attainment by academic resources and first institution type for all students based on high school and beyond, sophomore cohort (NCES 2000-194).

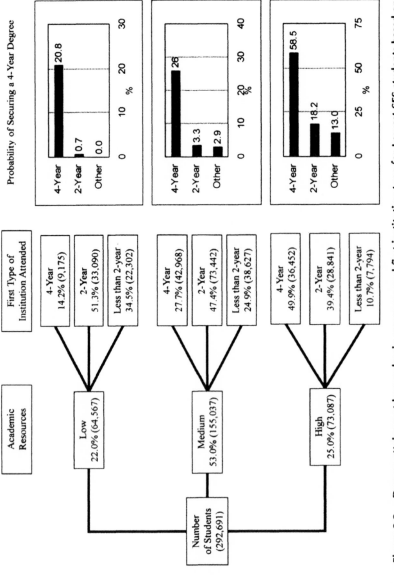

Figure 8.2. Degree attainment by academic resources and first institution type for Lowest-SES students based on High School and Beyond, Sophomore Cohort (NCES 2000-194).

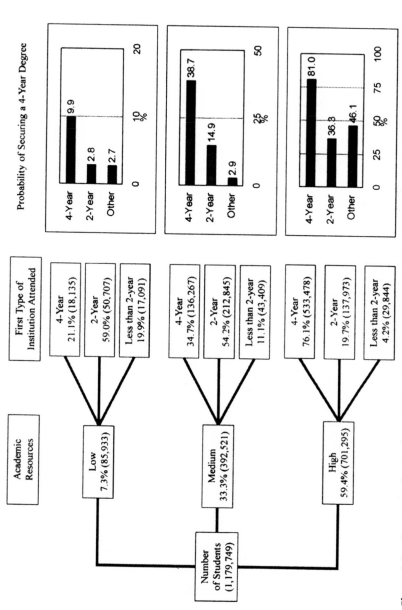

Figure 8.3. Degree attainment by academic resources and first institution type for Highest-SES students based on High School and Beyond, Sophomore Cohort (NCES 2000-194).

Table 8.1. First type of postsecondary institution attended, by SES

Socioeconomic status	First type of postsecondary institution attended		
	Less-than-two-year	*Two-year*	*Four-year*
Lowest	22.3%	47.8%	29.9%
Medium low	14.4%	49.5%	36.1%
Medium high	13.7%	42.5%	43.9%
Highest	3.9%	29.2%	66.9%
Overall	12.0%	40.4%	47.6%

Note: Estimates are based on the HSB/So panel weight PSEWT1 that estimates participation in postsecondary education and degree attainment for the whole 1980 population cohort of high school sophomores (n=2,155,164).

students, first institutional choice was almost exclusively confined to institutions offering an associate's degree or less. These findings are supported by the works of Blecher, Michael, and Hagedorn (2002), Hagedorn, Moon, Cypers, Maxwell, and Lester (2003), and McPherson and Schapiro (1998), who reported that low-income students were more likely to enroll in two-year institutions than are their wealthier peers.

Degree Completion Outcomes and SES

Within our study, students from high socioeconomic backgrounds were, overall, more likely to earn four-year degrees than their less advantaged peers. Within all but one path to degree completion, students from the highest socioeconomic backgrounds were more likely to secure a four-year degree than their disadvantaged peers, regardless of their academic preparation or port of entry. Nevertheless, the results are not entirely dismal for disadvantaged students—lowest-SES students who secured only minimal academic resources and enter a four-year institution were approximately 11 percent more likely to secure a four-year degree than their better-off peers who followed the same path.

Degree Completion Outcomes as a Function of Academic Resources and First Type of Institution Attended

In the aggregate (see figure 8.1), successful pathways to a bachelor's degree appear to follow a logical progression: students who obtain the highest levels of academic preparation during high school and who initially enroll at a four-year institution are most likely to earn a four-year degree. Seventy-eight percent of those students who pursued this path graduated with a bachelor's degree within ten years. Conversely, students with poor levels of academic preparation for college and who chose an institution other than a four-year college or university saw their chances of securing a bachelor's degree diminished. Just 2.3 percent of such students graduated with a four-year degree within a ten-year period of time.

Although initially enrolling in a four-year institution exerted a powerful effect on students' graduation outcomes, their academic preparation for college seemed to provide them increased chances to earn a bachelor's degree, regardless of their institutional port of entry. For example, while 30 percent of highly resourced students initially attending a two-year institution eventually secured a bachelor's degree, only 2.3 percent of two-year college students with low levels of academic resources achieved such degree attainment outcomes (see figure 8.1).

Moving Beyond Descriptive Statistics

While our descriptive examination of the high school class of 1982 confirms an SES-based gap in postsecondary degree attainment outcomes, we cannot yet single out which factors help lowest-SES students overcome their substantially low odds of degree completion. The next section, "Determinants of Degree Completion," examines critical factors enabling students to successfully earn a four-year degree.

DETERMINANTS OF DEGREE COMPLETION

A growing body of literature indicates that what happens to students *before and during* college helps explain their eventual four-year degree completion outcomes (Adelman, 1999, 2006; Astin, 1993; Cabrera, Nora, & Castañeda 1992; Gladieux & Swail, 2000; Pascarella & Terenzini, 2005; Terenzini, Cabrera, & Bernal, 2001; Swail, 1995; Tinto, 1997). Factors that influence students' four-year degree completion include: (a) background characteristics; (b) supports received in high school; (c) academic resources acquired prior to college; (d) degree attainment aspirations; (e) pathways to and through college; (f) collegiate experiences; (g) financial aid; and (h) parental responsibilities (Adelman, 1999, 2006; Cabrera & La Nasa, 2001; Cabrera, Nora, & Castañeda 1992; Hagedorn et al., 2003; Horn & Chen, 1998; Pascarella & Terenzini, 2005; Perna & Titus, 2005; St. John, Cabrera, Nora, & Asker, 2000; Velez & Javalgi, 1987). This section individually examines each predictor of low-income students' degree completion by providing a synopsis of past research, as well as descriptive statistics and regression analyses from our study's examination of the High School Sophomore Cohort of 1980.

Degree Completion and SES

Low-income students face a variety of unique barriers that prevent them from completing a four-year degree (Horn & Carroll, 2006; Terenzini, Cabrera, & Bernal, 2001). As we examined degree completion rates for the 1980 High School Sophomore Cohort, we found a moderate, positive association between a student's socioeconomic background and their chances of earning a bachelor's degree (r=0.335). More specifically, the gap in degree completion rates across SES quartiles substantially increased as one moved up the SES ladder; the highest-SES students were 44 percentage points more likely to earn a college degree than lowest-SES students (see figure 8.4).

Degree Completion and Supports Received in High School

When students receive key forms of support to go to college from their parents, they are more likely to develop college-going aspirations, become academically qualified for college, and apply to, enroll and successfully adjust in, and complete college (Cabrera & La Nasa, 2000, 2001; Cabrera, Nora, & Castañeda, 1992; Flint, 1992; Corwin & Tierney, 2007; Hossler, Schmit, & Vesper, 1999; McClafferty, McDonough, & Nunez, 2002; Perna, 2000; Perna & Titus, 2005; Stage & Hossler, 1989). Research shows that such support can manifest itself in different forms, including through providing motivational support, saving for college, and being involved in a child's school activities (Cabrera & La Nasa, 2001; Corwin & Tierney, 2007; Stage & Hossler, 1989; McClafferty, McDonough, & Nunez, 2002).

Some research suggests that the level of parental support students receive varies by their socioeconomic status. Parents experiencing financial dif-

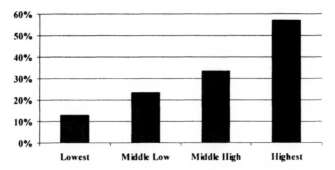

Figure 8.4. Observed probabilities of degree completion by 1993 for the High School Sophomore Cohort of 1980 (by SES). Estimates based on the High School and Beyond: 80 (sophomore cohort).

ficulties are less hopeful about their child's college prospects and are less involved in their children's educations (Cabrera & La Nasa, 2000; Crosnoe, Mistry, & Elder, 2002; Gutman & Eccles, 1999). Furthermore, parents of lesser means are also less likely to proactively save for their child's college education (Cabrera & La Nasa, 2000; Hossler & Vesper, 1993; Rowan-Kenyon, Bell, & Perna, 2008). Miller (1997) reported that less than 33 percent of low-income parents saved enough money to cover more than 10 percent of their children's college education costs. Overall, even though a vast majority of parents have high aspirations for their children to attend college, those with lower socioeconomic status levels are less likely to take any action to increase their child's chances of college-going (Cabrera & La Nasa, 2000; Catsambis & Garland, 1997; Cunningham, Erisman, & Looney, 2007; Hossler, Schmit & Vesper, 1999; Hossler & Vesper, 1993; Rowan-Kenyon, Bell, & Perna, 2008).

Our analysis of the HSS-1980 cohort revealed a positive relationship between students' SES and the extent to which they received support to go to college not only from their parents, but also from their high school personnel and high school friends. Ninety-three percent of highest-SES students reported their parents supported them to pursue a college degree, while only 69 percent of lowest-SES students received parental encouragement to go to college ($r=0.248$; see table 8.2). Similarly, while 77 percent of highest-SES students reported encouragement from high school professionals, only 61 percent of lowest-SES students reported receiving support from school sources ($r= 0.130$). Less than 50 percent of lowest-SES students were encouraged by their high school friends to earn a college degree, whereas more than three-fourths of highest-SES students received peer support to become a college graduate ($r= 0.216$).

Degree Completion and Academic Resources

Being academically qualified for college significantly increases a student's chances of graduating high school, applying to college, and successfully

Table 8.2. Differences in levels of support, by SES (proportion comparison)

Supports	Socioeconomic status (in quartiles)				F/χ^2	R
	Lowest	Middle-low	Middle-high	Highest		
Parental	68.8%	71.1%	83.6%	92.7%	131125.46, $p<.001$	.248
High school professionals	61.3%	63.5%	68.9%	76.7%	35994.37, $p<.001$	.130
Friends	47.7%	54.2%	64.9%	75.5%	98,770.08, $p<.001$	.216

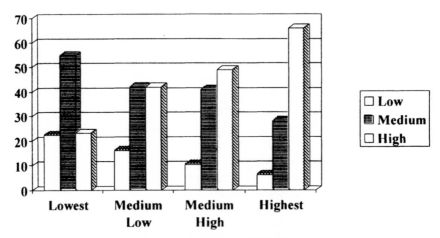

Figure 8.5. Academic resources among 1980 High School Sophomores (by SES). Estimates based on 1980 High School Sophomores (r=.216).

attaining a four-year degree (Adelman 1999, 2006; Cabrera & La Nasa, 2001; NACAC, 2008; Swail, Cabrera, Lee, & Williams, 2005). We found a moderate association between SES and academic resources among the HSS-1980 cohort (r=0.216). While 66 percent of highest-SES students possessed high levels of academic resources for college, merely 23 percent of lowest-SES students enjoyed the same level of academic resources (see figure 8.5).

Degree Completion & Attainment Aspirations

Aspiring to earn a four-year college degree enables middle and high school students and their families to ready themselves for college (Cabrera & La Nasa, 2000, 2001; Hossler, Braxton, & Coopersmith, 1988; Rumberger, 1995). Students aspiring to attain at least a four-year degree are predisposed to take the appropriate high school course curriculum, graduate high school, and apply to, enroll in, and complete college (Adelman, 1999; 2006; Cabrera & La Nasa, 2001).

Some research indicates students' SES levels moderate their degree aspirations (Terenzini, Cabrera, & Bernal 2001). We found significant SES-based differences in the four-year degree attainment aspirations among members of the HSS-1980 cohort. As students' SES levels increased, so did their chances of developing college completion aspirations by the time they reached the twelfth grade (r=0.335). While 70 percent of the lowest-SES students had no aspirations to attend college by their senior year in high school, 74 percent of highest-SES students had developed college-going aspirations by the twelfth grade. In other words, lowest-SES students were 44

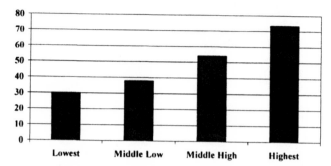

Figure 8.6. Degree aspirations for the 1980 High School Sopho-mores (by SES). Estimates based on the High School and Beyond: 80 (sophomore cohort). Panel weight PSEWT1 (r=.335).

percentage points less likely to aspire to a four-year degree than were their peers of greater means (see figure 8.6).

DEGREE COMPLETION AND PATHWAYS TO AND THROUGH COLLEGE

Mounting research shows that not all high school students follow the same, straightforward path to and through college (Adelman, 1999, 2006; Carroll, 1989; Goldrick-Rab, 2006; Hearn 1992). Examining the college paths of the HSS-1980 cohort, Carroll (1989) reported that one out of five students delayed entry into postsecondary education, initially entered less than four-year institutions, and enrolled in college on a part-time status. Additionally, Adelman (1999, 2006) determined that a considerable pro-portion of high school students delay entry into college, and that most col-lege students do not graduate within four years.

Our examination of the college paths followed by members of the HSS-1980 cohort shows lowest-SES students are indeed more prone to follow traditionally less successful paths to degree attainment. Only 30 percent of lowest-SES students entered higher education at a four-year institution, compared to 67 percent of highest-SES students (see table 8.1). Moreover, less than half of lowest-SES students maintained continuous enrollment in college, compared to more than 70 percent of highest-SES students. Simi-larly, while 41 percent of lowest-SES students dropped or withdrew from more than 10 percent of their college courses, 32 percent of highest-SES students engaged in this at-risk behavior (see table 8.3).

Table 8.3. Patterns of enrollment and coursework participation, by SES

Variable	Lowest	Middle-low	Middle-high	Highest	X^2	R
Continuous enrollment	48.4%	58.7%	59.5%	71.3%	44989.59 $p<.001$	0.147
Percentage of courses dropped, withdrew or left incomplete						
Less than 10%	58.9%	64.3%	62.0%	68.3%		
10–20%	14.7%	15.8%	14.8%	15.0%	17288.64	
More than 20%	26.4%	19.9%	23.2%	16.7%	$p< .001$	–.066

Degree Completion and Collegiate Experiences

Students who spend increased levels of time focusing on academics, by either working to maintain their grades or by engaging their faculty, are more likely to achieve eventual gains in critical thinking and other key competencies, as well as improved four-year degree completion outcomes (Astin, 1993; Cabrera, Colbeck, & Terenzini, 2001; Kuh, Douglas, Lund, & Ramin-Gyurnek, 1994; Pascarella & Terenzini, 2005). Students also benefit from being engaged and involved within their college environments. Levels of students' college engagement and involvement in out-of-class activities and jobs influence their cognitive and affective development (Kuh, Douglas, Lund, & Ramin-Gyurnek, 1994) and ability to adjust to their postsecondary institutions (Cabrera, Nora, & Castaneda, 1992; Hossler, 1984; Nora, Cabrera, Hagedorn, & Pascarella; 1996; Olivas, 1985; Pascarella & Terenzini, 2005; Stampen & Cabrera, 1986, 1988).

Our research uncovered three primary differences between the college experiences of the cohort's lowest and highest-SES students (see table 8.4). First, lowest-SES students earned lower college GPAs compared to highest-SES students. Second, lowest-SES students were 36 percentage points less likely to take college math courses, and 32 percentage points less likely to enroll in science courses than their highest-SES counterparts. These curricular choices set lowest-SES students at a disadvantage, both because students who take math and science courses are more likely to graduate from college (Adelman, 2006), and because some of the nation's fastest growing occupations require coursework or degrees in math or science (EOPCEA, 2009). Finally, the lowest-SES students were thirteen percentage points less likely than the highest-SES students to work at an on-campus job. This is concerning, because working on campus provides students access to members of

Table 8.4. Differences in collegiate experiences and curriculum patterns, by SES (means and proportions comparison)

| Variable | Socioeconomic status (in quartiles) | | | | F/X^2 | r |
	Lowest	Middle-low	Middle-high	Highest		
GPA	2.33	2.51	2.49	2.65	11143.99, $p<.001$	.112
Out of classroom experiences	3.61	3.64	3.65	3.83	9114.92, $p<.001$	.108
Quality of instruction	4.05	4.11	4.04	4.09	961.74, $p<.001$	.007
Counseling	3.36	3.44	3.31	3.43	1472.62, $p<.001$	.011
Campus facilities	3.97	3.97	9.97	4.06	1155.36, $p<.001$	.035
Institutional prestige	3.81	3.81	3.81	3.94	2451.29, $p<.001$	.051
Worked on campus	27.5%	32.9%	42.9%	40.7%	33522.06, $p<.001$	.119
Enroll in at least one Math course	23.7%	33.6%	41.5%	59.3%	164,528.54, $p<.001$	.264
Enroll in at least one Science course	24.4%	33.9%	41.1%	56.7%	134,332.16, $p<.001$	.239

the campus community as well as critical information and resources about their institution (Astin, 1993; Stampen & Cabrera, 1988).

Degree Completion and Financial Aid

Some researchers have examined college persistence and completion as the by-product of students' economic decisions (e.g., Manski & Wise, 1983; St. John, 1990; St. John, Andrieu, Oescher, & Starkey, 1994; Stampen & Cabrera, 1986, 1988). Under this scenario, a student persists to the extent to which the social and economic benefits of attending college outweigh the costs and benefits associated with alternative activities (i.e., working full-time). Higher costs of attendance relative to students' perceptions of their ability to pay could influence their decision to drop out, particularly if the costs of attending college far exceed future benefits (Becker, 1964). However, misunderstandings about college costs and ways to pay for college prevail among individuals from low-socioeconomic status levels

(Ikenberry & Hartle, 1998; Plank & Jordan, 2001). In fact, among a group of approximately one thousand surveyed high school graduates who had been academically qualified to, but did not, enroll in a four-year college, more than 80 percent reported financial concerns as the most significant barrier between them and a postsecondary education (Hahn & Price, 2008). Hall, Cabrera, and Bibo (2010) found that parents' concerns about the cost of college negatively influenced their children's own concerns about paying for college, their eventual college enrollment decisions, and the type of institution at which they initially enrolled.

Reduced tuition, direct grants, low interest loans, and subsidized work-study programs all seek to equalize, if not increase, the benefits of attending college relative to its costs (Bowen, 1977; Cabrera, Stampen, & Hansen, 1990; St. John, 1994). Research of the effect financial aid plays on degree completion is contradictory. Nora (1990), Voorhees (1987), and St. John (1990) found that all forms of federal support are equally effective in preventing students from dropping out. However, Stampen and Cabrera (1986, 1988) found persistence rates were highest when student aid packages included work-study programs. While Adelman (1999) reported that both grants and loans had a small but positive contribution to the probability of securing a college degree, Astin (1975) found that loans had negatively affected the college persistence outcomes of low-income students.

Not surprisingly, we found differences in the amount of financial aid received among students of varying SES levels. More than half of the lowest-SES students within the study received grants, whereas 36 percent of highest-SES students received this kind of financial aid (see table 8.5). This finding is consistent with Stampen and Cabrera's (1988) study of the way in which student aid was targeted in the early 1980s. While SES-based differences exist between student loan recipients ($r=0.059$), the gap between the lowest- and highest-SES students receiving loans only approximated five percentage points. Interestingly, in spite of the fact that lowest-SES students logically struggle more to pay for college than their wealthier peers,

Table 8.5. Financial aid factors, by SES

Variable	Lowest	Middle-low	Middle-high	Highest	X^2	r
Satisfied with cost of attending	60.0%	63.7%	59.1%	57.0%	4475.84, $p<.001$	.023
Received grants between 1982–1986	53.5%	44.6%	41.3%	36.2%	34095.21, $p<.001$	–.118
Received loans between 1982–1986	38.9%	36.5%	40.7%	33.6%	8343.610, $p<.001$	.059

they reported being relatively more satisfied with the costs associated with attending their college than the highest-SES students surveyed for the study.

Degree Completion and Parental Responsibilities

Having the responsibility of caring for a child while attending college is also associated with decreased outcomes of degree completion. Nora, Cabrera, Hagedorn, and Pascarella (1996) report that parental responsibilities often compete with students' academic and social opportunities at college, thereby lessening students' engagement in the college experience, their intellectual development, and subsequent persistence. Adelman (1999) adds that taking care of children while attending college lessens one's chances of completing a degree within ten years. While the above findings apply for college students as an aggregate group, the extent to which they hold true explicitly among lowest-SES students has not been examined.

Within our study's cohort, we found that lowest-SES students are most likely to have child care responsibilities (r=0.191). While 24 percent of lowest-SES students reported having to care for a child, only 6 percent of the highest-SES students within the study indicated similar parental responsibilities (see figure 8.7).

WHAT REALLY FACILITATES DEGREE COMPLETION?

The previous section identified a 44 percentage point gap in degree completion outcomes between lowest and highest-SES students, and individually described the multiple factors that played a significant role in influencing

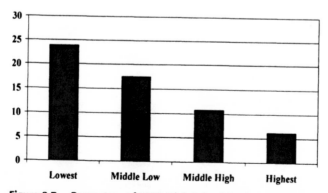

Figure 8.7. Percentage of 1980 High School Sophomore Cohort enrolled in college who had parental responsibilities by 1986 (by SES). Estimates based on the High School and Beyond:80 (sophomore cohort). Panel weight PSEWT1. (r=.191).

such a disparity. However, because such descriptive approaches do not take into account how such factors interact with one another, they cannot effectively capture each variable's net effect. In this section, we illustrate the results of a multiple logistic regression model that took into account the simultaneous interplay between factors influencing degree completion. The model's results uncovered that the study's descriptive statistics overestimated the role SES played in accounting for differences in degree completion outcomes between students of different backgrounds (see table 8.6 and figure 8.8). More importantly, the model's results identified which factors mattered most in facilitating the degree completion of all students, and lowest-SES students especially.

Supports Received in High School

Controlling for SES and other factors influencing students' degree attainment outcomes, receiving parental or peer support to go to college increased students' chances of earning a four-year degree by 4 and 5 percent, respectively (see table 8.6). Contradictory to our expectations, however, when we disaggregated our findings according to socioeconomic groups, we found that receiving such supports did not influence the degree attainment outcomes of lowest-SES students at a statistically significant level.

Academic Resources

Consistent with Adelman (1999), we found that students' academic resources had a substantial effect on their degree completion. Across all SES groups, students who possessed moderate or high levels of academic resources were 4 percent and 12 percent more likely to complete a college

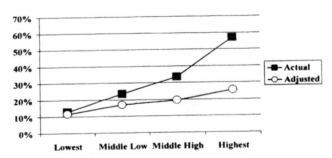

Figure 8.8. Adjusted probabilities of degree completion by 1993 for the 1980 High School Sophomore Cohort (by SES). Estimates based on the High School and Beyond:80 (sophomore cohort). Panel weight PSEWT1. (*r*=.335).

Table 8.6. Changes in the probability of degree completion

Factors	All	Socioeconomic Status			
		Lowest	Middle-low	Middle-high	Highest
SES					
Middle low	0.106*				
Middle high	0.149*				
Highest	0.235*				
Female	−0.044**	−0.076**	−0.052**	−0.043**	−0.022*
Ethnicity					
African American	–	–	−0.065*	−0.068*	0.112**
Hispanic	−0.038*	−0.055*	–	−0.088*	–
Asian American	0.192**	0.369**	–	0.105*	0.209**
High School Support					
From parents	0.041*	–	–	0.092*	–
From high school professionals	–	–	–	–	0.076*
From friends	0.052*	–	0.140*	0.152*	–
Academic Resources					
Moderate	0.044*	0.191*	–	0.081*	0.075*
High	0.120*	0.319*	–	0.274*	0.087*
Attainment Aspirations	0.229*	0.223*	0.425*	0.155*	0.255*
Type of First Institution Attended					
Two-year Institution	0.183*	0.461*	0.390*	–	0.253*
Four-year Institution	0.459*	0.686*	0.496*	0.311*	0.391*
Continuous Enrollment	0.230*	0.267*	0.377*	0.158*	0.224*
DWI Index					
10–20% of courses	−0.132*	–	−0.086*	−0.172*	−0.208*
At least 20% of courses	−0.267*	−0.124*	−0.156*	−0.270*	−0.364*
Number of Math Courses					
One course	0.274*	0.031*	0.422*	0.339*	0.193*
Two courses	0.292*	0.340*	0.296*	0.221*	0.296*
Three or more courses	0.419*	0.567*	0.622*	0.497*	0.268*
Number of Science Courses					
One course	0.206*	0.245*	0.219*	0.196*	0.085*
Two courses	0.208*	0.262*	0.249*	0.192*	0.151*
Three or more courses	0.287*	0.420*	0.355*	0.355*	0.148*
Collegiate Experiences					
Out-of-classroom	0.083*	–	0.157*	0.114*	0.037*
Quality of instruction	0.076*	0.148*	–	0.148*	0.027*
Counseling	0.009*	0.055*	–	0.022*	0.021*
Campus facilities	–	–	0.040*	–	–
Institutional prestige	0.012*	0.057*	0.023*	–	0.018*
Worked on campus	0.037*	0.019*	0.023*	0.092*	0.009*
College GPA	0.320*	0.279*	0.493*	0.190*	0.328*
Satisfaction with Costs	–	0.071*	–	–	–
Financial Aid					
Loans	0.104*	0.112*	0.296*	0.036*	0.051*
Grants/scholarships	0.070*	0.077*	0.099*	0.080*	0.085*
Parental Responsibilities	−0.221*	−0.126*	–	−0.229*	−0.458*

Note: Only delta-ps associated with significant betas are reported. See Table A3 for significant betas. *p<.01, **p<.001.

degree within ten years of graduating from high school than peers with low levels of academic resources (see table 8.6). Lowest-SES students benefit even more so from building their academic resources; those with moderate or high levels of academic resources were 19 percent and 31 percent more likely to earn a four-year degree than their peers of similar backgrounds with low academic resources (see table 8.6).

Attainment Aspirations

Across all SES quartiles, high school students with college degree aspirations were 23 percent more likely to achieve their attainment goals. While the effect of having college completion aspirations varies across SES groups, lowest-SES students benefit from holding such aspirations at essentially the same level as the entire population of students within the cohort (see table 8.6).

Pathways To and Through College

For all students, those who first enrolled in a four-year or two-year institution were 46 percent and 18 percent more likely, respectively, to earn a college degree than those who initially enrolled at an institution offering less-than-two-year degrees. Lowest-SES students who first enrolled in a two-year or four-year institution were 46 percent and 69 percent more likely to earn a four-year degree than their peers who initially enrolled in a less-than-two-year institution. This finding is especially important, because more than 22 percent of lowest-SES students within the study began their postsecondary education at a less-than-two-year college.

Among students within the study's cohort, those who did not maintain continuous college enrollment were 23 percent less likely to earn a bachelor's degree. Moreover, those who dropped, withdrew from, or failed to complete between 10 to 20 percent of their college coursework were 13 percent less likely to secure a four-year degree. Dropping, withdrawing from, or failing to complete more than 20 percent of college coursework reduced a student's chances to complete a degree by 27 percent (see table 8.6). Among lowest-SES students exclusively, failing to maintain a continuous enrollment in college was associated with a 27 percent decrease in attainment outcomes. However, dropping, withdrawing from, or failing to complete college courses had a lesser impact on lowest-SES students' completion than on their peers of greater means.

Collegiate Experiences

Most collegiate experiences had a positive impact on degree completion outcomes across all students within the study. Among these factors, however, students' academic performance in college (GPA) most significantly affected their four-year degree attainment rates. Across all SES groups, an increase in GPA improved students' chances of completing a four-year degree by 32 percent. That said, the impact of student GPA varied among SES groups. For example, increases in GPA increased degree completion by 28 percent among lowest-SES students, and 33 percent for highest-SES students (see table 8.6).

Students' curricular choices also played a crucial role in their degree attainment outcomes. Within the entire cohort of students within our study, those who took one college math course increased their degree completion by 27 percent. Moreover, those who enrolled in three or more math courses were 42 percent more likely to earn a four-year degree than peers who took no college math courses at all. Additionally, students who took a college science course increased their degree completion by 21 percent. Lowest-SES students seemed to disproportionately benefit from enrolling in math and science courses during college. For this group, taking one, two, or three or more college science courses increased their chances of degree completion by 25, 26, and 42 percent, respectively. Lowest-SES students taking one, two, or three or more college math courses increased their chances of degree completion by 3, 34, and 57 percent, respectively (see table 8.6).

Across SES groups, positive out-of-classroom activities and exposure to high-quality instruction each increased students' degree completion outcomes by 8 percent. Lowest-SES students within the study appeared to especially benefit from exposure to high-quality instruction; when enrolled in effectively taught courses, their four-year graduation rates increased by 15 percent. Working on campus also helped lowest-SES students persist to graduation. For every year a lowest-SES student worked on campus, his or her chances of completing a degree increased by 2 percent (see table 8.6).

Financial Aid

For all students within the study, those who received grants and loans were more likely to complete a four-year degree than peers who received no aid; receiving a grant increased students' degree completion by 7 percent, and receiving loans increased attainment by 10 percent. Lowest-SES students who received loans or grants increased their degree completion outcomes by 11 percent and 8 percent, respectively (see table 8.6).

Parental Responsibilities

College students who needed to care for a child or children were 22 percent less likely to complete a four-year degree than peers without any parental responsibilities. Interestingly, this negative effect was most strongly experienced by highest-SES college students with children, who were 46 percent less likely to earn a four-year degree than peers without such familial obligations. Conversely, lowest-SES students with parental responsibilities were only 13 percent less likely to complete their degrees than those who did not need to care for children during college (see table 8.6).

Joint Effects

While each of the aforementioned factors influences students' degree completion outcomes at a statistically significant level, the collective or joint effects of these variables can be even more powerful. For example, if a student maintained continuous enrollment *and* did not drop, withdraw from, or leave incomplete more than 10 percent of his or her courses, chances of degree completion increased by 35 percent.[2] The joint effect of academic performance and curricular choices is particularly noteworthy. For example, a student who was academically prepared, aspired for college, maintained a 'C' average in college, and took one college-level math and science course experienced a net increase in the probability of degree completion of 36 percent. If that same student had maintained a 'B' average, his or her chances of securing a degree increased to 68 percent.

DISCUSSION

Pathways to a Four-Year Degree

A high school graduate faces nine pathways to a college degree. These pathways result from several degrees of academic preparation for college and the type of postsecondary institution first attended. Not all paths are equally effective in leading to a four-year degree. For example, 78 percent of students with high academic resources and who initially enroll at a four-year college secure a bachelor's degree within a decade. Conversely, students with poor academic preparation who first enter a two-year institution only face a 10 percent chance of completing a bachelor's degree within ten years.

Additionally, certain pathways are less accessible to students from underserved backgrounds. Within the HSS-1980 cohort, the students who travelled along the most successful pathways to a four-year degree were most often from highest-SES backgrounds. On the other hand, the lowest-SES students within the study often followed pathways that least often led to their four-year degree attainment. Such divergences along the path to degree completion are primarily due to the fact that lowest-SES students are less likely to be academically prepared for college, and more likely to initially enroll in a two-year or less-than-two-year college. As such, more research needs to explore the influences behind such academic preparedness and institutional choice outcomes, and identify if and how these outcomes can be improved to promote degree completion among lowest-SES students.

Determinants of Degree Completion

By 1993, 13 percent of the lowest-SES students within the HSS-1980 cohort graduated from college with a baccalaureate degree. Over the same period of time, 57 percent of the cohort's highest-SES students graduated with a four-year degree. While students' SES explained a portion of their degree attainment outcomes, other, controllable factors played a greater role in predicting their eventual college completion. Such factors, which included students' academic resources, initial institution attended, support received during high school, degree attainment aspirations, continuous enrollment in college and courses, college experiences, and financial aid helped equalize degree completion outcomes between lowest- and highest-SES students within the study. Among lowest-SES students, gaining high levels of academic resources during high school, initially enrolling in a four-year college, and taking multiple college-level math and science courses most dramatically improved their chances of earning a four-year degree. More specifically, when such factors are improved collectively, students are even more likely to successfully complete college. As such, given that no single silver bullet exists to drastically change the college completion rates of lowest-SES students, policymakers and educational leaders must implement strategies and programs that take a multi-faceted approach to achieve these outcomes.

Additionally, it is critical to note that a student's path to degree completion begins in high school, if not sooner, when he or she accrues necessary academic resources for college. Moreover, during this period of time, a student can develop key aspirations to attain a college degree, and receive critical support from parents and peers to apply to, enroll in, and complete a college education. Therefore, intervention strategies must include key stakeholders from both the K-12 and postsecondary worlds to effectively ensure that more students, and especially those from lowest-SES backgrounds, earn four-year degrees. We also believe that improved partnerships and articulation agreements between high schools and colleges will enhance students' degree attainment outcomes. Indeed, more research on the effects of high school and college collaborations and partnerships on students' degree completion would certainly serve as a welcome complement to this study.

Limitations

Readers should bear in mind the following limitations when forming their own conclusions about the validity and usefulness of our findings.

Our conclusions are based on just one generation of students, who were high school sophomores in 1980. During the last thirty years, school reform initiatives, changes in the composition of financial aid, and substantial technological and economic transformations have produced new generations for which the determinants of transfer and degree completion may be qualitatively different. We can tell the story of one single cohort; we cannot presume all their experiences are applicable to subsequent groups of students.

Additionally, our study does not take into account some factors that likely affect students' college experiences, including their academic and intellectual development, institutional commitment, campus engagement, student effort, campus and classroom climates, frequency and quality of interactions with faculty and peers, exposure to different teaching practices, out-of-classroom experiences, and curricular quality (Astin, 1993; Cabrera, Colbeck, & Terenzini, 2001; Cabrera & Nora, 1994; Chickering & Reisser, 1993; Hurtado, Milem, Clayton-Pedersen, & Allen, 1999; Kuh, 2000; Kuh, Douglas, Lund, & Ramin-Gyurnek, 1994; Kuh, Pace, & Vesper, 1997; Nora & Cabrera, 1993; Pace, 1980; Pascarella, & Terenzini, 1980, 2005; Tinto, 1993, 1997). The lack of such measures, therefore, may lead to an underestimation of the effect of college experiences on degree completion. Though most of those measures were not available at the time the database was designed, future designers of national databases should consider their inclusion.

Finally, while our analyses highlight some of the characteristics that predict students' degree attainment, they offer only a glimpse as to why and how each factor plays a role in students' pathways to degree completion. As such, we believe that future research on this topic would greatly benefit from qualitative components that could effectively paint a picture of the complex process individual students undergo along the road to and through college.

Strengths

Our study uses degree completion as the measure of collegiate success. As shown by Adelman (1999, 2006), persistence to degree completion is a more valid and reliable measure of a student's success in college than is year-to-year persistence rate. Moreover, even though students benefit both economically and socially from attending some college, they reap significantly greater benefits from completing a degree (Baum, Ma, & Payea, 2010).

Additionally, this study builds upon extant works that promote the importance of focusing on bachelor's degree attainment, rather than other forms of degree or certificate completion (e.g., Adelman, 1999, 2006;

Advisory Committee on Student Financial Assistance, 2006, 2010; Baum, Ma, & Payea, 2010). Establishing a specific goal of four-year degree attainment is important for three reasons. First, four-year degree graduates are more likely to be employed than graduates of two-year or certificate programs (Baum, Ma, & Payea, 2010). Bachelor's degree recipients are also more likely to earn higher annual salaries, and earn more over the course of their lifetimes, than completers of other programs and degrees (Baum, Ma, & Payea, 2010). Perhaps most importantly, as we have illustrated in this study, students, and especially those from lowest-SES backgrounds, are more likely to persist and complete college when they initially enroll at a four-year institution (Advisory Committee on Student Financial Assistance, 2006, 2010).

We also believe that our study is methodologically strong for three specific reasons. First, because we used a database that allowed us to track a large, nationally representative sample of students, we believe that our findings can be generalized at a national level. Second, because our measures of student academic resources, enrollment patterns, curricular choices, financial aid, academic performance, satisfaction, and engagement are based on verifiable student records and surveys (Adelman, 1999), we are confident about the study's internal validity as well as the reliability of the relationships observed between these performance measures and students' degree completion outcomes. Third, our work moves beyond descriptive statistics, which often overestimate the connection between variables and fail to take into account the simultaneous effects of factors on a given outcome. Though commonly used to inform policymaking, descriptive statistics may overestimate to policymakers the importance of socioeconomic status as a determinant of transfer and degree completion. The real danger of using descriptive statistics as the basis of policy analysis is that the choice of variables automatically defines the problem and the solution. Rather, by employing a multiple logistic regression model that took into account the simultaneous interplay between factors influencing degree completion, we concluded that controllable factors beyond students' SES levels most significantly influenced their degree attainment outcomes.

Conclusions and Implications

Our study suggests that factors other than students' socioeconomic status play a larger role in helping them successfully navigate the pathway to college completion. As with countless generations, the path to a four-year degree for members of the HSS-1980 cohort began during high school, if not earlier (Cabrera & La Nasa, 2001; Hossler, Braxton, & Coopersmith, 1988; Wallace, Abel, & Ropers-Huilman, 2000). Additionally, students' academic, social, and extracurricular choices and experiences in college also greatly impacted their degree attainment outcomes. As such, it is critical for both policies and intervention programs to begin preparing students for college during grades K-12, and to continue supporting them through college, in order to promote their eventual degree completion outcomes. This section highlights suggestions, which can be adapted and implemented by middle and high schools, colleges, parents, policymakers, and national college access and success programs, which we believe will likely improve the four-year degree attainment rates of all students, and lowest-SES students especially.

During middle and high school, students' postsecondary and career aspirations can motivate them to secure the academic resources necessary to successfully complete a four-year degree. According to both Cabrera and La Nasa (2001) and Hossler, Braxton, and Coopersmith (1988), starting as early as the seventh grade, a student begins to establish his or her educational and occupational goals, and think about how the two might be related. For instance, a student who aspires to become a lawyer might learn that he or she will need to pursue both college and law school, and hone his or her analytical, reading, writing, public speaking, and logic skills to help prepare for the profession. Thus, while building and honing their career goals, students also often develop specific postsecondary aspirations, and learn what steps they must take during both middle and high school to realize their dreams. Schools can foster these outcomes by inviting parents or school alumni to speak about their work, and what qualifications their jobs require. Teachers can also explain the real-world relevance of a given topic or lesson by highlighting occupations that utilize such lessons or skills on a regular basis. Finally, schools can invite representatives from local colleges to talk about their various coursework and major offerings, and what careers graduates from these departments often pursue.

The quality and rigor of middle and high school curricula are intrinsically tied to students' academic preparation for college (Adelman, 1999, 2006; Horn & Nunez, 2000). Colleges, universities, and national postsecondary access programs can work with elementary and secondary schools in aligning curriculum with competencies, experiences, values, and skills deemed essential for future collegial work (Tierney, Corwin, & Colyar, 2005). Universities can also assist low-income school districts with faculty and resources to teach higher level math and science courses (Adelman, 1999). Additionally, in order to promote the implementation of college preparedness curricula, standardized tests should be designed to provide schools, teachers, students, and their parents with an accurate assessment of students' academic resources and preparedness for college (National Research Council, 1999; Kirst & Venezia, 2004).

Schools and postsecondary institutions can also partner together, and with national college access and success programs, to inform students about college and the college-going process. Such partnerships should be designed with at least three groups in mind: students, their families, and K-12 school personnel. College representatives can educate these populations about the benefits associated with college degree completion, provide advice on what middle and high school coursework and curricular tracks will best position a student to be academically prepared for college, and share critical information about the college application and financial aid processes. As a part of this learning process, students and families should also be informed of the different types of colleges and universities (i.e., four-year, two-year, and less-than-two year), what degrees, programs, and certificates each category of institution can offer, and the average graduation or degree completion rates among students who begin their postsecondary experiences at each institution. Additionally, through summer camps, summer bridge programs, and targeted visits, college officials can expose students and their parents to college campuses, classrooms, and social and residence areas. Making these opportunities available to middle and high school students will promote their early awareness about college and what steps they must take to increase their chances of qualifying for and successfully completing a four-year degree.

To promote students' academic performance, and, therefore, degree completion outcomes, university personnel should create environments and opportunities that engage students academically and socially within their institution (Astin, 1993, Kuh, Douglas, Lund, & Ramin-Gyurnek, 1994; Tinto, 1987, 1993). Learning communities, which seek to maximize student engagement in academically purposeful ways through collaborative learning, are an example of one strategy utilized by colleges and universities to successfully promote both student engagement and academic achievement outcomes (Gablenick, MacGregor, Matthews, & Smith, 1990; Lenning & Ebbers, 1999; Tinto, 1987, 1993). Our study also shows that taking college-level math and science courses significantly influences degree completion. While it may prove difficult to prescribe specific courses to a population of students with diverse academic interests, academic advisors could encourage students to explore majors and coursework in the STEM fields. Moreover, university leadership might incent faculty in math and the sciences to collaborate with colleagues from other departments to offer interdisciplinary learning opportunities.

Because students, and especially those from lower-SES backgrounds, are more likely to successfully earn a college degree when they have been awarded financial aid, colleges and universities need to carefully target both grants and loans to the students who need them most. Moreover, because our research concluded that students who work on campus are more likely to complete college, institutions should enhance their offerings of work-study opportunities as a form of financial aid.

Finally, both colleges and universities as well as policymakers should revise goals and measures that stress year-to-year persistence within one institution, and instead emphasize persistence to degree completion across the entire higher education system (Adelman, 1999, 2006). The use of year-to-year persistence rates as a criterion of success leads institutions to view student success through a very short-term lens. In fact, many institutions define their persistence rates according to the proportion of students who maintain enrollment from their freshman to sophomore years. By approaching students' progression through college in such a front-loaded manner, they may fail to implement the holistic, longitudinal supports that students require in order to succeed throughout college and earn a degree. This change in policy would also recognize the increasingly transient nature of today's college student population. As Adelman (1999) noted, while 43 percent of all college students persisted at the first institution they attended, 63 percent of students completed postsecondary degrees.

APPENDIX: METHODOLOGY

Model

This study is based on the expanded college-choice persistence model (Blecher, Michael, & Hagedorn, 2002; St. John, Cabrera, Nora, & Asker, 2000; St. John, Paulsen, & Starkey, 1996). Merging the college choice with the economic and student-institution fit perspectives, the nexus model posits that college persistence is the by-product of a longitudinal process linking factors that predispose high school students to select a college with his/her collegiate experiences and ability to pay for college. Using a 1987 national sample of college students, Paulsen and St. John (2002) found that college-choice factors and college experiences factors had varying effects on persistence depending upon the specific income-group under consideration. Though the expanded college-choice persistence model has examined within-year persistence, it is logical to expect that this model can also help us understand determinants of degree completion among students of different socioeconomic backgrounds. Adelman's (1999) seminal work of determinants of degree completion among members of the 1980 Sophomore cohort also guided the selection of variables. This study expands upon Adelman's in two important areas. It includes measures of collegiate curriculum; and it desegregates the analyses for four distinct SES-groups. This strategy facilitates the identification of trends that may be unique to socioeconomically disadvantaged students (Paulsen & St. John, 2002; Walpole, 2003). Our data analysis strategy was twofold. First, we examined the path to a four-year degree followed by members of the 1980

High School Sophomore Cohort. Second, we examined determinants of degree completion among four distinct SES groups.

Database

The sample for this study was drawn from the National Longitudinal High School and Beyond 1980 Sophomore Cohort (HS&B/So). Created by the National Center for Education Statistics (NCES), the database (CD#: 2000-194) follows almost fifteen thousand high school sophomores over an eleven-year span. In 1980, data were collected from high school sophomore students attending 1,015 schools. In the first follow-up (1982), high school seniors' responses were complemented with their high school transcripts. The third and fourth follow-ups took place in 1986 and 1992, respectively. In 1993, NCES collected college transcripts from all institutions students reported attending between 1982 and 1992 (Zahs, Pedlow, Morrissey, Marnell, & Nichols, 1995). Academic resources for college (ACRES), academic performance in college, collegiate curriculum, financial aid, and degree completion variables were all derived from students' high school and college transcripts.

Weight Employed in the Analyses

The NCES followed a stratified sample strategy in creating the HS&B/So whereby the original sample of tenth graders was adjusted to represent the 1980 census of all high school seniors (about 3.7 million). Subsequent weights reflect the number of individuals attending postsecondary institutions. In this study, we used the Postsecondary Education Participation Panel Weight (PSEWT1), which adjusts the HS&B/So data to reflect the number of 1980 high school sophomores who enrolled in postsecondary education (see table A1).

Table A1. Weighted and unweighted sample sizes and proportions

SES	Postsecondary education participation panel weight (PSEWT1)		UNWEIGHTED	
	N	%	N	%
Lowest	407,772	17.3	3967	27.9
Middle-low	526,214	22.3	3347	23.5
Middle-high	661,478	28.0	3443	24.2
Highest	764,332	32.4	3464	24.4
Total	2,359,796	100%	14,914	100%

As noted by Adelman (1999), standardized statistical packages such as SPSS significantly underestimate the sampling error when handling stratified samples. To correct for this problem we used the average design effect of 1.5 for adjusting the standard deviations of parameters used in logistic regression models. This value was chosen based on the recommendations contained in the High School and Beyond Fourth Follow-Up Methodology Report (Zahs et al., 1995). To minimize further type I error due to large sample sizes, all parameter estimates were tested using a *p*-value of 0.01.

Dependent Variables

Degree Completion.   Students who secured at least a bachelor's degree by 1993 were considered degree completers for this study. This variable was derived from NHDEG, which included a record of students' highest confirmed degree received by 1993 as indicated on college transcripts (Adelman, 1999).

Independent Variables

Socioeconomic Status.   This variable was built upon respondent's socioeconomic status (SESQ) at the time he or she was a tenth grader in 1980. Socioeconomic status, as defined by variables within NCES datasets, includes the following measures: parental education, parental occupation, items in the home (i.e., dishwasher, books, etc.), and family income. This variable ranged from 1 (Lowest-SES) to 4 (Highest-SES). As shown in table A.1, estimates of subjects across SES categories vary as a function of the weight under consideration.
Background.   Gender (PSEX) coded as 0 (Male) and 1 (Female) and ethnicity (RACE). Ethnic categories included White (1), African American (2), Hispanic (3), and Asian American (4). Native Americans, due to their small number, were excluded from the logistic regression analyses.
High School Support   Three dummy-coded indicators of whether the students felt supported to go to college by parents (PARENTE), high school teachers or counselors (HSPROF), and friends (FRIENDE) were used for this construct. PARENTE was derived from two items indexing whether respondents felt the father (FY63a) or the mother (FY63b) expected them to go on to college after high school graduation. Similar to parental encouragement, HSPROF was created from two items indicating whether the respondent felt teachers or counselors expected him or her to go on to college (FY63c and FY63d). FRIENDE was derived from highest expectations respondents' high school friends had for them in their education (FY63e). The selection of these variables is consistent with recent literature highlighting the role of family, high school teachers, high school counselors, and

friends on a student's college-choice decisions (e.g., Cabrera & La Nasa, 2001; King, 1996; Perna, 2000).

Academic Resources. Created by Adelman (1999), the academic resources index (ACRES) is a composite of multiple indicators of a student's high school academic performance and curriculum. It brings together a reduced but enhanced version of the SAT test students took in the twelfth grade along with high school rank, academic GPA, and measures of the intensity and quality of the high school academic curriculum. This index avoids problems associated with using "preparatory track" by capturing measures that are more valid of a student's effort and success in academically related areas. Furthermore, this measure is based on transcripts avoiding biases associated to self-reported data. Adelman (1999) found ACRES ranked highest among the predictors of degree completion for members of the High School Sophomore Cohort of 1980. Originally conceived in quintiles, we collapsed the two categories of both extremes in the variables creating academic resources in thirds: (1) low; (2) medium; and (3) high academic resources.

Attainment Aspirations. ASP82 is a dummy variable reflecting whether the high school senior aspired to attain for a four-year degree (1) or not (0).

Pathways To and Through College (Type of First Institution Attended & DWI Index). College pathways were indexed using three separate variables: first type of institution attended; continuous enrollment (NON-STOP); and the ratio of courses dropped, withdrawn from, or left incomplete in relation to those attempted (DWI#3). First type of institution attended was derived from TRIFA by forming three categories: (1) Less-than-two-year, (2) two-year, and (3) four-year. Used for the degree completion section, these variables were created from college transcripts (see Adelman, 1999).

Number of College Math and Science Courses. The number of college math and science courses taken by a student was derived through examination of course descriptions within transcript data (NCES 95-361). All course data that could not be positively categorized were dropped from further analyses. For both sections of the study, only courses where a student received credit were selected. Repeated courses, incompletes, withdrawals, or courses for which no credit was earned were dropped from the analysis.

Collegiate Experiences. Five indicators were used to measure the experiences of the student with the institution. The out-of-classroom experience scale is a composite of three Likert scale items assessing the extent to which the student was satisfied with: the college's social life (TY28b), cultural activities (TY28g), and sports and recreation facilities (TY28k). The alpha reliability for this scale is 0.64. The instructional quality scale is a composite of five Likert scale items indexing satisfaction with: curriculum (TY28i), acquisition of work skills (TY28c), quality of instruction (TY28j), quality of faculty (TY28a), and intellectual development (TY28h). The alpha reliability for this scale is 0.82. The Satisfaction with Campus Faculties (TY28f), Satisfaction with Counseling (TY28e), and Satisfaction with the Prestige of the Institution (TY28m) variables were each measured via a single Likert-item. Using the High School Senior Cohort of 1980, Cabrera (1987) found these items to show moderate correlations with Pascarella and Terenzini's (1980) scales of academic and social integration.

College Grade Point Average.   Analyses on degree completion employed overall undergraduate grade point average (GPA), which was derived from college transcripts (see Adelman, 1999).

Satisfaction with Costs.   Satisfaction with cost was derived from an item indexing a student's satisfaction with the cost of attending his or her college (TY28l). This variable was dichotomized to indicate satisfaction (1) or dissatisfaction (0) according to practices outlined in Cabrera, Stampen, and Hansen (1990) and Nora, Cabrera, Hagedorn, and Pascarella (1996).

Financial Aid.   Developed by Adelman (1999), the financial aid measure drew directly from student aid records, and signified whether the student received loans (loan8286) or grants (schl8286) within the 1982–1986 period.

Working on Campus.   This variables indexes the number of years the student reported working on campus on such activities as work-study, co-op placements, or teaching or research assistantships (Adelman, 1999).

Parental Responsibilities.   This variable signifies whether the student had children by 1986, six years after the first data collection (CHILD86).

Table A2 displays the descriptive statistics employed in the logistic regression analysis.

Logistic Regression

We relied on a series of logistic regression models to assess the effect of a number of factors on the probabilities of securing a baccalaureate degree within ten years. Logistic regression is an ideal method to model the effect of independent variables when the dependent variable under consideration is dichotomous. Moreover, logistic regression avoids violations to the assumption of homogeneity of variance and functional specification that Ordinary Least Squares (OLS) regression models are likely to produce (Aldrich & Nelson, 1986; Cabrera, 1994; Menard, 1995). Moreover, Press and Wilson (1979) proved the superiority of logistic regression for classification and prediction purposes in relation to discriminant analyses.

Interpretation of Logistic Regression Results

Baseline p—Observed Probability of the Dependent Variable.   The observed probability that 1980 high school sophomores will eventually

Table A2. Descriptive statistics for the variables employed in the degree completion logistic regression model

Variable	N	% Cell	Mean	S.D.
Degree completers				
Yes	842,493	35%		
No	1,566,633	65%		
SES				
Lowest	407,772	17.3%		
Middle low	526,214	22.3%		
Middle high	661,478	28.0%		
Highest	764,332	32.4%		
Gender				
Male	1,104,772	45.9%		
Female	1,304,354	54.1%		
Ethnicity				
Hispanic	148,991	6.3%		
African American	284,054	12.0%		
Asian American	43,241	1.8%		
White	1,893,474	79.9%		
High School Encouragement				
From parents	1,732,304	81.3%		
From high school professionals	1,462,415	68.9%		
From friends	1,340,736	63.1%		
Academic resources				
Low	264,253	12.6%		
Moderate	821,194	39.2%		
High	1,010,646	48.2%		
Degree aspirations				
Aspired for a college degree	1,245,822	52.4%		
Type of first institution attended				
Less than two-year	267,170	12.2%		
Two-year	894,437	40.8%		
Four-year	1,030,255	47.0%		
Continuous enrollment	1,309,733	61.8%		
DWI Index				
Less than 10%	1,421,202	64.1%		
10%-20%	331,286	14.9%		
More than 20%	465,666	21.0%		
Number of math courses				
None or missing	1,402,992	58.2%		
One	344,003	14.3%		
Two	255,648	10.6%		
Three or more	406,483	16.9%		
Number of science courses				
None or missing	1,416,027	58.8%		
One	267,874	11.1%		
Two	241,731	10.0%		
Three or more	483,496	20.1%		
Collegiate experiences				
Out-of-classroom experiences	1,797,614		3.70	0.778
Instruction quality	1,790,114		4.08	0.699
Counseling or job placing	1,808,262		3.39	1.078
Campus facilities	1,808,653		4.00	0.971
Institutional prestige	1,811,500		3.85	0.988
Worked on campus	1,397,574	59.3%		
College GPA	2,261,439		2.52	0.895
Satisfaction with cost	1,074,637	36.9%		
Financial aid				
Loans	887,943	36.9%	1.31	1.261
Grants	1,011,355	42.0%		
Parental Responsibilities	301,067	13.1%		

Note: Cases were weighted by the NCES panel weight PSEWT1.

secure a four-year degree by 1993 is 0.354, meaning that 35 percent of them graduated. Observed probabilities are also referred as "unadjusted probabilities." Baseline p serves as a benchmark to assist in assessing how much each independent variable contributes to the probability of the dependent variable.

Beta Weights.   In contrast to OLS, interpretation of logistic parameter estimates is not straightforward. Unlike OLS, the metric of individual coefficients is expressed in terms of logits rather than in terms of the original scale of measurement. This problem is particularly accentuated for categorical variables; the corresponding beta weights represent contrasts among categories summarized in terms of differences of logits. For instance, the SES effect of 0.962 displayed in table A3 indicates that highest-SES students, on average, are 0.962 logit units more likely to obtain a bachelor's degree than are lowest-SES students. To overcome this problem, logistic regression results are usually presented in terms of changes in probabilities and adjusted probabilities.

Delta-p.   Developed by Petersen (1985), delta-p reflects the incremental change in the dependent variable (e.g., completing a four-year degree) due to a unit change in the independent variable (e.g., college academic performance). The delta-p value of .320 associated with College GPA means that for every unit increase in GPA, the probability of degree completion increases by 32 percent.

Adjusted Probabilities.   Used to estimate corrected probabilities by holding constant the dependent variables at their mean value (Cabrera, 1994; Menard, 1995), adjusted probabilities control for factors that systematically affect a group in a consistent manner. For degree completion, we calculated the adjusted probabilities using the mean values and the logistic parameter estimates depicted in table A3 using the following formula (see Cabrera, 1994, p. 228).

$$P(Y) = \frac{\mathrm{Exp}\,(B_0 + B_1 X_1)}{1 + \mathrm{Exp}(B_0 + B_1 X_1)}$$

χ^2 **for the model.**   This value assesses whether the independent variables as a group are significantly associated with the dependent variable (Aldrich & Nelson, 1987).

Proportion of Correctly Predicted Cases (PCP).   Provides an overall indicator of fit of the logistic regression model paralleling the OLS proportion of variance explained with R^2. This measure involves a comparison between the number of cases that the model predicted as being either 0 (graduated) or 1 (did not graduate) against the total sample size. PCP represents the percent of cases correctly predicted by the model. PCP values greater than 55 percent signify a good fit of the model (see Cabrera, 1994).

Table A3. Effects of background, encouragement, academic resources, performance in college, remediation, collegiate experiences, financial aid, and family responsibilities on the probability of degree completion

Factor	All	Socioeconomic Status			
		Lowest	Middle-Low	Middle-High	Highest
SES[1]					
Middle low	0.439*				
Middle high	0.613*				
Highest	0.962*				
Female	-0.198**	-0.974**	-0.312**	-0.200**	-0.089*
Ethnicity[1]					
African American	0.004	-0.180	-0.404*	-0.323*	0.480**
Hispanic	-0.172*	-0.622*	0.270	-0.426*	0.042
Asian American	0.787**	1.903**	-0.285	0.446*	0.980**
High School Encouragement[1]					
From parents	0.176*	-0.744	0.171	0.391*	-0.138
From high school professionals	-0.036	-0.491	-0.376	-0.035	0.320*
From friends	0.223*	-0.272	0.669*	0.633*	-0.366
Academic Resources[1]					
Moderate	0.187*	1.154*	-0.821	0.347*	0.315*
High	0.497*	1.702*	-1.459	1.128*	0.370*
Collegiate Aspirations[1]	0.938*	1.300*	1.841*	0.644*	1.267*
Type of First Institution Attended[1]					
Two-year institution	0.748*	2.274*	1.689*	-0.075	1.257*
Four-year institution	2.074*	3.395*	2.177*	1.288*	2.916*
Continuous Enrollment[1]	0.942*	1.487*	1.634*	0.658*	1.068*
DWI Index[1]					
10-20% of courses	-0.653*	0.897	-0.561*	-0.949*	-0.847*

(continued)

Table A3. *(continued)*

Factor	All	Socioeconomic Status			
		Lowest	Middle-Low	Middle-High	Highest
Number of Math Courses[1]					
One course	1.125*	0.254*	1.829*	1.410*	0.886*
Two courses	1.203*	1.786*	1.302*	0.911*	1.583*
Three or more courses	1.826*	2.740*	2.971*	2.291*	1.358*
Number of Science courses[1]					
One course	0.844*	1.395*	0.993*	0.808*	0.361*
Two courses	0.852*	1.468*	1.116*	0.792*	0.668*
Three or more courses	1.181*	2.107*	1.541*	1.486*	0.655*
Collegiate Experiences[1]					
Out-of-classroom	0.346*	0.089	0.742*	0.479*	0.154*
Quality of instruction	0.319*	0.951*	0.072	0.616*	0.113*
Counseling	0.038*	0.420*	-0.335	0.095*	0.086*
Campus facilities	-0.120	-0.437	0.208*	-0.162	-0.118
Institutional prestige	0.054*	0.433*	0.126*	-0.102	0.074*
Worked on campus[1]	0.160*	0.156*	0.124*	0.390*	0.037*
College GPA[1]	1.329*	1.536*	2.162*	0.785*	1.895*
Satisfaction with Costs[1]	-0.309	0.525*	-0.415	-0.552	-0.390
Financial Aid					
Loans	0.433*	0.763*	1.304*	0.157*	0.213*
Grants	0.297*	0.561*	0.489*	0.341*	0.358*
Parental Responsibilities[1]	-1.276*	-3.864*	0.771	-1.439*	-2.353*
Intercept	-11.341	-17.616	-14.980	-10.366	-10.439
Number of cases	2,359,795	407,772	526,213	661,478	764,332
Baseline p	0.354	0.129	0.236	0.336	0.570
Model χ², df	675,788,35**	78,422,32**	155,395,32**	209,674,32**	209,081,32**
PCP	87.2%	92.8%	88.6%	86.4%	88.0%

*p<.01 **p<.001

[1]Effects of the variable were directionally tested.

Table A3 reports the logistic regression results for determinants of degree completion. Each case was weighted by the NCES panel weight PSEWT1. As already noted, the design effect of 1.5 was used to correct standard errors.

NOTES

The results reported in this chapter were produced thanks to a grant from the Association for Institutional Research (Contract No. 00-107). The opinions expressed herein do not necessarily reflect the opinions or policies of the funding organization, and no official endorsement should be inferred. We are most indebted to Clifford Adelman, Senior Associate with the Institute of Higher Education Policy, for his invaluable technical advice and knowledge. His own seminal work (Adelman, 1999) gave us the tools to work with the 1980 HSB/So. data. We also gratefully acknowledge the continuous guidance and support we received from Dennis Carroll, Aurora D'Amico, and Cynthia L. Barton.

1. Throughout this study, "academic resources" refers to Adelman's (1999) ACRES composite measure, which captured students' high school GPA and rank, aptitude test scores, and then created a composite measure, ACRES, capturing students' abilities, high school graduation rank, and quality and intensity of their high school curriculum. Adelman reported ACRES to be one of the best predictors of degree completion among for members of the 1982 High School Class. To facilitate comparison, ACRES quintiles were transformed into thirds (low, medium, and high) by collapsing the two quintiles at both ends of the scale. See methodology.

2. These values were derived using logistic regression equations, holding variables at their mean value. These equations are available from the first author upon request.

REFERENCES

Adelman, C. (1999). *Answers in the toolbox: Academic intensity, attendance patterns, and bachelor's degree attainment.* Washington, DC: U.S. Department of Education, Office of Educational Research and Improvement.

Adelman, C. (2006). *The toolbox revisited: Paths to degree completion from high school through college.* Washington, DC: U.S. Department of Education.

Advisory Committee on Student Financial Assistance (2006). *Mortgaging our future: How financial barriers to college undercut America's global competitiveness.* Washington, DC.

Advisory Committee on Student Financial Assistance (2010). *The rising price of inequality: How inadequate grant aid limits college access and persistence.* Washington, DC.

Aldrich, J. H. & Nelson, F. D. (1986). *Linear probability, logit, and probit models (3rd edition).* Beverly Hills, CA: Sage Publications.

Astin, A. W. (1975). *Preventing students from dropping out.* San Francicso: Jossey-Bass.

Astin, A. W. (1993). *What matters in college*. San Francisco: Jossey-Bass.

Baum, S., Ma, J., & Payea, K. (2010). *Education pays: The benefits of higher education for individuals and society*. Washington, DC: College Board.

Becker, G. S. (1964). *Human capital*. New York: National Bureau of Economic Research.

Berkner, L. K. & Chavez, L. (1997, October). *Access to postsecondary education for the 1992 high school graduates*. Statistical Analysis Report, NCES 98-105. Washington, DC: U.S. Department of Education, Office of Educational Research and Improvement, National Center for Education Statistics.

Blecher, L., Michael, W., & Hagedorn, L. (2002). *Factors related to the "system" persistence of students seeking the bachelor's degree at four-year institutions*. Paper presented at the 2002 annual meeting of the American Educational Research Association. New Orleans, Louisiana.

Bowen, H. R. (1977). *Investment in learning: The individual and social value of American higher education*. San Francisco: Jossey-Bass.

Bowen, W. G. & Bok, D. (1998). *The shape of the river: Long-term consequences of considering race in college and university admissions*. Princeton, NJ: Princeton University Press.

Bowen, W. G., Chingos, M. M., & McPherson, M. S. (2009). *Crossing the finish line: Completing college at America's public universities*. Princeton, NJ: Princeton University Press.

Braxton, J. M. (2000). *Reworking the student departure puzzle*. Nashville: Vanderbilt University Press.

Cabrera, A. F. (1987). *Ability to pay and college persistence*. Unpublished doctoral dissertation, University of Wisconsin, Madison, Madison, WI.

Cabrera, A. F. (1994). Logistic regression analysis in higher education: An applied perspective. In J. C. Smart (Ed.) *Higher education: Handbook for the study of higher education Volume 10*, pp. 225–256. New York, NY: Agathon Press.

Cabrera, A. F., Colbeck C. L., & Terenzini P. T. (2001). Developing performance indicators for assessing classroom teaching practices and student learning. *Research in Higher Education*, 42(3), 327–352.

Cabrera, A. F., Deil-Amen, R., Prabhu, R., Terenzini, P. T., Lee, C., & Franklin, R. F., Jr. (2006). Increasing the college preparedness of at-risk students. *Journal of Latinos and Education*, 5(2), 79–97.

Cabrera, A. F. & La Nasa, S. M. (2000). Understanding the college choice of disadvantaged students. *New Directions for Institutional Research*. San Francisco: Jossey-Bass.

Cabrera, A. F. & La Nasa, S. M. (2001). On the path to college: Three critical tasks facing America's disadvantaged. *Research in Higher Education*, 42(2), 119–150.

Cabrera, A. F., Nora, A., & Castañeda, M. B. (1992). The role of finances in the persistence process: A structural model. *Research in Higher Education*, 33(5), 571–593.

Cabrera, A. F. & Nora, A. (1994). College students' perceptions of prejudice and discrimination and their feelings of alienation: A construct validation approach. *The Review of Education, Pedagogy, and Cultural Studies*, 16(3–4), 387–409.

Cabrera, A. F., Stampen, J. O., & Hansen, W. L. (1990). Exploring the effects of ability to pay on persistence in college. *The Review of Higher Education*, 13(3), 303–336.

Carroll, C. D. (1989). *College persistence and degree attainment for 1980 high school graduates: Hazards for transfers, stopouts, and part-timers.* Survey Report # CS-89-302. Washington, DC: U.S. Department of Education, National Center for Education Statistics.

Catsambis, S. & Garland, J .E. (1997). *Parental involvement in students' education during middle school and high school.* Baltimore, MD: Center for Research on the Education of Students Placed At Risk.

Chickering, A. W. & Reisser, L. (1993). *Education and identity. Second edition.* The Jossey-Bass Higher and Adult Education Series. San Francisco: Jossey-Bass.

Choy, S. P. (2002). *Access & persistence: Findings from 10 years of longitudinal research on students.* Washington, DC: American Council on Education.

College Board. (2010). *Trends in student aid.* Washington, DC: College Board.

Corwin, Z. B. & Tierney, W. (2007). *Getting there—and beyond: Building a culture of college-going in high schools.* Los Angeles, CA: Center for Higher Education Policy Analysis.

Crosnoe, R., Mistry, R. S., & Elder, G. H. (2002). Economic disadvantage, family dynamics, and adolescent enrollment in higher education. *Journal of Marriage and Family, 64,* 690–702.

Cunningham, A. F., Erisman, W., & Looney, S. M. (2007). *From aspirations to action: The roles of middle school parents in marking the dream of college a reality.* Washington, DC: Institute for Higher Education Policy.

Darling-Hammond, L. (2004). Standards, accountability, & school reform. *Teachers College Record, 106*(6), 1047–1085.

Executive Office of the President Council of Economic Advisers (EOPCEA). (2009). *Preparing the workers of today for the jobs of tomorrow.* Washington, DC.

Flint, T. A. (1992). Parental and planning influences on the formation of student college choice sets. *Research in Higher Education, 33*(6), 689–708.

Flint, T. A. (1993). Early awareness of college financial aid: Does it expand choice? *Review of Higher Education, 16*(3), 309–327.

Gablenick, F., MacGregor, J., Matthews, R., & Smith, B. L. (Eds.) (1990, Spring). Learning communities: Creating connections among students, faculty, and disciplines. *New Directions for Teaching and Learning, 41.* San Francisco: Jossey-Bass.

Geiser, S. & Santelices, M. V. (2007). *Validity of high-school grades in predicting student success beyond the freshman year: High-school record vs. standardized tests as indicators of four-year college outcomes.* Berkeley, CA: Center for Studies in Higher Education, University of California, Berkeley.

Gladieux, L. E. & Swail, W. S. (2000). Beyond access: Improving the odds of college success. *Phi Delta Kappan, 82*(9), 688-692.

Goldrick-Rab, S. (2006). Following their every move: An investigation of social-class differences in college pathways. *Sociology of Education, 79,* 61–79.

Gutman, L. M. & Eccles, J. S. (1999). Financial strain, parenting behaviors, and adolescents' achievement: Testing model equivalence between African American and European American single- and two-parent families. *Child Development, 70*(6), 1464–1476.

Hagedorn, L. S., Moon, S. H, Cypers, S., Maxwell, W. E., & Lester. J. (2003). *Transfer between community colleges and four-year colleges: The all American game.* Paper presented before the annual meeting of the Association for the Study of Higher Education. Portland, OR.

Hahn, R. D. & Price, D. (2008). *Promise lost: College-qualified students who don't enroll in college*. Washington, DC: Institute for Higher Education Policy.

Hall, W. D., Cabrera, A. F., & Bibo, E. W. (2010, November). *The cost of concern: How parents' fears about paying for college influence their child's college enrollment behaviors*. Association for the Study of Higher Education, Indianapolis, IN.

Hearn, J. C. (1992). Emerging variations in postsecondary attendance patterns: An investigation of part-time, delayed, and nondegree enrollment. *Research in Higher Education, 33*(6), 657–687.

Heller, D. E. (2002). State aid and student access: The changing picture. In D.E. Heller (Ed.) *Condition of access: Higher education for lower income students* (pp. 97–112). Westport, CT: Praeger Publishers (ACE/Oryx Series on Higher Education).

Horn, L. & Carroll, C.D. (2006). *How 4-year college graduation rates vary with selectivity and the size of low-income enrollment (NCES 2007161)*. Washington, DC: U.S. Department of Education, National Center for Education Statistics.

Horn, L. J. & Chen, X. (1998). *Toward resiliency: At-risk students who make it to college*. Washington, DC: U.S. Department of Education.

Horn, L. & Nunez, A-M. (2000). *Mapping the road to college: First-generation students' math track, planning strategies, and context of support (NCES 2000153)*. Washington, DC: U.S. Department of Education, National Center for Education Statistics.

Hossler, D. (1984). *Enrollment management: An integrated approach*. New York, NY: The College Board.

Hossler, D., Braxton, J., & Coopersmith, G. (1988). Understanding student college choice. In J. Smart (Ed.) *Higher Education: Handbook of Theory and Research, Volume 5*. New York: Agathon.

Hossler, D., Schmit, J., & Vesper, N. (1999). *Going to college: How social, economic, and educational factors influence the decisions students make*. Baltimore: John Hopkins University Press.

Hossler, D. & Vesper, N. (1993). An exploratory study of the factors associated with parental saving for postsecondary education. *Journal of Higher Education, 64*(2), 140–165.

Hurtado, S., Milem, J., Clayton-Pederson, A., & Allen, W. (1999). *Enacting diverse learning environments: Improving the climate for racial/ethnic diversity in higher education*. Washington, DC: The George Washington University, Graduate School of Education and Human Development.

Ikenberry, S. O. & Hartle, T. W. (1998). *Too little knowledge is a dangerous thing: What the public thinks and knows about paying for college*. Washington, DC: American Council on Education.

King, J. E. (1996). *The decision to go to college: Attitudes and experiences associated with college attendance among low-income students*. Washington, DC: The College Board.

Kirst, W. & Venezia, A. (2004). *From high school to college: Improving opportunities for success in postsecondary education*. San Francisco: CA: Jossey-Bass.

Kuh, G. D. (2000). *The national survey of student engagement: The college student report*. Bloomington, IN: Indiana University Center for Postsecondary Research and Planning.

Kuh, G., Douglas, K. B., Lund, J. P., & Ramin-Gyurnek, J. (1994). *Student learning outside the classroom: Transcending artificial boundaries.* ASHE-ERIC Higher Education Report 23(8). Washington, DC: The George Washington University, Graduate School of Education and Human Development.

Kuh, G., Pace, R. C., & Vesper, N. (1997). The development of process indicators to estimate student gains associated with good practices in undergraduate education. *Research in Higher Education, 38*(4), 435–454.

Lankford, H., Loeb, S., & Wykoff, J. (2002). Teacher sorting and the plight of urban schools: a descriptive analysis. *Educational Evaluation and Policy Analysis, 24*(1), 37–62.

Lareau, A. (1987). Social class differences in family-school relationships: the importance of cultural capital. *Sociology of Education, 60,* 73–85.

Lee, V. E., & Eckstrom, R. B. (1987). Student access to guidance counseling in high school. *American Educational Research Journal, 24*(2), 287–310.

Lenning, Q. T. & Ebbers, L. H. (1999). *The powerful potential of learning communities: Improving education for the future.* ASHE-ERIC Higher Education Report 26(6). Washington, DC: The George Washington University, Graduate School of Education and Human Development.

Leslie, L. L. & Brinkman, P. T. (1986). Rates of return in higher education: An intensive examination. In J. C. Smart (Ed). *Handbook of theory and research* (pp. 207–234). New York: Agathon.

Lewis, G. L. (1989). Trends in student aid, 1963–64 to 1988–89. *Research in Higher Education, 30*(6), 547–562

Lohfink, M. M. & Paulsen, M. B. (2005). Comparing the determinants of persistence for first-generation and continuing-generation students. *Journal of College Student Development, 46*(4), 409–428.

MacPhail-Wilcox, B. & King, R. A. (1986). Resource allocation studies: Implications for school improvement and school finance research. *Journal of Education Finance, 11,* 416–432.

Manski, C. F. & Wise, D. A. (1983). *College choice in America.* Cambridge, MA: Harvard University Press.

McClafferty, K. A., McDonough, P. M., & Nunez, A. M. (2002, April). *What is a college culture? Facilitating college preparation through organizational change.* Paper presented at the annual conference of the American Educational Research Association, New Orleans, LA.

McDonough, P. M. (1997). *Choosing college: how social class and schools structure opportunity.* Albany, NY: State University of New York Press.

McDonough, P. M. & Calderone, S. (2010). The meaning of money: Perceptual differences between college counselors and low-income families about college costs and financial aid. *American Behavioral Scientist, 12,* 1703–1718.

McPherson, M. S. & Schapiro, M. O. (1998). *The student aid game: Meeting need and rewarding talent in American higher education.* Princeton, NJ: Princeton University Press.

Menard, S. (1995). *Applied logistic regression analysis.* Sage University Paper series on Quantitative Applications in the Social Sciences, 07-106. Thousand Oaks, CA: Sage.

Miller, E. I. (1997). Parents' views on the value of a college education and how they will pay for it. *Journal of Student Financial Aid, 27*(1), 20.

Murnane, R. J. & Levy, F. (1996). *Teaching the new basic skills: Principles for educating children to thrive in a changing economy.* New York: The Free Press.

The National Association for College Admission Counseling (NACAC). (2008). *State of college admission.* Arlington, VA.

National Center for Education Statistics. (1998). *High school and beyond sophomore cohort: 1980–92 postsecondary education transcripts; restricted file.* NCES 98-135. Washington, DC: U.S. Department of Education, Office of Educational Research and Improvement.

National Research Council. (1999). *Testing, teaching, and learning: A guide for states and school districts.* Committee on Title I Testing and Assessment, Richard F. Elmore and Robert Rothman, editors. Board on Testing and Assessment, Commission on Behavioral and Social Sciences and Education. Washington, DC: National Academy Press.

Nora, A. (1990). Campus-based aid programs as determinants of retention among Hispanic community college students. *Journal of Higher Education, 61*(3), 312–331.

Nora, A., Cabrera, A. F. (1993). The construct validity of institutional commitment: A confirmatory factor analysis. *Research in Higher Education, 34*(2), 243–262.

Nora, A. & Cabrera, A. F., Hagedorn, L. S., & Pascarella, E. T. (1996). Differential impacts of academic and social experiences on college-related behavioral outcomes across different ethnic and gender groups at four-year institutions. *Research in Higher Education, 37*(4), 427–752.

Oakes, J. (1985). *How schools structure inequality.* New Haven, CT: Yale University Press.

Olivas, M. A. (1985). Financial aid packaging policies: Access and ideology. *Journal of Higher Education, 56*(4), 462–475.

Pace, R. C. (1980, April). *Measuring the quality of undergraduate education.* Paper presented at the annual meeting of the American Educational Research Association, Los Angeles.

Pascarella, E. T. & Terenzini, P. T. (1980). Predicting freshman persistence and voluntary dropout decisions from a theoretical model. *Journal of Higher Education, 51*, 60–75.

Pascarella, E. T. & Terenzini, P. T. (2005). *How college affects students, 2nd edition.* San Francisco: Jossey-Bass.

Paulsen, M. B. & St. John, E. P. (2002). Social class and college costs: Examining the financial nexus between college choice and persistence. *Journal of Higher Education, 73*(2), 189–236.

Perna, L. W. (2000). Differences in the decision to attend college among African Americans, Hispanics, and Whites. *Journal of Higher Education, 71*(2), 117–141.

Perna, L. W. (2002). Precollege outreach programs: Characteristics of programs serving historically underrepresented groups of students. *Journal of College Student Development, 43*(1), 64–83.

Perna, L. W. & Titus, M. A. (2005). The relationship between parental involvement as social capital and college enrollment: An examination of racial/ethnic group differences. *The Journal of Higher Education, 76*(5), 485–518.

Petersen, T. (1985). A comment on presenting results from logit to probit models. *American Sociological Review,* 50(1), 130–131.

Plank, S. B. & Jordan, W. J. (2001). Effects of information, guidance, and actions on postsecondary destinations: A study of talent loss. *American Education Research Journal,* 38(4), 947–979.

Press, S. J. & Wilson, S. (1979). *Choosing between logistic regression and discriminant analysis.* Santa Monica, CA: Rand Corp.

Rowan-Kenyon, H. T., Bell, A. D., & Perna, L. W. (2008). Contextual influences on parental involvement in college going: Variations by socioeconomic class. *The Journal of Higher Education, 79*(5), 564–586.

Rumberger, R. W. (1995). Dropping out of middle school: A multilevel analysis of students and schools. *American Educational Research Journal. 32*(3), 583–625.

St. John, E. P. (1990). Price response in persistence decisions: An analysis of the high school and beyond senior cohort. *Research in Higher Education, 31*(4), 387–403.

St. John, E. P. (1994). *Prices productivity, and investment: Assessing financial strategies in higher education.* ASHE-ERIC Higher Education Reports, No. 3. Washington, DC: George Washington University.

St. John, E. P., Andrieu, S., Oescher, J., & Starkey, J. B. (1994). The influence of student aid on within-in year persistence by traditional college-age students in four-year colleges. *Research in Higher Education, 35*(4), 455–480.

St. John, E. P., Cabrera, A. F., Nora, A., & Asker, E. H. (2000). Economic influences on persistence reconsidered. How can finance research inform the reconceptualization of persistence models? In J. M. Braxton (Ed.) *Reworking the student departure puzzle.* Nashville: Vanderbilt University Press.

St. John, E. P., Paulsen, M. B., & Starkey, J. B. (1996). The nexus between college choice and persistence. *Research in Higher Education, 37*(2), 175–220.

Stage, F. K. & Hossler, D. (1989). Differences in family influences on college attendance plans for male and female ninth graders. *Research in Higher Education, 30*(3), 301–315.

Stampen, J. O. & Cabrera, A. F. (1986). Exploring the effects of student aid on attrition. *Journal of Student Financial Aid, 16,* 28–40.

Stampen, J. O. & Cabrera, A. F. (1988). The targeting and packaging of student aid and its effect on attrition. *Economics of Education Review, 7*(1), 29–46.

Swail, W. S. (1995). *The development of a conceptual framework to increase student retention in science, engineering, and mathematics programs at minority institutions of higher education.* Unpublished doctoral dissertation, George Washington University, Washington, DC.

Swail, W. S., Cabrera, A. F., Lee, C., & Williams, A. (2005). *Latino students and the educational pipeline: A three-part series.* Stafford, VA: Educational Policy Institute.

Terenzini, P. T., Cabrera, A. F., & Bernal, E. M. (2001). *Swimming against the tide: The poor in American higher education.* College Board Research Report No. 2001-1. New York: The College Board.

Tierney, W. G., Corwin, Z., & Colyar J. E. (2005). *Preparing for college: Nine elements of effective outreach.* Albany, NY: SUNY Press.

Tinto, V. (1987). *Leaving college: Rethinking the causes and cures of student attrition.* Chicago: University of Chicago Press.

Tinto, V. (1993). *Leaving college: Rethinking the causes and cures of student attrition, 2nd Edition.* Chicago: The University of Chicago Press.

Tinto, V. (1997). Classrooms as communities: Exploring the educational character of student persistence. *The Journal of Higher Education, 68,* 599–623.

U.S. Department of Education. (2008). *A nation accountable: Twenty-five years after a nation at risk.* Washington, D.C.

Useem, E.L. (1992). Middle schools and math groups: Parents' involvement in children's placement. *Sociology of Education, 65,* 263–279.

Velez, W. (1985). Finishing college: The effects of college type. *Sociology of Education, 58,* 191–200.

Velez, W. & Javalgi, R. G. (1987). Two-year college to four-year college: The likelihood of transfer. *American Journal of Education, 96*(1), 81–94.

Venezia, A., Kirst, M. W. & Antonio, A. L. (2003). *Betraying the college dream: How disconnected K-12 postsecondary education systems undermine student aspirations.* Stanford University: Stanford Institute for Higher Education Research.

Voorhees, R. (1987). Toward building models of community college persistence: A logit analysis. *Research in Higher Education 26*(2), 115–129.

Wallace, D., Abel, R., & Ropers-Huilman, B. (2000). Clearing a path for success: Deconstructing borders through undergraduate mentoring. *The Review of Higher Education, 24*(1), 87–102.

Walpole, M. (2003). Socioeconomic status and college: How SES affects college experiences and outcomes. *The Review of Higher Education, 27*(1), 45–73.

Willingham, W. W., Pollack, J. M., & Lewis, C. (2000). *Grades and test scores: Accounting for observed differences.* Princeton, NJ: Educational Testing Service.

Wimberly, G. L. & Noeth, R. J. (2005). *College readiness begins in middle school.* Iowa City, IA: ACT.

Zahs, D., Pedlow, S., Morrissey, M., Marnell, P., & Nichols, B. (January, 1995). *High school and beyond: fourth follow-up: Methodology report.* Chicago: National Opinion Research Center.

9

Online Student Retention

Daniel W. Salter

Perhaps the best place to start this discussion is to clarify what this chapter is not. It is not a review of the increasing use of technology in teaching, the explosion of online courses and programs, or the emergence of virtual universities. Higher education is moving past that tipping point, and the focus needs to turn to what these changes may mean in current and future terms. No attempt to develop an extensive taxonomy of the characteristics of online students is made, either. If the ability to access the Internet defines "being online," then nearly all students could be considered online students . . . or soon will be. Nowadays, the online environment touches every aspect of a student's academic career, from pre-enrollment to post-graduate (Floyd & Casey-Powell, 2004), and future editions of this book may well include a chapter on retaining the non-online student, as a special consideration.

Discussion of learning outcomes related to different instructional formats is also not included. With entire journals devoted to this topic, two trends already seem apparent: (1) online and real-time deliveries of courses are not *that* different; and (2) a blended approach may be best. Also worth noting: by the time research has been conducted and published on implementing a particular technology, a new one is waiting to take its place. Finally, little review is offered on what is currently known about students as people. The ability to watch a course lecture streamed to an iPad while seated in the back of a bus, as opposed to watching it live from the back of a lecture hall, does not change the developmental needs that that student has, such as a quest for identity or finding a purpose in life.

With those parameters established, the goal of this chapter is relatively simple: to have a conversation about the *current* challenges to understanding retention in this liminal time when being an online student is still considered as something different from just "being a student." Arguably, the notion of online student could be viewed as consistent with the Jungian premise of an archetype (Hopcke, 1989), an idea with structure and affect, but needing content and meaning. And because of this archetypal quality, an attempt to define and discuss what many would consider a universally recognized concept these days in higher education, may open a door to scholarly hubris and insights into a writer's own academic shadow. Retaining online students is an important and challenging goal, however, and worth the risks.

THE ONLINE STUDENT

Many terms have been used to describe the same basic phenomenon (Yoon, 2003). For purposes of this discussion, one simple approach to crafting a working definition is to break the term into the two words that form it. A *student* is someone who is being educated, and education is the process of teaching a student. Although such a definition may seem pretty fundamental, the Internet has given everyone the capacity to learn from a distance, and increasing numbers of universities are making their content freely available through outlets like iTunes University (www.apple.com/education/itunes-u/). Because the focus of this book is on college students, however, the term will be constrained to include individuals involved in the formal higher education process.

As noted, the notion of *online* may soon be an unnecessary and redundant adjective, in an age where the Internet is becoming embedded in all aspects of students' lives (Ogan, Ozakca, & Groshek, 2007). Nearly every adult has access to a computer, many have smart phones, and a billion people will likely be registered with Facebook by the time this chapter is published (McCarthy, 2010). At this point in time, however, higher education has not reached an academic singularity, where everyone is connected in every way. Instead, a major presenting challenge of providing distance education is the fact that both the digital natives and digital immigrants (Prensky, 2001) are enrolling in online courses and programs, taught by both digital types, all of whom are differentially equipped for this journey. Hence, while higher education is in this transition, an online instructor's e-mail inbox may contain both an invite to be friended on Facebook and a request for more information on how to save a file to a hard drive.

Within this large group of students who could be described as online is a group of particular interest to this conversation: the fully online students. Without a doubt, retaining the residential student who opts to take the online section of a general education course is no small challenge. But these days, the ability to take one's entire academic program in the distributed environment of distance education presents a situation in which everyone must re-examine his or her assumptions about the student experience and how to support the process, and acknowledge the paradoxes. For example, many online students pick this approach because of the convenience and access it offers, not because of the fact that it is technology-based (which can become a liability for some students). Fortunately, this conversation has already commenced.

A FRAMEWORK

Rather than a foray into the various models of student retention, this chapter stands on the scholarly shoulders of Bean's (2005) earlier identification of nine themes of college student retention. His work provides a very tenable framework for organizing many of the current challenges of working with online students. In this synthesis, he noted that student retention can be framed in at least four ways—theoretical, policy, institutional, and individuals—and that any one or more have guided studies and practice in this domain. Then, drawing on over two decades of research and his own deep understanding of the issues, he highlighted those aspects that seem most germane. With some nuancing, all seem to hold true for online students.

In some essential ways, the actions and goals of the college student have not changed in centuries, so the broader differences between online and non-online students would be expectedly minimal. But in some key ways, as discussed below, the academic environment for achieving those goals has changed. What does not seem clear at this juncture is whether technology and the Internet comprise a new class of variables to retention models or simply a new form of the recognized ones. Perhaps educators are always looking for the new-new thing, and some thinkers consider technology to be a new phenomenon (Yoon, 2003). Other scholars (e.g., Sutton & Nora, 2009) seem to argue that technology is not a new class of variable in retention models, but a new expression of the recognized ones that effect student persistence. The reality most likely lies between these two views.

THEMES OF RETENTION

Intentions

Bean's (2005) discussion of the influence of intentions on retention speaks quite well to the online student experience. Although intention-to-leave has high predictive value to departure, he noted that knowing this fact does not necessarily explain *why* a student makes the choice to withdraw. However, intention may be one of the more pronounced differences for the online student as compared to other students, when considering why online students enroll in these types of programs in the first place (Boston, Díaz, Gison, Ice, Richardson, & Swan, 2009). Ironically, in a time when fewer students can afford to go to college just to "see what it's about," precisely this tactic appears to be the motivation behind the enrollment of students in online programs. Therefore, the noticeably lower retention rate in distance education makes some sense in this context of experimentation, and is the reason why the notion of persistence may need to be reframed (Park, Boman, Dean Care, Edwards, & Perry, 2008).

For example, to obtain a PhD from a residential program at a school like The Ohio State University, many doctoral students must quit their full-time jobs and relocate themselves (and families) to a place like Columbus, Ohio. New doctoral students in an online program, such as one at Walden University, can stay where they live and continue to work, with minimal disruption to their personal and professional lives: very convenient for them . . . but maybe too convenient, from a retention standpoint. The Ohio State student who has a change of heart and wants to transfer to the University of Michigan will have another series of challenges and disruptions. The Walden student, who still intends to get a PhD but wants a different school, need only pull up a web browser to start the process of re-enrolling in the next school down the virtual street, such as Cappella University. Both groups of students have an intention to obtain a doctoral degree, but the ease of enrolling and attending a virtual university becomes its biggest liability from a retention standpoint. An online student has the convenience of enrolling in a program to try out both doctoral education and the online delivery of it, either of which may be a reason to reconsider the choice. The new residential doctoral student may feel "pot committed," as they say in high-stakes poker, before the game has even started, making her or him easier to retain.

Although many other distinctions between these two types of students are relevant to understanding retention and are discussed below, differences related to intention relate to the needed shift in understanding of retention and persistence (Park et al., 2008). When the constraints of time and place no longer apply, a student can log into the course management systems of multiple universities, thus extending the "anywhere, anytime" nature of distance education to include "any school." Even faculty see how the rules are changing, and some are forming boutique colleges (Berg, 2011) that augment the increasingly available academic resources on the Internet, such as the Khan Academy (www.khanacademy.org). Looking ahead, higher education can expect increased demands for the portability of earned credit, a continued rise in e-portfolios, along with countless tense meetings for accrediting bodies and governing agencies, who are already facing the swirling student phenomenon (Boston et al., 2009). The ability to "piece together" a degree from multiple sources challenges the notion of the institution as being a variable in retention models and the tracking of persistent students.

Relationship to the Institution

Fully online students attend an institution that allows them to complete most, if not all, of their academic expectations virtually. The types of institutions vary widely, and taxonomies have been developed to capture all these differences (Meyer, 2009). What does not seem broadly understood at this point in the process is how online students' attitudes about these institutions, many of which are only a few decades old, impact their attachment and subsequent retention. Connection and sense of community are key to a virtual institution (Heyman, 2010), but how a school achieves these bonds can be different, even within the online milieu. Consider the following schools.

The Pennsylvania State University has a rich history and tradition as a research university, with a vast alumni group spread across the planet, nationally ranked athletic programs, a bit of a reputation as a "party school," and a nationally recognized distance education division (thebestcolleges.org, 2011). The success of this online program was built on the resources already available in faculty expertise, along with the university's name recognition; and conceivably, a World Campus student can graduate from Penn State without ever having been to Happy Valley. Because their online students may see themselves as part of this larger system, however, it's likely easier for them to feel attached to Penn State, even if they have never participated in the range of events that define its character as a institution. They are Penn State.

The University of Phoenix is one of the higher-profile virtual universities that offer students the opportunity to complete a degree at a distance. They also have alumni across the planet, but with enrollments nearly four times greater than the entire Penn State commonwealth system. What the U. of P. does not have is the wooded campus in central Pennsylvania, where alumni return to take pictures with their newly graduated grandchildren by the statue of the Nittany Lion. Instead, they have a marketing department that wisely saw the need to establish institutional identity with their comprehensive "I am a Phoenix" ad campaign. What better "mascot" for a university that serves such a large population of returning adult students? And what better way to build this sense of attachment in this group of students than through the television commercials, web ads, and building-sized banners in major sites across the country?

Psychological Processes and Key Attitudes

Students seem to want more online opportunities and seem to be satisfied with those choices (Sher, 2008). But the strategy of offering an anytime, anywhere education to any student (at any institution) could seem daunting when acknowledging that all aspects of the student experience can affect their retention. That is, to have two thousand residential students "captured" in a residence hall complex allows an institution to provide a somewhat consistent student experience (even including diet). If those two thousand students were spread across the globe, the only characteristics that may be shared among this group of online learners are enrollment in that institution and the desire to obtain a degree in this manner. But are these groups of students different as learners?

One view is that a good student is a good student, no matter the learning modality that is used (Yip, 2009), and many of the recognized aspects of studenthood that have seemed related to retention also influence online learners, including learning styles (Harrington & Loffredo, 2010; Mupinga, Nora & Yaw, 2006; Zacharis, 2010); emotional intelligence and personality (Berenson, Boyles & Weaver, 2008); self-regulation and discipline (Heyman, 2010); locus of control (Morris, Wu, & Finnegan, 2005), and so forth. If any themes are noticeable, online students need to be just a little more capable with these attributes than their residential peers to succeed; and the digital immigrants seem to share some characteristics that are often ascribed to first-generation college students—one in particular.

Of all the personal variables that Bean discussed in his review, self-efficacy seems especially important to the online student experience (Vuong, Brown-Welty, & Tracz, 2010). Street (2010) even recommended screening for it. The "trying it out" phase, which some online students use, can certainly offer the opportunity to develop a sense of being able to succeed. A key point of online efficacy is the relation that students have with the technology that allows them to participate in distance education. It is not enough to make it available; online students also need to see technology as useful to their education (Christensen, Anakwe, & Kessler, 2001; McWright, 2003) and to be given a chance to address any previous negative interactions with it (Pattison, 2003). As noted, the digital natives and immigrants are both attending college, so attitudes about technology and its usefulness will continue to shift as that distribution changes. In the short run, the immigrants may continue to struggle somewhat (Boston et al., 2009), but for the natives who have never known a world without computers, "the more, the more" (Ogan, Ozacka, Groshek, 2007, p. 175).

Another key attribute is the ability to communicate in the current higher education climate (Junco, Merson, & Salter, 2010), and one area where the differences between synchronous and asynchronous processes may constitute a unique variable to understanding retention (Ortiz-Rodríguez, Telg, Iran, Roberts, & Rhoades, 2005). The research on social-psychological dimensions of online communication seems to be mixed, and an area needing more exploration (Hu, 2009). Asynchronous forms, such as discussion board postings or even e-mail, allow people to reflect and prepare the best responses to communicate their intentions, but remove the subtle nonverbal cues that people use. On the other hand, synchronous communication, such as group online chat or using Skype, is more cognitively challenging (Hu, 2009) and relies on unfamiliar tools. At this point in time, educators may not fully understand the important differences between giving an approving smile to a student when returning a paper with a perfect score in the real-time classroom, and using some type of emoticon smiley—e.g., :-)—when uploading that same paper to a course dropbox. While commonplace in many real time classes, even the simple act of introducing oneself in an online course seems to support completion (Nistor & Neubauer, 2010).

Academics

"Dr. Smith, we'd like you to teach your course online next term." Anecdotally, the first wake-up call for these conscripted faculty is the work required to revamp and realign their syllabi and course assignments. Simply adding a little HTML code won't do it. An upside of the migration to distance education has been the emerging science that supports online delivery of courses. As a matter of fact, people now earn academic degrees in subjects such as educational technology and hold positions that support faculty adjusting to these types of demands throughout the education spectrum. These same scholars are producing *volumes* of research on the online student/faculty/classroom dynamic and, given the continual influx of new technologies, plenty of work awaits them. For example, at this point, longitudinal research on the impact of tablet computing is only just beginning.

As Bean (2005) suggests, improving the delivery of the educational product serves to help students remain at an institution, so it would be difficult to argue against research that improves the student experience in online courses. The issue will continue to be, "What actually helps?" Like many people perhaps, some educators wait to see what shiny new "how did I ever live without this?" thing Apple Computer has come out with before settling on a technology plan. The caution in this situation would be to not assume that every new technology supports the academic experience and retention. For example, one e-book website (www.bookboon.com) recently suggested that students want iPads, seeing them as adding value to their experience, but, paradoxically, don't want to read electronic texts on a device created exactly for this purpose. Even more "classic" technologies, such as online chat, may unintentionally produce negative outcomes in some students (Hu, 2009). Most sobering, universities are already looking at alternative forms of communication to replace the older new technologies that students no longer use so much, such as e-mail (Junco, Merson, & Salter, 2010).

Dr. Smith's second wake-up call is how much more work teaching an online course can be. A professor can ask a probing question in a real-time class, take answers from a few students, maybe seek follow-up from a few more, and then must move on to the next topic. Although time for more discussion would be nice to have, the real-time course may only meet for an hour. In the asynchronous environment, a single probing question gets a response from *all* students, along with two or three reactions to that response from each student. That classic admonition to new faculty, "Don't give an assignment you aren't prepared to grade," would seem especially relevant to online education. In the real-time class, Dr. Smith can ask a dozen or more probing questions. In an online class, even two discussion board prompts can be potentially arduous to read, depending on the class size. Importantly though, the marginal student, who may be at increased risk for dropping the course, would have a much more difficult time "hiding in the back of the room" in a course with required discussion postings, and therefore be more easily identified for an earlier intervention to support success in the course and program.

A third wake-up call for Dr. Smith is the change in the non-class-time demands. The anytime-anywhere quality of online education places a set of expectations on faculty and staff to be available in a similar way. It is not uncommon in the halls of Academe to hear a professor complain, "The student e-mailed me a question at 10 A.M., and then again at 11 A.M., asking why I had not responded to the first e-mail." Bean highlighted the spotty research on advising, and the online environment would seem to introduce some new considerations, many of which relate back to the earlier conversation in this chapter about communication (Floyd & Casey-Powell, 2004; Nichols, 2010). Still, for the student who is stuck on a statistics problem at 3 A.M., the immediacy of video conversation, where a professional advisor-tutor can watch the shared computer screen and walk the student through the solution, certainly shows potential to meet students' immediate needs and to break down the physical distance in distance education.

Social Factors

Of all the components to Bean's synthesis, the role that social factors play in online student retention is probably the one for which the research is only beginning to provide insights into a situation that still seems to be evolving (e.g., real-time, group video conferencing is possible but not yet the norm). Overcoming the social distance in distance education seems to be a significant challenge that is not fully understood (Boston et al., 2009), and may well be another new variable to retention models. Assuming that online students are no different socially from any other human beings, however, the question is better focused on how to help online students to establish a social presence and to cope with the isolation that is often attributed to distance education: their "e-solation," as it were (e.g., Appana, 2008).

Actually, with the larger society, education is caught in a proliferation of these online analogues of common social domain concepts, such as "friends," "like," and "networking" (some of which have become plot devices in motion pictures!). What seems to be a trend at this point in time is that paradoxes are the norm. As Bean notes, development of social skills is a key developmental challenge for traditionally aged students, yet these digital natives also seem to be the ones who most readily take advantage of what technology offers, as seen in the meteoric rise of Facebook. Older students, the digital immigrants, may have different needs socially than an eighteen-year-old student, as theory would predict. Yet one of the fastest growing demographics on Facebook comprises women over the age of fifty-five (Smith, 2009). Video chatting, while a potentially powerful social technology that is becoming more widely available, may actually turn out to be too personal and cumbersome for students (Kleiner, 2011). Most telling of the challenge here, perhaps, Bean specifically highlights the role of friends in the lives of students, in 2005, before education (and the world) fully began to understand how Mark Zuckerberg would redefine that concept.

Early indications are positive and supportive of the view that these technologies can be employed to support the social experience of online students and potentially influence their retention. Distance orientation courses appear to offer the same types of presocialization as real-time experiences, even if they do compete with the time available to participate in one (e.g., Bishop & White, 2007; Scagnoli, 2001) and improve student satisfaction (Pattison, 2003). Technologies that connect students socially, such as instant messaging and texting, seem to be meaningful, especially for students who might otherwise feel isolated on a residential campus (Junco, Merson, & Salter, 2010) and the growing group of students who eschew e-mail. Twitter helps students succeed in class (Junco, Heiberger, & Loken, 2010), as does blogging (Hsu & Wang, 2011). For people concerned with retention through the social experience of the virtual campus, the challenges would seem to lie in keeping pace with what's available and making them work.

At this writing, icons for links to Facebook, Twitter, YouTube, and iTunes University can be found on the bottom of the main website of Harvard University (www.harvard.edu), along with countless other university portals. Although social media may appear to be an easy solution to the challenge of e-solation and retention of online students, it's quite possible that higher education may not have a complete answer to that question before the variables shift again. When Bean's chapter from 2005 was published, Facebook was just moving out of the university environment and YouTube had just launched; Twitter launched the following year and iTunes University the year after that. The iPhone was only a vague rumor among the Apple acolytes, and devices like the iPad were seen mainly on the Starship *Enterprise*. So, even if research were able to determine fully whether friending a university has long-term impact on retention, in the next year or so, will it soon matter?

Organizational Factors

A troubling meme made its way through the inboxes of many distance administrators a few years ago. Reportedly, nearly 40 percent of fully online students quit their programs without ever having had contact with anyone at the university. They just left. Whether true or not (as not everything on the Internet is grounded in fact), that statistic "felt right" in light of the experiences of these individual administrators. The information on which online students leave and why is not as "clean" as it could be, given the multiple definitions in distance education and methodological challenges (Park et al., 2008), although one study found that the ability to access and install the necessary materials and software was the most common reason why many online students stopped before they even got started (Muse, 2003). No doubt, it is hard to create an organizational response to such a challenge when why-they-leave and where-they-go are not known.

For all their differences in formation and organization (Meyer, 2009), most virtual universities currently look and function much like their counterparts in the real-time world, which makes sense for a number of reasons. To deliver a product like a college degree in a distributed environment, a certain comfort lies in the traditional structures and roles of a university or college. Beyond student and faculty expectations, the accrediting bodies that work with institutions that offer online programs are also challenged to assess and assure quality. And at this juncture, student services for online students appear to function and be organized largely the same as those for residential students, even in the completely virtual environment. The paradigm does not seem to have shifted yet, and online analogues of most services can be seen (online orientation, online advisors, online career counseling, etc.).

The "take home message" at the end of this chapter is a conclusion that the traditional structure of higher education institutions may not survive the challenge of a technologically connected student body. And while student support services based on sound interventions undeniably make a positive and measurable contribution to student retention, online students are especially sensitive to the lack of support (Nichols, 2010), even if they often don't notice their presence and positive impact. If there's a retention lesson for student services in the years ahead, the experiences of the academic side of the institution, such as those of Dr. Smith above, may be instructive. The techniques used in traditional classrooms do not always "translate" into the online environment (Yoon, 2011), and the co-curricular environment is likely no different. New thinking is in order (Clay, Rowland, & Packard, 2009; Nichols, 2010).

The External Environment

As countless school children across the nation are learning, distance education is slowly killing the dream of ever having another snow day. Their parents and grandparents, on the other hand, are taking advantage of the anytime-anywhere promise of distance education . . . and in droves. Certainly, forces beyond the control of students can affect their retention, and often an institution can do little to fix the student's problem, online or not (Tello, 2007). Interestingly though, some of the examples that Bean gives as external factors are situations in which online delivery might actually serve to improve retention, such as a job relocation, changes in one's personal relationships, or even natural disasters: any challenge in which location and time would constrain a real-time education. As a matter of fact, these heroic tales of success in the face of adversity have become part and parcel of the online education narrative. For example, a doctoral student at Walden University, diagnosed with a life-threatening disease during her studies, was able to complete her degree from her hospital bed. To watch her family accept the degree on her behalf was a powerful, "the rules have changed" moment for many educators in the auditorium.

These moments of inspiration and success must be tempered by the downside of this type of access, however. Changing jobs is different from losing a job, and an education still continues to be seen as a means to improve one's situation. The market for working adult enrollments is big, especially in comparison to graduating high school students, and the competition for their tuition has been, in a word, fierce. In the year leading up to finishing this chapter, a few schools in the for-profit sector, which primarily offer online degrees to this cohort, have been "called on the congressional carpet," as it were, for their practices. The veracity of these claims notwithstanding—and it would surely be a mistake to use a single descriptor for such a large and diverse group of institutions—the public's trust in higher education is undoubtedly eroded by the airing of concerns about recruitment violations and financial aid abuses. As the political discourse around the higher education environment intensifies, coupled with the financial challenges discussed below, the theme of trust that transcends Bean's observations becomes especially relevant. It is so hard to know the direct impact of a university's reputation being dragged through media on students' choices to remain at a particular school or even to continue pursuing further education, online or not.

The Student's Background

Bean (2005) discusses many fundamental relationships between students' backgrounds and their retention that would seem directly applicable to online students, such as support, parental educational goals, and income. He also notes that not all institutions have the luxury of picking the students that they know will ultimately succeed. For online students, some institutions have made it their mission to recruit the nontraditional students and those individuals not typically served by higher education (Meyer, 2009), thereby diversifying the types of students that require retention strategies. Arguably, the single, middle-class student coming to college directly out of high school (about which more is known than any other type of student) is only a small category in the population of online students.

One area of particular interest, mentioned in a previous section, is online education for students with disabilities (Richardson, 2009). In many ways, advances in technology (e.g., real-time captioning, text readers) have allowed access to a higher education to countless people who would not have had the chance even a decade ago. Certainly, the online environment removes the challenges of physically attending a class, and asynchronous assignments provide students, with or without disabilities, the added time they may need to reflect and respond (Grabinger, 2010). New opportunities are not immune to the old challenges of any technology used in education, however. At this point in time, tablet computing is a new-new technology that holds potential to revolutionize education one more time, and yet concerns about access have already emerged (Wieder, 2011). As the computing bandwidth expands, more real-time technologies (e.g., video conferencing) will be available and woven into delivery of online courses and programs. How these advancements will affect the experience of students with disabilities will need continued consideration.

Money and Finance

The economy interacts with higher education, certainly, and the financial benefits and costs of being in the online education sector are beyond the scope of a chapter on retaining students. The growth of enrollments in for-profit virtual universities suggests that people, beyond the investors, have seen distance education as potentially lucrative [actually, profit has become the dirty little secret of eLearning, as many traditional schools also see its impact on the bottom line (Wagner, 2011)]. However, the US economy is still struggling to find its way out of a recession, and it's hard to know if this enrollment growth can be sustained in virtual education. Further, traditional institutions are seeing dramatic cuts to operating budgets, and the increasing costs of tuition have invigorated the ongoing question about the return-on-investment of a college degree. Even the term "higher education bubble" has become commonplace in the media over the past couple of years (Cronin & Horton, 2009).

So, Bean's (2005) observation about the "complicating factors" (p. 234) in the role of money in retention may have been unintended understatement. Most factors he identifies in this trend seem completely relevant to all students, online or not, especially the pragmatic challenge of running out of money (Morris, Wu, & Finnegan, 2005). Logic suggests that students with financial resources also have the social capital that supports their success, and delivery format of the degree would seem to have little influence on those types of resources. Less clear is whether an online education is just inherently cheaper to deliver and/or to complete. Planned upgrades to software, hardware, and the user are key components of university budgets . . . and those of students as well.

SUMMARY

To summarize the presenting themes in retention of online students, at this time, three can be offered. First, when considering the various aspects of studenthood, being online seems largely an extension of what is currently known about being a successful student, and those variances will likely shrink as the digital immigrants are assimilated and/or move through the system. Second, all the individuals who are charged with delivering and supporting the online academic experience, many of whom are digital immigrants themselves, will continue to be challenged by the tension in using what they know works and incorporating newer solutions. With the possible exceptions of copying machines and overhead projectors, much of the non-online delivery of course content has not changed much in centuries. Like the computers that built it, however, advances in the field of educational technology seem to be following the spirit of Moore's law (doubling in capacity every two years). That is, if it has not done so already, the speed of technological change will soon surpass researchers' ability to inform the community about which ones truly support student success.

Perhaps the biggest challenge in the years ahead, from a retention standpoint, will be to the institutions that deliver a higher education. Will they be retained? Knowledge is becoming less codified in the faculty, and students can access it from any convenient web browser or smart phone, thus erasing any requirement that an "education" occur within a particular place and timeframe. Further, when students can construct a degree from attending multiple online universities, including one or more outside of their home country, institutional attachment and relevance will begin to fall away. Educators need look no further than the example of iTunes and how it changed the music industry to see what *may* be ahead. Will students be able to buy various faculty "hits" and not an academic program's entire album (curriculum)? If so, then companies like Google, with technologies that could potentially track student learning across the Internet, may be the future source of retention statistics.

REFERENCES

Appana, S. (2008). A review of benefits and limitations of online learning in the context of the student, the instructor, and the tenured faculty. *International Journal on E-learning, 7*(1), 5–22. Retrieved May 29, 2011, from www.editlib. org/?fuseaction=Reader.ViewFullText&paper_id=22909.

Bean, J. P. (2005). Nine themes of college student retention. In A. Seidman (Ed.), *College student retention: Formula for student success* (pp. 215–243). Westport, CT: Praeger.

Berenson, R., Boyles, G., & Weaver, A. (2008). Emotional intelligence as a predictor for success in online learning. *International Review in Open and Distance Learning, 9*(2), 1–16. Retrieved May 16, 2011, from www.irrodl.org/index.php/irrodl/article/viewArticle/385.

Berg, J. (2011, May 30, 2011). It's his very own college, and welcome to it. *Chronicle of Higher Education.* Retrieved from http://chronicle.com/article/Its-His-Very-Own-College-and/127588/.

Bishop, M. J., & White, S. A. (2007). The Clipper Project: Exploring whether early engagement through web-based instruction can help ease high school students college transition. *Journal of College Student Retention: Research, Theory and Practice, 9*(3), 357–376. doi: 10.2190/CS.9.3.f.

Boston, W., Díaz, S. R., Gibson, A. M., Ice, P., Richardson, J., & Swan, K. (2009). An exploration of the relationship between indicators of the community of inquiry framework and retention in online programs. *Journal of Asynchronous Learning Networks, 13*(3), 67–84. Retrieved May 16, 2011, from http://apus.academia.edu/documents/0108/7762/v13n3_8boston.pdf.

Christensen, E. W., Anakwe, U. P., & Kessler, E. H. (2001). Receptivity to distance learning: The effect of technology, reputation, constraints, and learning preferences. *Journal of Research on Computing in Education, 33*(3), 263–279. Retrieved May 17, 2011, from www.umsl.edu/technology/frc/pdfs/receptivity_to_distance_learning.pdf.

Clay, M. N., Rowland, S., & Packard, A. (2009). Improving undergraduate online retention through gated advisement and redundant communication. *Journal of College Student Retention: Research, Theory and Practice, 10*(1), 93–102. doi: 10.2190/CS.10.1.g.

Cronin, J. M., & Horton, H. E. (May 22, 2009). Will higher education be the next bubble to burst? *Chronicle of Higher Education.* Retrieved from http://chronicle.com/article/Will-Higher-Education-Be-the/44400

Floyd, D. L., & Casey-Powell, D. (2004). New roles for student support services in distance learning. *New Directions for Community Colleges, 2004,* 55–64. doi: 10.1002/cc.175.

Grabinger, S. (2010). A framework for supporting postsecondary learners with psychiatric disabilities in online environments. *Electronic Journal of e-Learning, 8*(2), 101–110. Retrieved May 20, 2011 from www.editlib.org/?fuseaction=Reader .ViewFullText&paper_id=22909.

Harrington, R., & Loffredo, D. A. (2010). MBTI personality type and other factors that relate to preference for online versus face-to-face instruction. *Internet and Higher Education, 13*(1–2), 89–95. doi: 10.1016/j.iheduc.2009.11.006.

Heyman, E. (2010). Overcoming student retention issues in higher education online programs. *Online Journal of Distance Learning Administration, 13*(4). Retrieved May 20, 2011 from www.westga.edu/%7Edistance/ojdla/winter134/heyman134 .html.

Hopcke, R. H. (1989). *A guided tour of the Collected Works of C. G. Jung.* Boston: Shambhala.

Hsu, H.-Y., & Wang, S. (2011). The impact of using blogs on college students' reading comprehension and learning motivation. *Literacy Research and Instruction, 50*(1), 68–88. doi: 10.1080/19388070903509177.

Hu, M. (2009). Will online chat alleviate mood loneliness? *Cyberpsychology, Behavior, and Social Networking, 12*(2), 219–223. doi: 10.1089/cpb.2008.0134

Junco, R., Heiberger, G., & Loken, E. (2010). The effect of Twitter on college student engagement and grades. *Journal of Computer Assisted Learning, 27*(2), 119–132. DOI: 10.1111/j.1365-2729.2010.00387.x.

Junco, R., Merson, D., & Salter, D. W. (2010). The effect of gender, ethnicity, and income on college students' use of communication technologies. *Cyberpsychology, Behavior, and Social Networking, 13*(6), 619–627. doi: 10.1089/cyber.2009.0357.

Katz, Y. J. (2000). The comparative suitability of three ICT distance learning methodologies for college level instruction. *Educational Media International, 37*(1), 25–30. doi: 10.1080/095239800361482.

Kleiner, K. (2011, May 15). Why don't we video chat more often? [online article]. Retrieved from: http://singularityhub.com/2011/05/15/why-dont-we-video-chat-more-often/.

McCarthy, C. (July 21, 2010). Who will be Facebook's next 500 million? [online article]. Retrieved from http://news.cnet.com/8301-13577_3-20011158-36.html.

McWright, B. L. (2003). Educational technology at a distance: Is access to technology enough? *The Quarterly Review of Distance Education, 4*(2), 167–176. Retrieved May 16, 2011. from http://eric.ed.gov/ERICWebPortal/recordDetail?accno=EJ670106.

Meyer, K. A. (Ed.), 2009. Lessons learned from virtual universities. *New Directions for Higher Education,* 146 (Summer).

Morris, L., Wu, S. S., & Finnegan, C. L. (2005). Predicting retention in online general education courses. *American Journal of Distance Education, 19*(1), 23–36. doi: 10.1207/s15389286ajde1901_3.

Mupinga, D. M., Nora, R. T., & Yaw, D. C. (2006). The learning styles, expectations, and needs of online students. *College Teaching, 54*(1), 185–189. doi: 10.3200/CTCH.54.1.185-189

Muse, H. (2003). The web-based community college student: An examination of factors that lead to success and risk. *Internet and Higher Education, 6*(3), 241–261. doi: 10.1016/S1096-7516(03)00044-7.

Nichols, M. (2010). Student perceptions of support services and the influence of targeted interventions on retention in distance education. *Distance Education, 31*(1), 93–113. doi: 10.1080/01587911003725048.

Nistor, N., & Neubauer, K. (2010). From participation to dropout: Quantitative participation patterns in online university courses. *Computers & Education, 55*(2), 663–672. Elsevier Ltd. doi: 10.1016/j.compedu.2010.02.026.

Nora, A., & Snyder, B. P. (2009). Technology and higher education: The impact of e-learning approaches on student academic achievement, perceptions and persistence. *Journal of College Student Retention: Research, Theory and Practice, 10*(1), 3–19. doi: 10.2190/CS.10.1.b.

Ogan, C. L. O., Ozakca, M., & Groshek, J. (2007). Embedding the Internet in the lives of college students: Online and offline behavior. *Social Science Computer Review, 26*(2), 170–177. doi: 10.1177/0894439307306129.

Ortiz-Rodríguez, M., Telg, R. W., Irani, T., Roberts, T. G., & Rhoades, E. (2005). College students—perceptions of quality in distance education: The importance of communication. *The Quarterly Review of Distance Education, 6*(352), 97–105.

Park, C. L., Boman, J., Dean Care, W., Edwards, M., & Perry, B. (2008). Persistence and attrition: What is being measured? *Journal of College Student Retention: Research, Theory and Practice, 10*(2), 223–233. doi: 10.2190/CS.10.2.g.

Pattison, S. A. (2003). The effect of an orientation on distance-program satisfaction. *Journal of College Student Retention, 5*(2), 205–233.

Prensky, M. (2001). Digital natives, digital immigrants. *On the Horizon, 9*(5): 1–6. Retrieved May 25, 2011 from www.scribd.com/doc/9799/Prensky-Digital-Natives-Digital-Immigrants-Part1.

Richardson, J. T. E. (2009). The attainment and experiences of disabled students in distance education. *Distance Education, 30*(1), 87–102. doi: 10.1080/01587910902845931.

Scagnoli, N. I. (2001). Student orientations for online programs. *Journal of Research on Technology in Education, 34*(1), 19–27. Retrieved May 17, 2011, from http://eric.ed.gov/ERICWebPortal/recordDetail?accno=EJ645725.

Sher, A. (2008). Assessing and comparing interaction dynamics, student learning, and satisfaction within web-based online learning programs. *MERLOT Journal of Online Learning and Teaching, 4*(4), 446–458. Retrieved May 20, 2011 from http://jolt.merlot.org/vol4no4/sher_1208.pdf.

Smith, J. (February, 2, 2009). Fast growing demographic on Facebook: Women over 55. *Inside Facebook: Tracking Facebook and the Facebook platform for developers and markets.* [online article]. Retrieved from www.insidefacebook.com/2009/02/02/fastest-growing-demographic-on-facebook-women-over-55/.

Street, H. (2011). Factors influencing a learner's decision to drop-out or persist in higher education distance learning. *Online Journal of Distance Learning Administration, 13*(4). Retrieved May 20, 2011 from www.westga.edu/%7Edistance/ojdla/winter134/street134.html.

Sutton, S. C., & Nora, A. (2009). An exploration of college persistence for students enrolled in web-enhanced courses: A multivariate analytic approach. *Journal of College Student Retention: Research, Theory and Practice, 10*(1), 21–37. doi: 10.2190/CS.10.1.c.

Tello, S. F. (2007). An analysis of student persistence in online education. *International Journal of Information and Communication Technology Education, 3*(3), 47–62. IGI Publishing. Retrieved May 17, 2011, from http://0-wcubookstore.wcu.edu .wncln.wncln.org/WebFiles/PDFs/Tello_Interaction.pdf.

thebestcolleges.org (2011). *Top 25 online colleges of 2011* [online article]. Retrieved from www.thebestcolleges.org/top-online-schools/.

Vuong, M., Brown-Welty, S., Tracz, S. (2010). The effects of self-efficacy on academic success of first-generation college sophomore students. *Journal of College Student Development, 51*(1), 50–64. doi: 10.1353/csd.0.0109.

Wagner, E. (2011). The "dirty little secret" of online learning. *eLearning Roadtrip* [online article]. Retrieved from http://elearningroadtrip.typepad.com/ elearning_roadtrip/2011/09/the-dirty-little-secret-online-learning.html.

Wieder, B. (May 26, 2011). Education department clarifies e-reader accessibility rules. CHE.

Yip, M. (2009). Differences between high and low academic achieving university students in learning and study strategies: A further investigation. *Educational Research and Evaluation, 15*(6), 561–570. doi: 10.1080/13803610903354718.

Yoon, S.-won. (2003). In search of meaningful online learning experiences. *New Directions for Adult and Continuing Education, 100*, 19–30. doi/10.1002/ace.116/ abstract.

Zacharis, N. Z. (2010). The impact of learning styles on student achievement in a web-based versus equivalent face-to-face course. *College Student Journal, 44*(3), 3–6.

10

Student Persistence and Degree Attainment beyond the First Year in College

Existing Knowledge and Directions for Future Research

Amaury Nora and Gloria Crisp

Persistence decisions are considered to be the products of longitudinal processes of varied lengths in students' lives (Tinto, 1975, 1993) that are influenced by different variables/constructs, including academic and social integration, different sources and forms of support, student finances, and even discriminatory behaviors and gestures (e.g., Bean, 1980; Bean & Metzner, 1985; Cabrera, Nora, & Castaneda, 1992; Nora & Cabrera, 1996; Nora, Cabrera, Hagedorn, & Pascarella, 1996; Pascarella & Terenzini, 1979; Reason, 2009; Singell & Waddell, 2009; St. John, Cabrera, Nora, & Asker, 2001; Tinto, 1975). Although much is known about why some students leave college and others persist, nearly all of the research and theory developed over the past thirty-five years has focused on explaining students' decisions to withdraw from college during the first year, as this is the point in time when institutions typically lose the largest percentage of students (US Department of Education, 1998, 2000).

It has been suggested that intense focus on the first year in college has shifted problems with attrition from the first year to subsequent years, even when students successfully engage during their initial collegiate experience. For instance, an analysis of a nationally representative sample of students drawn from the Beginning Postsecondary Students Longitudinal Study (BPS: 04/06) who began their postsecondary education during the 2003–2004 academic year reveals that while 12 percent of the entering cohort dropped during the first year of college, 16 percent withdrew during the second year, and 6 percent dropped out prior to earning a degree or certificate during year three.

Many of the factors that have been found to impact retention among students during the first year of college are thought to carry over to subsequent years, culminating in a decision to withdraw from college. It is also reasonable to assume that the strength and direction of the factors influencing dropout behavior may change over time (Ishitani & DesJardins, 2002–2003). However, very little research to date has focused on the identification or measurement of variables that influence students' persistence decisions beyond the first year (Pascarella & Terenzini, 2005). An understanding of how time affects students' decisions to withdraw from college is therefore needed in order to develop effective interventions that reduce students' risk for leaving college prior to graduation (DesJardins, Ahlburg, & McCall, 1999; Ishitani, 2008).

The intent of this chapter is to provide an overview of research specific to students' persistence decisions beyond the first year in college. We begin with a brief overview of persistence theory and offer a conceptual framework to explain the longitudinal nature of student persistence. Because very little has been investigated for the time period following a student's first year, we present a description of a nationally representative sample of students who withdrew from college during the second and third years of college, followed by a synthesis of existing inferential work. We conclude with specific recommendations for future research to expand our understanding of students' decisions to remain enrolled in college beyond the first year.

THEORETICAL FRAMEWORKS
GUIDING PERSISTENCE RESEARCH

To provide a context for comparison with what is known regarding the first-year experience, the conceptual framework for this chapter will be guided by current theoretical perspectives used in studying the persistence of undergraduate students. As previously mentioned, much of what is known regarding student persistence has been focused on students prior to the second year (e.g., Braxton & Lien, 2000; Nora, 2004; Nora & Cabrera, 1996; Nora, Cabrera, Hagedorn, & Pascarella, 1996). Many of these studies have used different, yet overlapping, frameworks including Tinto's (1975) model of student integration, Bean's (1985) student attrition model, Astin's (1984, 1999) student involvement perspective, and Nora and Cabrera's (1996) student adjustment model. Studies by Braxton and Brier (1989), Rendon (1994), Hurtado and Carter (1997), Pascarella and Terenzini (1990) and others have modified and added an array of factors, all found to impact the decisions of college students to remain enrolled in college or to decide to drop out, temporarily or permanently. Among those efforts is research by Nora and associates (e.g., Cabrera, Nora, & Castaneda, 1992, 1993; Nora & Cabrera, 1996; Nora & Garcia, undated; Nora & Lang, undated; Nora, 2002,

2004). The culmination of those efforts has led to the conceptualization of the student engagement model (Nora, 2004) displayed in Figure 10.1.

SECOND- AND THIRD-YEAR WITHDRAWAL AMONG FTIC UNDERGRADUATE STUDENTS

Although a limited amount of descriptive work has been conducted to explore the characteristics of students who do and do not persist in college beyond the first year (e.g., Bartlett & Abell, 1995; DuBrock, 1999; Horn & Kojaku, 2001), much of this work has been limited to a description at a single institution or to national data that tracked students who attended college almost two decades ago (e.g., Smith, 1995). The following section provides what we believe to be the most comprehensive and current description of student persistence through the second and third years of college. Data were analyzed from the Beginning Postsecondary Students Longitudinal Study (BPS: 04/06), which were drawn from a variety of sources including institutional records, National Student Clearinghouse enrollment records, and student interviews to capture students' background characteristics, high school academic experiences, college enrollment behavior, and outcomes. Table 10.1 provides demographic, pre-college, and college data for: (1) the entire entering cohort of students who first began their postsecondary education in 2003–2004 (as a comparison); (2) students who withdrew from college without earning a degree during the second year; and (3) students who withdrew without earning a degree during year three.

Demographic Profile

Entering Cohort. Females comprised the majority (58 percent) of students who entered postsecondary education during the 2003–2004 year (n = 18,650[1]). White students represented 63 percent of the sample, while 14 percent classified themselves as African American, 13 percent as Hispanic or Latino, and 5 percent as Asian American. The remaining 5 percent of students indicated they were more than one race or desired not to disclose their ethnicity. The average age of students was twenty-two years, and 9 percent of the cohort was married during the 2003–2004 academic year. The majority of students expected to earn a graduate degree (55 percent) and 85 percent of the cohort intended to obtain a bachelor's degree or higher. Nearly 80 percent of students received some form of financial aid during the first year of college and almost a third (31 percent) had delayed enrolling in college for at least some period of time following high school. Many students were the first in their family to attend college, as only 40 percent

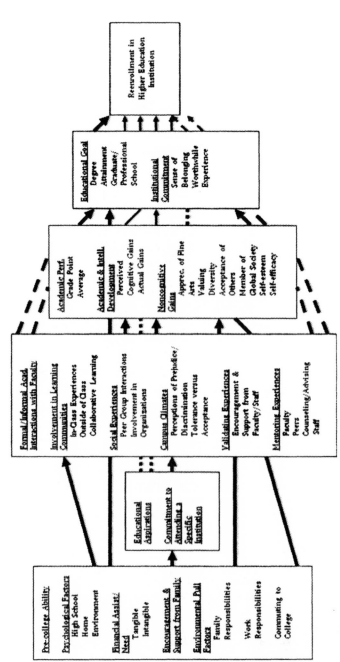

Pre-college Factors &
Pull-Factors

Initial Commitments

Academic & Social
Experiences

Cognitive & Non-
Cognitive Outcomes

Final Commitments

Persistence

Figure 10.1.

of the cohort had at least one parent who had earned a four-year college degree or higher.

Students Who Withdrew during the Second Year of College. Roughly 16 percent of the entering cohort persisted during the first year of college but then withdrew before the end of the second year (n = 2,950). These students were demographically similar to the entire entering cohort in terms of gender and the percentage who received financial aid. However, consistent with analyses of other national, state, and institutional data (e.g., Swail, Redd, & Perna, 2003), students who withdrew from college during the second year were more likely to be African American or Hispanic and less likely to be white or Asian American when compared to the ethnic distribution of the entering cohort. Moreover, students who withdrew during the second year were slightly older (average age twenty-three years old compared to twenty-two) and more likely to be married. Also consistent with the persistence literature (e.g., Cabrera, Nora, & Castaneda, 1993; Nora, Castaneda, & Cabrera, 1992), students who withdrew during the second year had lower educational aspirations (22 percent did not intend to earn a bachelor's degree compared to 15 percent), and/ or were more likely to have delayed entering into college following high school (46 percent versus 31 percent). Furthermore, students who withdrew during the second year were more likely to have a mother and father who had not completed college (57 percent versus 45 percent) when compared to the entering cohort.

Students Who Withdrew during the Third Year of College. Six percent of the entering cohort persisted during the first and second years of college but then withdrew before the end of the third year (n = 1,040). These data suggest that white and Asian American students are less likely to withdraw from college during the third year. In fact, less than 1 percent of the students who withdrew during the third year were Asian American, even though that group represented 5 percent of the entering cohort. Similar to data from the second year, a greater proportion of African American and Hispanic students withdrew from college during year three. Eighteen percent of the students who withdrew in year three were Hispanic, compared to only 13 percent of the entering cohort. The average age of students who withdrew in year three was twenty-two, and 11 percent of the students who withdrew were married (compared to 9 percent of the entering cohort). Interestingly, overall this group of students was more demographically similar to the entering cohort than the students who withdrew during the second year in terms of degree aspirations, parental education, and delaying enrollment into college. For instance, 38 percent of the students who dropped out of college during year three did not immediately enroll in college following high school (compared to 31 percent in the entering cohort).

Table 10.1. Persistence to the second and third years of college: Percent of column total or mean and standard deviation

	Entire 03/04 cohort (n = 18,650[a])	Students who withdrew without a degree in year 2 (n = 2,950)	Students who withdrew without a degree in year 3 (n = 1,040)
Demographic Characteristics			
Gender			
Female	58%	58%	57%
Male	42%	42%	43%
Ethnicity			
White	63%	56%	57%
African American	14%	19%	16%
Hispanic	13%	17%	18%
Asian American	5%	3%	< 1%
Other or more than one race	5%	5%	5%
Age	22(7.2)	23(7.4)	22(6.9)
Marital Status			
Married	9%	12%	11%
Not married or separated	91%	88%	89%
Highest degree expected in 2003–2004			
Less than a bachelor's degree	15%	22%	13%
Bachelor's degree	30%	35%	37%
Graduate degree	55%	43%	50%
Received financial aid in 2003–2004	78%	79%	77%
Delayed enrollment into college	31%	46%	38%
Parents' highest education level			
Did not graduate college	45%	57%	49%
Attended 2 years or associate's	12%	13%	15%
Bachelor's degree	21%	15%	19%
Graduate degree	19%	11%	14%
Do not know	3%	3%	3%

Pre-College Experiences			
High school GPA			
Less than 2.0	2%	5%	3%
2.0 to 2.9	20%	27%	25%
3.0 to 3.4	26%	23%	27%
3.5 to 4.0	27%	11%	15%
Missing data	24%	34%	29%
Highest mathematics course in HS			
Algebra II	24%	28%	28%
Trigonometry/Algebra II	15%	12%	13%
Pre-Calculus	17%	11%	14%
Calculus	15%	5%	9%
Missing or not valid	30%	44%	36%
Earned college credits in HS	25%	14%	18%
College Experiences			
First institution level			
Community or technical college	51%	71%	60%
4-year university	49%	29%	40%
First Institution Type			
Public	63%	60%	67%
Private not-for-profit	23%	14%	18%
Private for-profit	14%	26%	16%
Enrollment Intensity in 2003-04			
Full-time	77%	72%	72%
Part-time	13%	19%	17%
Mixed	10%	9%	11%
Hours worked per week	17(16.1)	20(16.9)	19(16.4)
Enrolled in developmental courses	20%	23%	25%
GPA 2003–2004	2.94(.82)	2.76(.92)	2.76(.89)

ᵃ Data are rounded to the nearest 10 per IES guidelines.
Note: Percentages may not sum to 100% due to rounding.

Profile of Pre-College Experiences

Entering Cohort. There was much variance in the high school grade point average (GPA) of students who first entered post-secondary education during the 2003–2004 year. Slightly more than one-fourth of students (27 percent) in the entering cohort earned a GPA between 3.5 and 4.0; 26 percent earned a GPA between 3.0 and 3.4; a fifth (20 percent) earned a GPA between 2.0 and 2.9; and only 2 percent of the entering cohort had a GPA that was less than 2.0. There was also a great deal of variation with regard to the highest mathematics course taken during high school, with the majority of students (24 percent) completing only algebra II, 15 percent completing a course that combined trigonometry and algebra II, 17 percent completing a pre-calculus course, and 15 percent completing calculus. A fourth (25 percent) of students in the entering cohort earned college credit while they were still enrolled in high school. As shown in Table 10.1, sizeable amounts of data were missing for the above-mentioned pre-college variables and it is unclear whether these data were missing at random.

Students Who Withdrew during the Second Year of College. Roughly in keeping with existing persistence theory and literature (e.g., Bean, 1985; Nora & Cabrera, 1996; Nora, 2004), the students who withdrew during the second year of college had lower levels of academic performance during high school when compared to the entire 2003–2004 cohort. Only 11 percent of students who withdrew during the second year had a GPA that ranged between 3.5 and 4.0 (compared to 27 percent in the entire cohort). Similarly, although nearly half of the data were missing, data for the high school mathematics course variable would suggest a positive relationship between taking advanced mathematics courses during high school and persistence during the second year of college. For instance, only 5 percent of the students who withdrew during the second year had completed calculus while in high school, and 28 percent of the students who withdrew only completed an algebra II course. These findings are consistent with analyses using other nationally representative data (e.g., Horn & Kojaku, 2001). Finally, only 14 percent of the students who withdrew during the second year of college had completed college credit during high school (compared to 25 percent of the entering cohort).

Students Who Withdrew during the Third Year of College. In general, the students who withdrew during the third year of college had lower high school GPAs, were less academically prepared for college mathematics courses, and were less likely to have earned college credits during high school when compared to the entire entering 2003–2004 cohort. However, similar to several demographic findings, data with regard to pre-college experiences suggest that students who withdrew during the third year were somewhat more representative of the entire cohort than students who withdrew during the second year. For instance, 27 percent of the entire entering cohort had a high school GPA that ranged between 3.5 and 4.0, compared to 15 percent of students who withdrew during the third year and 11 percent of students who withdrew during the second year. Additionally, 25 percent of the 2003–2004 cohort earned college credit during high school compared to 18 percent of the students who withdrew in year three and 14 who withdrew during the second year of college.

Profile of College Experiences

Entering Cohort. Nearly half (49 percent) of the entering cohort began their postsecondary education at a four-year institution while 51 percent began at a community or technical college. The majority (63 percent) of students enrolled at a public institution, 23 percent attended a private not-for-profit, and 14 percent enrolled at a private for-profit college or university. Three fourths (77 percent) of entering students enrolled in college full-time, 13 percent enrolled part-time, and the remaining 10 percent of students enrolled a combination of part- and full-time during their first year in college. Students in the entering cohort worked an average of seventeen hours per week, although there was a substantial amount of variance (*SD*=16.1 hours). A fifth (20 percent) of the entire cohort enrolled in one or more developmental courses during the first year of college. The average GPA for the 2003–2004 academic year was 2.94 (on a 4.0 scale).
Students Who Withdrew during the Second Year of College. Students who attended a technical or community college during their first year in college were substantially more likely to withdraw during the second year of college when compared to students who initially enrolled at a four-year institution. In fact, nearly three-fourths of the students who withdrew during the second year attended a two-year or technical school (compared to 51 percent of the entering cohort). Further, data suggest that students who attend proprietary institutions are at greater risk of withdrawing during the second year, as a greater proportion (26 percent) of students attending for-profit institutions withdrew during the second year when compared to the entering cohort (14 percent).

Also consistent with prior research on first-year persistence, students who attended college part-time were more likely to withdraw during year two. Nearly one fifth (19 percent) of students who dropped out of college during year two attended part-time during the first year compared to 13 percent of students in the entering cohort. Interestingly, there was little difference (10 percent compared to 9 percent) between the proportion of the entering cohort and the percentage of students who attended a combination of part- and full-time during the first year of college. Perhaps the indecision represents the commitment on the part of the student to earn a college degree and, while they may not be able to exclusively attend college full-time, their goal or desire is to attend full-time and persist.

Students who withdrew during the second year reported working an average of twenty hours per week (*SD* = 16.9 hours). A slightly greater proportion of students who dropped out of college during year two enrolled in developmental courses (23 percent compared to 20 percent of the entering cohort). Finally, the average first-year GPA of students who withdrew during year two was 2.76 compared to an average GPA of 2.94 for the entire cohort, consistent with literature that indicates that a student's academic performance during the first year impacts subsequent enrollment decisions. **Students Who Withdrew during the Third Year of College.** Roughly speaking, students who withdrew during the third year of college were found to be similar to students who withdrew in year two in terms of enrollment intensity (i.e., part- or full-time), hours worked, and first-year GPA. Two-thirds (67 percent) of the students who withdrew during year three attended a public institution compared to only 63 percent of the entire cohort. At the same time, students who attended private institutions were less likely to withdraw from college during year three (18 percent compared to 23 percent of students in the entire entering cohort). It is also notable that only 16 percent of the students who withdrew during year three attended for-profit institutions compared to the large proportion who withdrew during year two (26 percent). This finding adds to the existing criticism surrounding for-profit institutions.

Another observable difference between the students who withdrew during the second and third years was specific to institutional level. While community college and technical students were still more likely to withdraw from college compared to four-year students, only 60 percent of the students who withdrew during year three were two-year students compared to 71 percent in year two. Finally, these data suggest that students who enroll in developmental courses may be at particular risk of withdrawing during the third year, as a fourth (25 percent) of the students who withdrew during year three were developmental students compared to 23 percent who withdrew in year two and 20 percent of students in the entire cohort.

SUMMARY OF RESEARCH FINDINGS—STUDENT ATTRITION BEYOND THE FIRST YEAR

There is a growing body of inferential work that utilizes multivariate analyses to examine student persistence beyond the first year. In addition to traditional regression techniques, researchers engaged in this line of work have begun utilizing survival analysis, also known as event history modeling, to model how time impacts students' decisions to withdraw from college. According to Ishitani (2008), survival analysis offers several advantages for studying persistence beyond the first year in college, including analyzing a dichotomous variable (i.e., persisted or withdrew), more appropriately than using linear regression techniques. Survival analysis allows researchers to understand departure behaviors/experiences that are unique to specific time periods beyond the first year. It also allows for an examination of the impact of variables that change values over time (e.g., grade point average) on student attrition. Moreover, event history modeling allows for an examination of different forms of departure (e.g., stopout, transfer) in a single dataset. The following section provides a synthesis of findings to date organized around the factors that have been found to increase the odds of student attrition beyond the first year of college, including: (1) demographic characteristics; (2) financial assistance; (3) pre-college behaviors/ experiences; (4) social and academic experiences; (5) environmental pull factors; (6) student commitment; and (7) institutional characteristics.

Demographic Characteristics

Findings suggest that numerous demographic characteristics may influence the timing of a student's withdrawal from college including gender, ethnicity, parental education, socioeconomic status, student's and parents' educational goals, delayed enrollment in college, transfer status, and even the size of a student's hometown. For instance, Ishitani's (2003) investigation of the longitudinal effects of being a first-generation student on attrition using a sample cohort of students who enrolled at a four-year comprehensive public institution in the Midwest reveals that female students were 61 percent more likely to withdraw during the fourth year when compared to male students. Moreover, Ishitani's (2006) more recent work involving a survival analysis of a nationally representative sample of students using data from the National Education Longitudinal Study of 1988 (NELS:88) and NELS:1988–2000 Postsecondary Education Transcript Study (PETS:2000) suggest that females may be at particular risk of dropping out of college during the second and fourth years.

Current findings indicate that a student's ethnicity may also influence persistence decisions beyond the first year in college including earlier work by DesJardins, Ahlburg, and McCall (1999), who utilized event history modeling to study the temporal dimensions of student attrition at a large research university. Results indicate that African American students had a higher risk of dropout in year three than white students. In addition, Ishitani's work (2003, 2006) found that non-Asian minority students were more likely to leave college during the second year, when compared to white students. In contrast, work by Titus (2004, 2006) has utilized hierarchical generalized linear modeling (HGLM) analyses to identify institutional-level variables (after taking student variables into account) that increase the chance of students persisting to the third year of college. His analyses involving a nationally representative sample of first-time, full-time, degree-seeking students attending four-year institutions fail to find a relationship between third-year persistence and numerous demographic characteristics including ethnicity, gender, and socioeconomic status.

Several studies have identified a relationship between the parental education levels and/or socioeconomic status and subsequent decisions to remain enrolled in college beyond the first year. For instance, Ishitani and DesJardins (2002–2003) found that for students who come from low-income families, a mother's educational attainment significantly impacts student persistence in second-to-third-year re-enrollment and in third-to-fourth year return of students. Not surprisingly, being raised in a low-income family was found to more negatively influence student persistence at the end of the second and third years than it was in the first year. It is to be expected that circumstances associated with a family living in a low-income situation would put undue pressure on the student to withdraw and help with family expenses. For those students coming from a low-income family, however, the impact of a mother's educational attainment had the largest effect on reducing student attrition in second- to third-year rates. Specifically, at the end of the second year, students whose mothers had attained an undergraduate degree were 57 percent more likely to re-enroll for a third year than students whose mothers did not complete a college education. Evidence to support the role of parental education and/or socioeconomic status on students' decisions to remain enrolled in college through the second or third year of college is also provided by Crisp and Nora (2009) and Ishitani (2003).

Financial Assistance

Consistent with literature focusing on first-year persistence (e.g., Cabrera, Nora, & Castaneda, 1992; Nora & Cabrera, 1996; Nora, Cabrera, Hagedorn, & Pascarella, 1996), research has suggested that receipt of financial aid may increase the odds that a student will remain in college. More specifically, research demonstrated that students were nearly twice as likely to persist between the second and third years if they received financial aid (DuBrock, 1999; Ishitani & DesJardins, 2002). Ishitani and DesJardins (2002) found that receiving financial aid reduced the risk of attrition the most in the third year. In contrast, needy students (operationally defined as receiving Pell Grants) were less likely to continue to the second year and were even less likely to return for the third year (DuBrock, 1999). Similar findings have also been found for at-risk populations including Hispanic community college students (Crisp & Nora, 2009), first-generation college students

(Ishitani, 2006), and cohorts of low-income, minority, and female science, engineering, and math (SEM) majors (Fenske, Porter & DuBrock, 2000).

Current findings also suggest that the impact of financial aid may vary according to the form of assistance received. For instance, findings by Dowd and Coury (2006) indicate that community college students' decisions to persist to the second year were negatively related to the receipt of loans. Similarly, Fenske, Porter and DuBrock (2000) found that SEM majors who received financial aid packages that included a combination of loans and grants in the second and third years of college were less likely to persist. There is also evidence to suggest that the receipt of loans is most likely to reduce attrition in year three and also beyond the fourth year (DesJardins, Ahlburg & McCall, 1999). In addition to the ability to pay for books, tuition, fees, and other education expenses, Nora and Cabrera (1993) found that an intangible benefit of financial assistance is reduced stress among students associated with meeting the many costs of a higher education.

An overlapping factor with student finances is the residency status of the student as it relates to out-of-state tuition. According to research by DuBrock (1999), not being able to establish residency in a state and having to pay non-resident tuition has a significant negative effect on student persistence in the first two years of college. Specifically, undergraduates classified as out-of-state students were found to be 1.93 times less likely to return for a second year and 2.04 times less likely to return for a third year (DuBrock, 1999). It is thought that the exceptionally high cost of tuition may outweigh any perceived benefits to students attending college outside their home state.

Pre-College Factors/Experiences

The role of high school curriculum in impacting students' decisions to remain in college has been documented. For instance, Horn and Kojaku (2001) found that the level of a high school curriculum undertaken by a student was strongly related to third-year persistence in college. Specifically, at the beginning of the third year, 87 percent of the students who had completed an advanced high school curriculum were still enrolled in an institution of higher education compared to only 62 percent that simply completed a core curriculum. Crisp and Nora (2009) also found that persistence during the second and third years of college among Hispanic community college students was uniquely influenced by the level of mathematics courses taken during high school.

Mixed findings have been found with regard to the role of academic achievement during high school on student persistence beyond the first year of college. DuBrock (1999) found that high school grade point average (GPA) exerted a significant impact on student persistence into both the second and third years. Results indicated that a student with a GPA that was one-tenth of a point higher was 8 percent more likely to persist to the second year. Additionally, the increased odds of persisting with a higher high school GPA was 7 percent between the second and third years, 8 percent between the third and fourth years, and 6 percent between the fourth and fifth years of college. Work by Ishitani (2006) has also indicated that high school achievement influences students' decisions to remain in college beyond the first year. More specifically, his findings reveal that students who are in the lowest or third quintile class ranking were most likely to withdraw from college during the third year and students in the fourth quintile were most vulnerable during the second year. In contrast, research by DesJardins, Ahlburg, and McCall (1999) failed to find a significant relationship between high school rank percentile and student attrition beyond the first year (controlling for other factors including test scores and GPA).

Differences in academic ability as measured by standardized test scores have been shown to influence withdrawal decisions beyond the first year in college. Ishitani and DesJardins (2002) found that, over time, high-ability students (those with SAT scores in the highest quartile) were at a lower risk of withdrawing relative to students who scored in the lower three quartiles. Previous to the publication of these findings, DesJardins, Ahlburg, and McCall (1999) found that students who scored high on the ACT were also less likely to withdraw during the second year of college when compared to students with lower ACT scores. Also previously, DuBrock (1999) had established that students who had total SAT scores of 1010 or less and had persisted to the fourth year were found to be significantly more likely to graduate or persist to the fifth year.

Inferential work specific to persistence beyond the first year of college also suggests that additional pre-college factors, including delaying enrollment in college, transfer status, and even the size of a student's hometown, may be related to the timing of student withdrawal from college. Crisp and Nora (2009) found that the persistence during the second and third years of college among Hispanic community college students was uniquely influenced by students' decisions to delay enrollment in college immediately following high school. These findings substantiated those by Ishitani (2006) which indicated that attrition during the second year was related to delayed enrollment among first-generation college students. As to the issue of transfer, DesJardins, Ahlburg and McCall (1999) found that transfer students were more likely to persist in the second year when compared to students who began at the university as freshmen.

Finally on the topic of pre-college factors, work by Ishitani (2003) indicates that students from larger towns were significantly less likely to withdraw during the second year when compared to students from mid-sized towns. We suggest that coming from larger towns and school districts may have rendered those students better equipped to handle negative campus climates, larger class sizes, differing values, and invalidating classroom experiences, while students coming from smaller or mid-sized towns may have difficulty transitioning from a sense of a small community and friends to one much more intimidating.

Educational aspirations have also been found to positively impact student attrition beyond the first year. Specifically, low educational aspirations were found to have the strongest negative effect on student retention in the first year (Ishitani & DesJardins, 2002). Work by Titus (2004) reveals that the educational goals of students subsequently served to decrease the odds of withdrawal to the third year in college. Also, Ishitani (2006) found that students whose parents were unsure about their educational expectations for their child were most likely to withdraw during the second year. Additionally, students whose parents did not expect them to graduate from college were most likely to withdraw in the third year, followed by the second year.

Social and Academic Integration

Early work on student persistence (e.g., Bean, 1980; Bean & Metzner, 1985; Pascarélla & Terenzini, 1979, 1980) centered on a student's social integration into his or her environment. Throughout the years, the influence of this factor on students' persistence decisions has been confirmed and substantiated among different student groups at a variety of institution types (e.g., Nora, 1993, 2004). Very little is known with regard to these aspects for students beyond the first year, however. A single institutional report found that the students receiving appropriate assessment as they entered college, seeking and receiving counseling (both academic as well as personal), and attending an official orientation session provided by the institution, were significant factors associated with persistence to the second and third years (Maack, 2002). The integration of students in classroom discussions, collaborative learning experiences, and study groups are all part of an underlying process affecting the adjustment of students to college, their academic performance, and their decisions to remain enrolled to graduation. While these factors are not fully representative of the academic and social experiences identified in the literature, they do represent valid proxies for those components. Moreover, more recent findings by Allen, Robbins, Casillas, and Oh (2008) reveal that social connectedness and commitment to college have direct positive effects on retention to the third year of college.

Researchers have also used academic performance during college as a measurement of academic integration. Although findings by DesJardins, Ahlburg, and McCall (1999) suggest that a student's grades might have a relatively stronger impact on reducing attrition in year one than beyond the first year of college, findings from other studies point to a lingering negative impact of poor academic performance on attrition during the second and/or third years (e.g., Allen, Robbins, Casillas & Oh, 2008; Bradburn, 2002; Crisp & Nora, 2009; Ishitani & DesJardins, 2002; Maack, 2002). For instance, work by Titus (2004) reveals that the probability of students persisting to the third year increased eight percentage points with a one standard deviation increase in college GPA. Similarly, Titus's more recent work (2006) found that academic performance in college is positively related to third-year persistence for students attending four-year institutions. Furthermore, findings by Ishitani and DesJardins (2002) indicate that students may be at a higher risk of dropping out of college in year two if their first-year GPA is below 2.0.

Environmental Pull Factors

Very early retention work established that environmental influences in different forms have a negative impact on a student's ability to successfully engage in academic and social activities on campus, subsequently affecting academic performance and the desire to remain enrolled in college (e.g., Bean, 1985; Nora, 1987; Nora & Wedan, 1993). Factors that have been found to "pull" students away from college include living off campus, working more than twenty hours per week on or off campus, and taking a reduced course load (i.e., part-time enrollment). Findings by Crisp and Nora (2009) demonstrate the negative influence of environmental factors, such as working full-time and not enrolling full-time, on persistence through the second and third years among Hispanic community college students. Similarly, DuBrock's (1999) work beyond the first year revealed that students who had on-campus jobs and were permitted to remain in close proximity to faculty and an academic environment were more likely to persist well beyond the first year. Students who could afford to live on campus were much more likely to persist beyond the first year. More specifically, students living on campus were found to be 1.73 times more likely to return the second year and 1.38 times more likely to persist to the third year in college. Similarly, Titus's work (2004, 2006) found that both living on campus and student involvement had a positive influence on persistence during the third year of college. Moreover, Titus (2004) found that a deviation increase in the number of hours worked per week increased the odds that students would persist by three percentage points. In contrast, persistence to the third year was not found to be related to the number of hours a student worked per week or working off campus in Titus's (2006) later work.

Institutional Characteristics

Current work on student persistence beyond the first year in college has begun to consider the role of institutional characteristics on students' decision to remain in college. For instance, findings by Crisp and Nora (2009) indicate that Hispanic students' decisions to remain in college during the third year were influenced by whether students attended a Hispanic-serving institution. Moreover, research findings reveal that institutional type may have a significant impact on students' decisions to remain in college beyond the first year. Ishitani (2006) found that students who attended non-selective institutions were at greater risk for not persisting during the first four years of college when compared to students attending selective institutions. Students attending non-selective institutions were most likely to withdraw from college in the fourth year. In contrast, attending a private institution was found to be positively related to persistence in the first five years of college. More specifically, first-generation students who attended a private college were 30 percent less likely to withdraw from their institutions in the second year, and 54 percent less likely in their third year, as compared with students who attended public four-year universities.

SUGGESTIONS FOR FUTURE RESEARCH

The literature on first-year persistence has provided a fairly robust picture of the process of students transitioning from home and high school to post-secondary education. While each student is unique and each institution offers opportunities for a unique set of experiences, it has been informative to have an aggregate understanding of the transition and adjustment process and how the interconnectedness of different academic, social, and environmental factors in that longitudinal process points students toward persistence. Beyond the first year, however, it may be especially important for institutions to gather and examine data on their individual students and their experiences. Factors pushing students forward or pulling students back become more localized in the experiences students have at a given institution, specifically as those experiences interact with personal circumstances (e.g., financial, familial, occupational).

At the time of this writing, data from the newest BPS cohort follow-up 04:09 were not available. For that reason, the profile on students for this chapter extends only through the first three years in college. Because graduation on time (traditionally considered as four years) is not reality, future research must extend its analysis of data that demonstrate how the characteristics and experiences of students who withdraw during years four, five, or six might be different from those students enrolled in the first three years in college. More importantly, comparisons can be made between those who, despite the length of time, graduated and who did not.

Ishitani (2006) suggests that the time-varying effects of variables in current models of student persistence should be taken into account to more fully understand the departure of students from college. As more and more longitudinal data become available, or the norm, more appropriate and sophisticated statistical tools can be utilized to derive parameter estimates that more truly capture reality. The carryover effects of variables from one time period to another, the changes in student's characteristics, beliefs, and behaviors over time, and the cumulative effects of specific factors on student outcomes will address the misspecification of current models in the literature. The issue is not that those models of student persistence have not provided researchers with valuable information, but rather that even with the best of models there is still much more to be learned.

In years past, one criticism of studies examining the dropout behavior of college students has centered on the emphasis on student outcomes, excluding the incorporation of theoretical perspectives and frameworks. Comparisons simply focused on reporting the differences in dropout rates, transfer rates, and graduation rates between those who re-enrolled and those who walked away from higher education. The field is at a point where profiles of different groups such as dropouts, transfer students, stopouts, and those involuntarily withdrawn because of their academic records can be much more informative. Now, comparisons among those groups can not only focus on their academic performance and degree attainment but can provide a fuller understanding of those outcomes in relation to academic and social interactions, commitments to earning a college degree, behaviors in the classroom and on campus, and psychosocial experiences while enrolled in college. Researchers must now examine student withdrawal behavior within a specific and discrete time frame, allowing for a comparison of conceptual frameworks among those that withdrew from college all together, managed to transfer or not, or were academically dismissed. These tests of model invariance can help to uncover the underlying structural patterns among sets of interrelated factors that ultimately will inform practice and policy in higher education.

NOTE

1. Data are rounded to the nearest 10 per IES guidelines.

REFERENCES

Allen, J., Robbins, S. B., Casillas, A., & Oh, In-Sue. (2008). Third-year college retention and transfer: Effects of academic performance, motivation, and social connectedness. *Research in Higher Education, 49*, 647–664.

Astin, A. (1984). Student involvement: A developmental theory for higher education. *Journal of College Student Personnel, 25*, 297–308.

Astin, A. W. (1999). Student involvement: A developmental theory for higher education. *Journal of College Student Development, 40*(5), 518–529.

Bartlett, C. & Abell, P. (1995, February). *Understanding the transfer Student—Or are we?* Symposium conducted at the Annual National Transfer and Articulation Symposium, Tucson, AZ.

Bean, J. (1980). Dropouts and turnover: The synthesis and test of a causal model of student attrition. *Research in Higher Education, 12*, 155–187.

Bean, J. (1985). Interaction effects based on class level in an explanatory model of college student dropout syndrome. *American Educational Research Journal, 22*, 35–64.

Bean, J. & Metzner, B. (1985). A conceptual model of nontraditional undergraduate student attrition. *Review of Educational Research, 55*, 485–540.

Bradburn, E. M. (2002). Short-term enrollment in postsecondary education: Student background and institutional differences in reasons for early departure, 1996–1998. Postsecondary Education Descriptive Analysis Reports. *National Center for Education Statistics* (Publication No. NCES-2003-153).

Braxton, J. & Brier, E. (1989). Melding organizational and interactional theories of student attrition: A path analytic study. *Review of Higher Education, 13*, 47–61.

Braxton, J. M. & Lien, L. A. (2000). The viability of academic integration as a central construct in Tinto's interactionalist theory of college student departure. In J. Braxton (Ed.), *Reworking the student departure puzzle.* Nashville: Vanderbilt University Press.

Cabrera, A. F., Nora, A., & Castaneda, M. B. (1992). The role of finances in the student persistence process: A structural model. *Research in Higher Education, 33*(5), 571–594.

Cabrera, A. F., Nora, A., & Castaneda, M. B. (1993). College persistence: The testing of an integrated model. *Journal of Higher Education, 64*(2), 123–139.

Crisp, G., & Nora, A. (2009). Hispanic student success: Factors influencing the persistence and transfer decisions of Latino community college students enrolled in developmental education. *Research in Higher Education, 51*, 175–194.

DesJardins, S. L., Ahlburg, D. A., & McCall, B. P. (1999). An event history model of student departure. *Economics of Education Review, 18*(1999), 375–390.

Dowd, A. C. & Coury, T. (2006). The effect of loans on the persistence and attainment of community college students. *Research in Higher Education, 47*(1), 33–62.

DuBrock, C. P. (1999, May). *Financial aid and college persistence: A five-year longitudinal study of 1993 and 1994 beginning freshmen students.* Symposium conducted at the AIR 40th Annual Forum, Cincinnati, OH.

Fenske, R. H., Porter, J. D., & DuBrock, C. P. (2000). Tracking financial aid and persistence of women, minority, and needy students in science, engineering and mathematics. *Research in Higher Education, 41*(1), 67–94.

Horn, L. & Kojaku, L.K. (2001). High school academic curriculum and the persistence path through college: Persistence and transfer behavior of undergraduates 3 years after entering 4-year institutions. *National Center for Education Statistics* (Publication No. NCES 2001-163). Retrieved April 4, 2004 from NCES Website: http://nces.ed.gov/pubs2001/2001163.pdf

Hurtado, S. & Carter, D. (1997). Effects of college transition and perceptions of the campus racial climate on Latino college students' sense of belonging. *Sociology of Education, 70*, 324–345.

Ishitani, T. T. (2003). A longitudinal approach to assessing attrition behavior among first-generation students: Time-varying effects of pre-college characteristics. *Research in Higher Education, 44*(4), 433–449.

Ishitani, T. T. (2006). Studying attrition and degree completion behavior among first-generation college students in the United States. *The Journal of Higher Education, 77*(5), 861–885.

Ishitani, T. T. (2008). How to explore timing of intervention for students at risk of departure. In T. T. Ishitani (Ed.), *Alternative perspectives in institutional planning: New directions for institutional research, 137.* San Francisco: Jossey-Bass.

Ishitani, T. T. & DesJardins, S. L. (2002–2003). A longitudinal investigation of dropout from college in the United States. *Journal of College Student Retention, 4*(2), 173–201.

Maack, S. C. (2002). *Whatever happened to students who entered in the Fall 1995? Persistence at Rio Hondo College.* (ERIC Document Reproduction Service No. ED466878). Retrieved April 4, 2004 from http://www.eduref.org

Nora, A. (1987). Determinants of retention among Chicano college students: A structural model. *Research in Higher Education, 26*(1), 31–59.

Nora, A. (1993). Two-year colleges and minority students' educational aspirations: Help or hindrance. In J. C. Smart (Ed.), *Higher education: Handbook of theory and research,* Vol IX. NY: Agathon Press.

Nora, A. (2002). A theoretical and practical view of student adjustment and academic achievement. In W. Tierney & L. Hagedorn (Eds.), *Increasing access to college: Extending possibilities for all students.* Albany: State University of New York Press.

Nora, A. (2004). The role of habitus and cultural capital in choosing a college, transitioning from high school to higher education, and persisting in college among minority and non-minority students. *Journal of Hispanic Higher Education, 3*(2), 180–208.

Nora, A., & Cabrera, A. F. (1993). The construct validity of institutional commitment: A confirmatory factor analysis. *Research in Higher Education, 34*(2), 243–262.

Nora, A. & Cabrera, A. F. (1996). The role of perceptions of prejudice and discrimination on the adjustment of minority students to college. *Journal of Higher Education, 67*(2), 119–148.

Nora, A., Cabrera, A. F., Hagedorn, L., & Pascarella, E. T. (1996). Differential impacts of academic and social experiences on college-related behavioral outcomes across different ethnic and gender groups at four-year institutions. *Research in Higher Education, 37*(4), 427–452.

Nora, A., Castaneda, M. B., & Cabrera, A. F. (November, 1992). Student persistence: The testing of a comprehensive structural model of retention. Paper presented at the annual conference of the Association for the Study of Higher Education, Minneapolis, MN.

Nora, A. & Garcia, V. (undated). *The role of perceptions of remediation on the persistence of developmental students in higher education.* Unpublished manuscript, University of Houston, Houston, TX.

Nora, A. & Lang, D. (undated). *Precollege psychosocial factors related to persistence.* Unpublished manuscript, University of Houston, Houston, TX.

Nora, A. & Wedam, E. (1993). *Off-campus experiences: The pull factors affecting freshman-year attrition on a commuter campus.* Unpublished manuscript, University of Illinois at Chicago, Chicago, IL.

Pascarella, E. & Terenzini, P. T. (1979). Student-faculty informal contact and college persistence: A further investigation. *Journal of Educational Research, 72,* 214–218.

Pascarella, E. T. & Terenzini, P. T. (1980). Predicting freshman persistence and voluntary dropout decisions from a theoretical model. *Journal of Higher Education, 51,* 60–75.

Pascarella, E. & Terenzini, P. T. (1990). *How college affects students: Findings and insights from twenty years of research.* San Francisco: Jossey-Bass.

Pascarella, E. & Terenzini, P. (2005) *How college affects students (Vol. 2): A third decade of research.* San Francisco: Jossey-Bass/Wiley.

Reason, R. D. (2009). An examination of persistence research through the lens of a comprehensive conceptual framework. *Journal of College Student Development, 50*(6), 659–682.

Rendon, L. I. (1994). Validating culturally diverse students: Toward a new model of learning and student development. *Innovative Higher Education, 19*(1), 23–32.

Singell, L. D. & Waddell, G. R. (2009). Modeling retention at a large public university: Can at-risk students be identified early enough to treat? *Research in Higher Education, 51,* 546–572.

Smith, T. Y. (1995, May). *The retention status of underrepresented minority students: An analysis of survey results from sixty-seven U.S. colleges and universities.* Symposium conducted at the AIR 35th Annual Forum, Boston, Massachusetts.

St. John, E. P., Cabrera, A. F., Nora, A., & Asker, E. H. (2001). Economic perspectives on student persistence. In J. Braxton (Ed.), *Rethinking the student departure puzzle.* Nashville: Vanderbilt University Press.

Swail, W. S., Redd, K., & Perna, L. (2003). Retaining minority students in higher education: A framework for success. In A. Kezar (Ed.), *ASHE-ERIC Higher Education Report: Volume 30, Number 2.* Hoboken, NJ: Wiley Periodicals, Inc.

Tinto, V. (1975). Dropout from higher education: A theoretical synthesis of recent research. *Review of Educational Research, 45,* 89–125.

Tinto, V. (1993). *Leaving college: Rethinking the causes and cures of student attrition.* Chicago: University of Chicago Press.

Titus, M. A. (2004). An examination of the influence of institutional context on student persistence at 4-year colleges and universities: A multilevel approach. *Research in Higher Education, 45*(7), 673–699.

Titus, M. A. (2006). Understanding the influence of the financial context of institutions on student persistence at four-year colleges and universities. *The Journal of Higher Education, 77*(2), 353–375.

U.S. Department of Education, National Center for Education Statistics (1998). *Stopouts or stayouts? Undergraduates who leave college in their first year* (NCES 1999-087). Washington, DC: Author.

U.S. Department of Education, National Center for Education Statistics. (2000). *Descriptive summary of 1995–96 beginning postsecondary students: Three years later* (NCES 2000-154). Washington, DC: Author.

11

Moving from Theory to Action

A Model of Institutional Action
for Student Success

Vincent Tinto

Despite many years of research on student retention and attempts at theory building, there is still much to do. Though significant strides have been made in constructing the broad dimensions of a theory of institutional departure, there is still a good deal of disagreement, if not confusion, over the details of such a theory. More importantly, there has been little significant development of a theory of action that would provide institutions of higher education guidelines for the development of policies, programs, and practices to enhance student persistence. Consequently, while it can be said that we now know the broad dimensions of the process of student leaving, we know very little about a theory of action for student persistence. The goal of this chapter is to lay out the broad outlines of such a theory and show how it might be used to guide institutional action.

To do so, we first must consider the nature of the current debate about existing retention theories, in particular as they are exemplified in the preceding chapters. We do so because understanding some of the challenges researchers and theorists face will not only help build a more effective theory of student departure, but also aid our pursuit of a useful theory of institutional action.

REFLECTION ON CURRENT DEBATES OF A THEORY OF INSTITUTIONAL DEPARTURE

Defining Student Leaving.   One of the challenges we face in developing social theory, regardless of its focus, lies in the complexity of defining the

251

very object of our concern, namely human behavior. We continue to struggle with the question of how we should define the human act. Is it what an external observer sees or what the actor intends? So too in considering student leaving, we have yet to be clear on what constitutes leaving. Is it the act that is seen by an institutional observer or is it what the leaver intends? Though an institutional observer (e.g., administrator) may rightly feel that any departure represents a type of failure, if only because of the loss of revenue as described by John Schuh and Ann Gansemer-Topf in chapter 5, the departing individual may understand his or her departure quite differently. Among other possibilities, the leaver may understand his or her leaving as enabling entry to another institution (transfer). In that case, it may be seen as a positive rather than a negative act.[1] It may also be the case that some students leave to take on a job or accept a promotion that was in fact the goal of their initial entry. In this case, their attendance has led to the successful achievement of an occupational goal.[2] For other persons, leaving may represent a response to external commitments that pull them away from the institution. They would have preferred to stay but were obliged to leave at least for a period of time. For some this may result in stopout, while for others it may mean the end of their educational pursuit. In either case, their leaving may be seen as a form of involuntary behavior that has little to do with their experience on campus.

Among the various behaviors an institutional observer may define as institutional departure, there are likely to be a range of behaviors that are quite different in character, intent, and causation. Unfortunately, most studies of institutional departure and, by extension, attempts to construct and/or test theories of institutional departure, have typically lumped together under the label "leaving" what often are very different behaviors.[3] The result is not only limited explained variance, but also conceptual confusion that yields muddled if not contradictory and sometimes nonsensical conclusions. This, in effect, is the point Tom Mortenson makes in chapter 2.

There are other challenges. Researchers have often ignored Weber's observation that the terms we employ in constructing social theory, such as social status, are abstractions that cannot be understood without specific reference to the behaviors and contexts from which they are derived. Nor can they be separated from the meanings individuals attach to their behaviors. People do not have social status. They have, among other things, income, education, occupation, and material possessions. Social status is merely an abstraction that allows us to talk about how the sum of those possessions can be used to understand patterns of human behavior. At the same time, though our analyses of human behavior often assume that people understand and respond to social status in very much the same ways, we know that this is not the case. We make that assumption to simplify what would otherwise be very complex analyses.

The same can be said of the abstractions *academic* and *social integration*. The fact is that students are not integrated. They interact with a range of people and situations on campus, both academic and social, and they derive meaning from those interactions in ways that may lead them to feel at home and/or a member of a place or community. They feel they "belong." Of course, others may, in the process of interaction, come to feel at odds with those who make up the institution or feel that they are not welcomed by people in the institution. They feel as if they do not belong or that others do not want them to belong. This is what Hurtado and Carter (1996) were getting at in their use of the term "hostile climate." In the final analysis, what matters in students' decisions to stay or leave are not their interactions, as objectively defined, but how they understand and draw meaning from those interactions. For researchers, what matters are not the abstractions we use such as academic or social integration, but how we define and in turn measure the behaviors from which abstractions are drawn and the meanings different people derive from those interactions.

Why does this matter? It matters because what we end up using for our construction of and/or tests of theory are data that reflect a series of decisions involving both conceptualization and measurement that may vary from study to study and may differentially represent differing behaviors. Though studies may be using the same abstraction, such as academic integration or what is now referred to as academic engagement, their data are often drawn from very different measures. The result is once more conceptual confusion that further muddies the water.

What's my point? My point is simply that we still have much to do as we seek to develop a more powerful theory of institutional leaving that captures the full range of behaviors that are lumped under the umbrella term of "student leaving." This does not mean our existing theories are seriously flawed. Quite the contrary: we have more than ample evidence to support the broad outlines of existing theories of student institutional departure. Rather it argues that those theories are, in their current form, only rough predictors of leaving as currently measured. In their present formulation, they can tell us only so much about the forces shaping student leaving.

More importantly, theories of student leaving can tell us only so much about the forces shaping student persistence. Leaving is not the mirror image of staying. Knowing why students leave does not tell us—at least not directly—what institutions can do to help students stay and succeed. In the real world of action, what matters are not our theories, but how they help us address pressing issues of retention and persistence, especially among low-income and underrepresented students.[4] Unfortunately, current theories of student leaving are not well suited to that task. This is the case not only because they focus on leaving, but also because they utilize abstractions and variables that are not clearly within the immediate control of the institution to influence. Take for instance the concept of academic integration. Though the concept may be useful to a theorist, it does not tell a practitioner what she or he would do to achieve academic integration. What is needed is a model of student retention and, in turn, a model of institutional action that provides institutions guidelines for the development of effective policies, procedures, and programs that enhance the retention of their students, especially those who continue to fare less well in higher education, namely, low-income and underrepresented students.

Moving Toward a Model of Institutional Action

Our goal here is modest. Rather than propose a full model of institutional action—that is beyond the scope of this chapter—we will identify some of the major elements that such a model must include. We do so in the expectation that future work will begin to fill in the gaps and move toward the development and testing of a useful model and in turn theory of institutional action for student success.[5]

In moving toward the identification of a possible model of institutional action, we will focus on the conditions within institutions in which we place students rather than on the attributes of students themselves or the events external to the institution that may also shape decisions to stay or leave. This is because it is too easy to see the absence of student success as solely the responsibility of students or of external forces beyond institutional control. Too often we tend to "blame the victim" and avoid seeing our own actions as at least partially responsible for the problems we face.

This is not to say that individual attributes or external events do not matter. Of course they do. In some cases they matter greatly. We all know stories of students who, by sheer drive of personality, succeed against what are for most students seemingly insurmountable barriers. Yet there are other students who do not succeed even when placed in settings that favor success. Nevertheless, though some might argue otherwise, student attributes such as personality, drive, or motivation are, for the great majority of institutions, largely beyond immediate institutional control.[6] The same can be said of events external to the institution. Though we know that family, work, and other matters may influence staying and leaving, such events are not easily within the ability of institutions to influence. This is not the case, however, for the conditions or environments in which students are placed. Such environments are already within institutional control, reflecting as they do past decisions, and can be changed if institutions are serious in their pursuit of student success. Since our focus is on institutional action, it makes sense to begin our search for a model of action with those aspects of institutional environment that shape student success that are within the capacity of institutions to change.

What are these conditions? What does research on student success tell us about the conditions within universities that promote success?[7] What it tells us is that there are at least four conditions that capture the nature of settings in which students are most likely to succeed. These are expectations, support, feedback, and involvement or engagement.[8]

Expectations

First, expectations are a condition for student success. Students fare best in environments that provide clear and consistent expectations for what is required to succeed in college. As importantly, students are more likely to succeed in settings that do so while holding high expectations for their ability to meet those requirements. Quite simply, no student rises to low expectations. Regrettably, it is too often the case that universities expect too little of students, especially during the critical first year of college. Indeed, a recent national study by Kuh (2003) indicates that first-year students spend less time on their studies out of class than what we deem necessary for successful learning. They simply do not study enough. It is my view that this is the case in part because we do not expect enough of them nor construct educational settings that require them to study enough.

At the same time, universities will sometimes hold differing expectations for differing students. This may be expressed in the labels we use to describe groups of students, as for instance contained in the term "remedial" students, or more subtly, but no less effectively, in the way we treat differing students as sometimes happens among faculty and students of different gender or ethnicity. However expressed, research is clear that students quickly pick up expectations and are influenced by the degree to which those expectations validate their presence on campus. This is precisely what Rendon (1994) was referring to in her research on validation and success of nontraditional, first-generation college students and what Solorzano, Ceja, and Yosso (2000) were referring to in their study of microaggressions.

Expectations can also be expressed in concrete ways through formal and informal advising. Knowing the rules and regulations and the informal networks that mark campus life are part and parcel of student success. Yet it remains the case that formal advising remains a "hit and miss" affair; some students are lucky and find the information they need, while others are not. The same can be said of the informal advising, the sharing of accumulated knowledge that goes on within a campus among and between faculty, staff, and students. Again, some students are able to locate that knowledge, often through informal networks of peers, while others are not (Attinasi, 1989).

Advising is particularly important to the success of the many students who either begin college undecided about their major and/or change their major during college.[9] The inability to obtain needed advice during the first year or at the point of changing majors can undermine motivation, increase the likelihood of departure, and for those who continue, result in increased time to degree completion. Though students may make credit progress, they do not make substantial degree-credit progress.

Support

Second, support is a condition that promotes student success. Research points to three types of support that promote success: academic, social, and financial. As regards academic support, it is unfortunately the case that more than a few students enter the university insufficiently prepared for the rigors of university study. For them, as well as for others, the availability of academic support, for instance, in the form of developmental education courses, tutoring, study groups, and academic support programs such as supplemental instruction, is an important condition for their continuation in the university. So also is the availability of social support in the form of counseling, mentoring, and ethnic student centers. Such centers provide much-needed support for individual students and a safe haven for groups of students who might otherwise find themselves out of place in a setting where they are a distinct minority. For new students, these centers can serve as secure, knowable ports of entry that enable students to safely navigate the unfamiliar terrain of the university.

As regards the nature of support, research has demonstrated that support is most effective when it is connected to, not isolated from, the learning environments in which students are asked to learn. Nowhere is such support more important than in the classrooms of the institution, for it is success in those places of learning that form the building blocks upon which student success in college is built. Supplemental instruction, for instance, provides academic support that is directly attached to a specific class in order to help students succeed in that class. As a support strategy, it is most often used for key first-year "gateway" courses that are foundational to coursework that follows in subsequent years.

Assessment and Feedback

Third, assessment and feedback are conditions for student success. Students are more likely to succeed in settings that assess student performance and provide faculty, staff, and students frequent feedback about their performance. Here I refer not only to entry assessment of learning skills and early warning systems that alert institutions to students who need assistance, but also to classroom assessment techniques such as those described by Angelo and Cross (1993) and those that involve the use of learning portfolios. These techniques are not to be confused with testing but with forms of assessment, such as the well-known "one-minute" paper, that provide students and faculty information on what is or is not being learned in the classroom. When used frequently, such techniques enable students and faculty alike to adjust their learning and teaching in ways that promote learning. When implemented in portfolio form that requires continuous reflection, assessment can also deeply enrich learning.

Involvement

Fourth, involvement, or what is now referred to as engagement, is also a condition for student success (e.g. Astin, 1993; Tinto, 1993). Quite simply, the more students are academically and socially involved, the more likely are they to persist and graduate. This is especially true during the first year of university study when student membership is so tenuous yet so critical to subsequent learning and persistence. Involvement during that year serves as the foundation upon which subsequent affiliations and engagements are built.

Nowhere is involvement more important than in the classrooms and laboratories of the campus, again especially during the first year of college. This is the case for two reasons. First, the classroom may be the only place students meet each other and the faculty. Lest we forget, most students commute to college and a majority work while in college. For them and for many others, if involvement does not occur in those smaller places of engagement, it is unlikely it will easily occur elsewhere. Second, learning is central to the college experience and is the root source of student success. Involvement in classroom learning, especially with other students, leads to greater quality of effort, enhanced learning, and in turn heightened student success (Tinto, 1997). Even among students who persist, students who are more involved in learning, especially with other students, learn more and show greater levels of intellectual development (Endo & Harpel, 1982). It is for these reasons that so much of the literature on institutional retention, student learning, and development speaks of the importance of involvement and building educational communities that involve all, not just some, students (Carini, Kuh, & Klein, 2008; Tinto, 1993).

To sum up, students are more likely to succeed when they find themselves in settings that provide clear and high expectations for their success, provide needed academic, social, and financial support, provide frequent feedback, and actively involve them, especially with other students and faculty in learning.

MOVING TOWARD A THEORY OF INSTITUTIONAL ACTION

Two observations should be made about the current discussion. First, it argues that student learning is central to student success and by extension that, without learning, students are not successful regardless of whether or not they persist. The more students learn, the more value they find in their learning, the more likely they are to stay and graduate. This is true not only for those students who enter college academically underprepared, but also for the more able and motivated students who seek out learning and are, in turn, more likely to respond to perceived shortcomings in the quality of learning they experience on campus.

Second, our discussion leaves open, for the moment, the definition of success other than to imply that without learning there is no success and that at a minimum success implies successful learning in the classroom. By extension it argues that one way of understanding student success as it may be influenced by institutional action is to see it as being constructed from success in one class at a time, one upon another in ways that lead to academic progress. A model of institutional action, whatever its final dimensions, must therefore treat student learning as part and parcel of the process of student success and that success, however it is defined and measured, must have at its core success in individual classes.

What then might a model of institutional action for student retention look like? Following upon the prior discussion, Figure 11.1 describes some

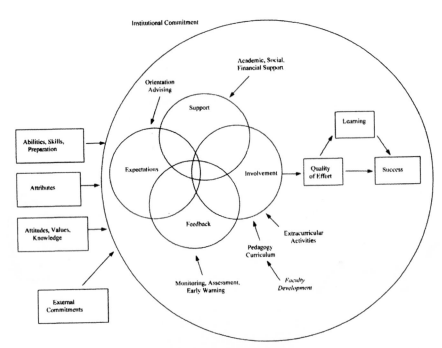

Figure 11.1. Elements of a Model of Institutional Action.

of the elements that such a model would contain and some of the institutional actions that would shape those elements.[10]

Students enter an institution with a variety of attributes (e.g., gender, social class, race, ethnicity), abilities, skills, and levels of prior academic preparation (e.g., academic and social skills), and attitudes, values, and knowledge about higher education (e.g., goals, commitments, motivations, and expectations). At the same time, they participate in a range of external settings (e.g., family, work, community) each of which have their own demands on the student's time and energies. They enter an institution with specific attributes (e.g., level, mode of control, size, location, and resources). As argued here, student attributes and external environments are, for all practical purposes, considered fixed and not immediate objects of institutional action.[11]

What are not fixed are the expectational climates established by members of the institution (faculty, staff, administrators, and other students); the academic, social, and financial supports provided by the institution; the feedback that is provided to and about students by the institution; and the educational and social activities that shape student academic and social involvements.

As depicted, the model argues that institutional commitments provide the overarching context for institutional action. Everything else being equal, institutions that are committed to student success are more likely to generate that success than institutions whose commitment to students may be of lower order than other competing commitments (e.g., research, athletics). Institutional commitment to student success in turn sets the tone for the expectational climate for success that students encounter in their everyday interactions with the institution, its policies, practices, and various members (faculty, staff, administrators, and other students). As importantly, it captures the willingness to invest the resources and provide the incentives and rewards needed to enhance student success. Without such commitment, programs for student success may begin, but rarely prosper over the long term.

Within these nested climates, students encounter varying degrees of academic, social, and financial support, are provided varying types of feedback about their progress, and experience educational settings whose structure and practices result in differing degrees of academic and social involvement. These act together to influence the quality of student effort (Pace, 1982) that in turn influences student learning, and both influence student success. That success and success in other classes generate credit and degree credit progress and, for some students, eventual degree completion.

The institution acts in a variety of ways through its policies, practices, and programs to shape those conditions. Though there are many possible courses of action, Figure 11.1 notes several that must be part of any institutional strategy for student success. Two deserve comment here, namely, actions that shape pedagogy and curriculum and those that attend to faculty development. The former actions play a direct role in shaping the learning environment within the classroom and, in turn, patterns of social and academic involvements within the classroom. Faculty development plays a direct role in influencing pedagogy and curriculum and an indirect but very important role in student involvements and, therefore, student learning and success. Faculty development practices may also influence assessment practices and help shape the way support is provided to students.[12]

Several observations should be made about the model. First, it sees student effort and learning as central to student success. Second, it sees the classroom as the critical ground upon which student success is played out. This is especially true for non-residential campuses and for commuter students because in those settings and for those students, the classroom may be the only place where students engage faculty, staff, and other students in learning. Third, it is a model that seeks to highlight those aspects of institutional environments that are amenable to direct institutional action that have been shown to influence student success. As such, the model posits a chain of causation linking institutional action to environments in which students participate to student success. Fourth, it argues that student success is most likely when all four conditions apply and are linked in such a way that each is supportive of the others.

TRANSLATING THEORY INTO ACTION: A CASE STUDY

To repeat, the model of institutional action presented here argues that students are more likely to succeed when they find themselves in settings that are committed to their success; hold high expectations for their success; provide needed academic, social, and financial support; provide frequent feedback; and actively involve students with other students and faculty, especially in learning. The key concept is that of educational community and the capacity of institutions to establish educational communities that involve all students as equal members.

Unfortunately, the educational experiences of most students are not involving, the time they spend on task disturbingly low (Kuh, 2003). Learning, especially in the critical first year of college, is still very much a spectator sport in which faculty talk dominates and where few students actively participate. Most students experience learning as isolated learners whose learning is disconnected from that of others, where the curriculum is experienced as a set of detached, individual courses, one separated from another in both content and peer group, one set of understandings unrelated in any intentional fashion to the content learned in other courses. Though specific programs of study are designed for each major, courses have little academic or social coherence. It is little wonder that students seem so uninvolved in learning. Their learning experiences are not very involving.

PEDAGOGIES OF ENGAGEMENT

What should universities and colleges do? How should they reorganize themselves and construct educational environments that promote student learning? Fortunately, there are a number of pedagogical, curricular, and support strategies for which evidence supports the claim that they can enhance student persistence and learning. These include the use of cooperative or collaborative learning and problem- or project-based learning strategies that require students to work together in cooperative groups; service learning, where students engage in service activities that are connected to learning in the classroom; the use of learning communities that require students to enroll in courses together and share the experience of learning a common coherent curriculum; classroom assessment techniques that provide students and faculty frequent feedback about student learning; and the use of supplemental instruction strategies where academic assistance is connected to specific courses and to specific student academic needs.

Though these reforms are different, they share a number of common attributes that capture the underlying sources of their success. First, they all focus on student learning and the places in which students are asked to learn. They are either located in classrooms or directed toward the task of learning in the classroom. Second, they all stress shared, connected learning and the importance of educational community. Students are asked to learn together in a coherent manner and form communities that provide social as well as academic support. Third, when assistance is provided, it is typically connected to the classroom, not isolated from it. In this way, assistance is contextualized in ways that enable students to utilize assistance for learning in the settings in which they are attempting to learn.

Learning Communities and Student Success

Of these various possibilities, I will focus here on learning communities because accumulating evidence suggests that they offer a particularly effective way of addressing the learning needs of a range of students while also providing a structure for collaboration among faculty and between faculty and student affairs professionals (Taylor et al., 2004; Zhao & Kuh, 2004). Equally important, for the purposes of the present discussion, they provide institutions an integrated way of directing support, feedback, and involvement to the critical task of learning in the classroom.

Learning communities have a number of characteristics (Gablenick, MacGregor, Matthews, & Smith, 1990). First, they require students to enroll in two or more courses together. In this way, students are asked to share the experience of taking courses together. But the courses students take are not random or coincidental. They must be linked by an organizing theme or problem that gives meaning to their linkage. This is the case because an important attribute of learning communities is that they serve to build academic as well as social connections between what otherwise would be discrete academic and social experiences. Their purpose is to promote a deeper, richer multidisciplinary learning that is typically not possible when courses are unrelated one to another. To do so, learning communities require the faculty and sometimes staff who teach in them to collaborate. The point of doing so is to ensure that the experience of the learning community provides for an academic coherence that crosses the borders of the linked courses. Finally, an increasing number of learning communities are altering the way students experience learning so that students not only share the curriculum, but share as well the experience of learning the shared curriculum together. Faculty and staff are turning away from reliance on traditional lecture methods toward more active learning strategies such as cooperative learning, collaborative learning, and problem- or project-based learning.

Research has shown that learning communities, in particular those that are fully integrated, yield a number of important benefits for students (Tinto, 2000; Zhao & Kuh, 2004). First, students tend to develop supportive peer groups and find personal support via the interactions that occur within those groups. As one student noted in an interview, the learning community in which she was enrolled was "like a raft running the rapids of her life." Second, students in learning communities tend to spend more time together, in particular more time studying together. And they do so in ways that extend beyond the borders of the classroom. As one student observed, "class continued even after class." The result is that students study more after class and they do so with other students with whom they share the learning community. Third, in finding more support and spending more time studying, students in learning communities become more involved in a range of learning activities, learn more, and persist more frequently than do students in more traditional learning settings (Tinto, 1997, 2000; Zhao & Kuh, 2004). And this is true for regularly admitted students as well as those who enter academically underprepared for college work (Malnarich et al., 2004; Tinto, 1998). Finally, and perhaps most importantly, students in learning communities, in particular those that employ active learning strategies, speak of "learning better together." They come to experience and, in turn, value the power of environments that provide for a multi-lensed, multi-voice learning experience that requires students to "think, re-think, and even re-re-think" about what they are learning. As one student noted, "you not only learn more, you learn better" (Tinto, 2003).

One of the many virtues of learning communities is that they can be applied to a variety of majors and fields of study and can be adapted to the needs of varying groups of students. For instance, they are being adapted to the needs of undecided students as well as those who require academic assistance (Malnarich et al., 2004; Tinto, 1998). In the latter case, one or more of the linked courses is a developmental level or study skills course such that the skills acquired in the study skills course can be directly applied to the content course to which it is linked (Engstom & Tinto, 2008). In residential campuses, some learning communities have moved into the residence halls. These "living-learning communities" combine shared coursework with shared living. However structured, the power of these and other arrangements is that they enable the institution to integrate the provision of academic assistance to the social and academic needs of students in ways that is connected to their needs as learners. In other words, as a form of institutional action, learning communities enable institutions to reshape several important conditions, each of which impacts student learning and, in turn, student success.

It should also be observed that one of the other benefits of learning communities is that they provide an academic structure within which collaboration among faculty and between faculty and professional staff is possible, and indeed often required (Engstrom & Tinto, 2000; Taylor, et al., 2004). For learning communities to succeed, faculty must work together to ensure that the linked courses provide a coherent, shared learning experience that is tailored to the needs of the students the community serves. In this way, learning communities can have an indirect yet powerful impact upon student success because they help reshape the nature of institutional arrangements and patterns of affiliation that in turn impact the experiences of students and eventually their success.

CLOSING THOUGHT

Though we have learned much over the past thirty years on why students leave colleges, we have not yet fully explored what institutions can do to help more students stay and succeed. More importantly, we have yet to develop an effective model of institutional action that provides institutions guidelines for the development of policies, programs, and practices to enhance student success. The goal of this book, in particular this chapter and that by Alan Seidman, is the development of such a model.

NOTES

1. Indeed, more than a few students enter institutions with the unstated goal of transferring to another institution before graduation.

2. Lest we forget, a sizable proportion of students enter higher education with no intention of completing a college degree. They may enter with the sole intent of obtaining a better job.

3. Given the likely variations in the patterning of differing types of leaving behaviors at different institutions, researchers who use multi-institutional data to study departure may inadvertently compound the problem by combining and/or comparing studies that reflect quite different patterns of leaving.

4. The term retention reflects the perspective of the institution such that institutions retain students. Persistence reflects the perspective of the individual who may persist to completion though it may involve transfer to one or more institutions.

5. This is not to say that researchers have ignored this matter. In addition to a range of studies on the impact of specific programs on student success, e.g., Bowles and Jones's (2003) study of supplemental instruction—several authors have written about strategies to increase retention; e.g., Braxton, Hirschy, and McClendon (2004). But only Swail, Redd, and Perna (2003) have sought to develop a comprehensive framework for student retention, specifically for minority students.

6. Not surprisingly, many institutions see this issue as one of recruitment, of attracting more able and motivated students who themselves are more likely to graduate. But there are only so many able and motivated students, and it seems every university is seeking to attract the same group of students. In any event, such efforts leave untouched the learning environment and do little to ensure that the experience of students will in any way be changed by attracting more able students.

7. Here the term "research" must be understood more broadly as accumulated knowledge that includes research, institutional studies, and shared experience of many practitioners. Such "research" is often more reliable than the research cited in some of the chapters in this volume because it involves the accumulation of evidence from differing sources and methodologies of knowledge making.

8. Also see Laird, Chen, and Kuh (2008).

9. It is estimated that among four-year college students nearly two-thirds either begin undecided or change their majors at least once during college.

10. See Tinto (2010).

11. For the purposes of the present discussion, the timeframe for institutional action is considered that which applies to the experiences of any entering student cohort, that is, three to five years. The longer-term timeframe that would encompass several cohorts and therefore reflect long-term institutional actions not considered in this discussion.

12. The fact remains that, as compared to elementary, middle, and high school teachers, faculty in higher education are the only faculty in education not trained to teach their own students. This is not to say that there are not many talented faculty in two- and four-year colleges. Rather, it is to say that most faculty in higher education are not trained in those practices that have been shown to help students learn and succeed in classrooms.

REFERENCES

Angelo, T. and P. Cross (1993). *Classroom assessment techniques: A handbook for college teachers.* San Francisco: Jossey-Bass.

Astin, A. (1993). *What matters in college? Four critical years revisited.* San Francisco: Jossey-Bass.

Attinasi, L. C. Jr. (1989). Getting in: Mexican American student's perceptions of university attendance and implications for freshman year persistence. *Journal of Higher Education,* 60, 247–277.

Baumgart, N., and Johnston, J. (1977). Attrition at an Australian university: A case study. *Journal of Higher Education, 48*(5): 553–570.

Bowles, T. J., and J. Jones. (2003). The effect of supplemental instruction on retention: A bivariate probit model. *College Student Retention: Research, Theory, and Practice,* 5, 431–439.

Braxton, J., A. Hirschy, and S. McClendon. (2004). *Understanding and reducing college student departure.* San Francisco: Jossey-Bass.

Carini, R., G. Kuh, and S. Klein (2006). Student engagement and student learning: Testing the linkages. *Research in Higher Education,* 47, 1–32.

Endo, J. and R. Harpel (1982). The effect of student-faculty interaction on students' educational outcomes. *Research in Higher Education,* 16, 115–135.

Engstrom, C. and V. Tinto. (2000). Building collaborative partnerships with student affairs to enhance student learning. In M. Barr (ed.) *Handbook for Student Affairs Administrators.* San Francisco, Jossey Bass.

Engstrom, C. and V. Tinto. (2008). Learning better together: The impact of learning communities on the persistence of low-income students. *Opportunity Matters.* 1, 5–21.

Gablenick, F., J. MacGregor, R. Matthews, and B. L. Smith. (1990). *Learning communities: Creating connections among students, faculty, and disciplines* (Vol. 41). San Francisco: Jossey-Bass.

Hurtado, S., and Carter, D. (1996). Latino students' sense of belonging in the college community: Rethinking the concept of integration on campus. In F. Stage, et al. (eds.), *College students: The evolving nature of research,* Needham Heights, MA: Simon & Schuster Custom Publishing, 123–36.

Kuh, G. (2003). What we're learning about student engagement from NSSE. *Change,* 35, 24–32.

Laird, T., D. Chen, and G. Kuh (2008). Classroom practices at institutions with higher-than-expected persistence rates: What student engagement data tell us. In J. Braxton (ed.). *New Directions for Teaching and Learning, 115,* Fall, 85–99.

Malnarich, G., Sloan, B., van Slyck, P., Dusenberry, P., and Swinton, J. (2003). *The pedagogy of possibilities: Developmental education, college-level studies, and learning communities.* Olympia, WA: Washington Center for Improving the Quality of Undergraduate Education, in cooperation with the American Association for Community Colleges.

Pace, R. C. (1982). *Achievement and the quality of student effort.* Higher Education Research Institute, Graduate School of Education, University of California, Los Angeles.

Pascarella et al. 1986. Orientation to college and freshman year persistence/withdrawal decisions. *Journal of Higher Education,* 57(2): 153–175.

Rendon, L. (1994). Validating culturally diverse students: Toward a new model of learning and student development. *Innovative Higher Education, 19,* 13–52.

Solorzano, D., M. Ceja, and T. Yosso. (2000). Critical race theory, racial microaggressions and campus racial climate: The experiences of African American college students. *Journal of Negro Education, 69,* 60–73.

Swail, S., K. Redd, and L. Perna. (2003). *Retaining minority students in higher education: A framework for success.* San Francisco: Jossey-Bass.

Taylor, K., W. Moore, J. MacGregor, and J. Lindblad. (2004). *Learning community research and assessment: What we know now.* Olympia: The Washington Center for Improving the Quality of Undergraduate Education at The Evergreen State College.

Terenzini, P, Lorang, W., and Pascarella, E. (1981). Predicting freshman persistence and voluntary dropout decisions: A replication. *Research in Higher Education* 15 (2): 109–27.

Tinto, V. (1993). *Leaving college: Rethinking the causes and cures of student attrition.* (2nd ed.). Chicago: The University of Chicago Press.

Tinto, V. (1997). Classrooms as communities: Exploring the educational character of student persistence. *Journal of Higher Education,* 68, 599–623.

Tinto, V. (1998). Adapting learning communities to the needs of remedial education students. Paper presented at the Rethinking Remedial Education Symposium, Stanford University.

Tinto, V. (2000). Linking learning and leaving: Exploring the role of college classrooms in student departure. In J. Braxton (Ed.), *Reworking the student departure puzzle* (pp. 81–94). Nashville: Vanderbilt University Press.

Tinto, V. (2003), *Learning better together.* Higher Education Monograph Series, No. 2. Higher Education Program, Syracuse University.

Tinto, V. (2010). From theory to action: Exploring the institutional conditions for student retention. *Higher Education: Handbook of Theory and Research.* Vol. XXV. 51–90.

Zhao, C. and G. Kuh (2004). Adding value: Learning communities and student engagement. *Research in Higher Education, 45,* 115–138.

12

Taking Action

A Retention Formula and Model for Student Success

Alan Seidman

For intervention programs and services to be successful they must be powerful enough to effect change (Seidman, 2004)

$Ret = Early_{ID} + (E + In + C)_{IV}$; that is, Retention = Early$_{Identification}$ + (Early + Intensive + Continuous)$_{Intervention}$ (Seidman, 2004)

The study of college student retention has a long and distinguished history (see chapter 1, "Past to Present: A Historical Look at Retention"). Over the years, colleges and universities have designed programs and services to help retain students by trying to ease student transition into the academic and social systems of the institution. These programs and services consist of orientation programs (Green, 1987), counseling and student development (Conklin, 2009; Seidman, 1992a, 1992b), assessment, remedial and academic support services (Crockett, 1984; Silverman, 2010; Silverman & Seidman, 2011–2012; Seidman, 1995, 1993), and the development of educational communities within the classroom Tinto, 1997, 1998; (Tinto et al., 1994), among others. Yet in spite of the implementation of these programs and services, the retention data reveal that students are not retained at a higher rate than they were twenty or more years ago (see chapter 2, "Measurements of Persistence").

Perhaps without these programs and services the retention and graduation rates would be worse. Or perhaps we are at a point that, regardless of what is provided to students, retention rates will not increase significantly or will stay within a narrow band. I believe we can do better and improve term-to-term retention and graduation rates without having to spend a lot of taxpayer or student tuition dollars to do so.

What This Chapter Is and What It Is Not

Although there are references throughout the chapter (many of them dated, since there has been nothing really new published on how to increase retention), it is *not* a research-oriented chapter. Rather it is a "how-to" chapter. That is, this chapter will describe the Seidman Formula and Success Model, which is easy to comprehend and implement and which will really help a student achieve his or her academic and personal goals. This chapter will provide a practical guide that, if implemented, can actually help students succeed.

For too long the educational community has been arguing and bickering over whose theory is the best, what terminology to use when talking about student success (integration vs. engagement, retention, attrition), what individual programs or services provide the best bang for the buck. The arguments continue: how to increase the retention and graduation rates of specific groups; e.g., minorities, specific economic groups, different age sectors, undergraduate, graduate, etc. It is time to stop bickering over definitions and who has the best this-and-that program. It is time to take action and stop trying to receive credit. Our society and the public demand it, and colleges should accede to the demand forthwith. With this in mind, therefore, the reader will have to be the judge and decide whether it is worthwhile to implement the Seidman Formula and Success Model.

It really is a very simple concept to understand and to implement when you come right down to it. $Ret = Early_{ID} + (E + In + C)_{IV}$. That is, Retention equals Early Identification plus (Early plus Intensive plus Continuous) Intervention (Seidman, 2005; Silverman, 2010; Silverman & Seidman, 2011–2012). And it applies to *all* students: right out of high school, adults, and retirees; from any economic status, culture, or religion; brick-and-mortar institutions, Internet delivered programs, hybrid institutions, undergraduate, or graduate schools.

The literature, however, gives the impression or implies that a student can have a successful college experience if he chooses a college carefully and if the college is compatible with his individual characteristics. That is, if a student's background, both academic and social, and a college's characteristics, both academic and social, are similar, there is a likelihood of student success. Also, if a college provides a structure that integrates or engages (you pick the term) the student into the formal and informal academic and social systems of the college, the student has a higher likelihood of success.

This is consistent with the Tinto (1987, 1993) retention model, which posits that individual pre-entry college attributes (family background, skill and ability, prior schooling) form individual goals and commitments; the individual's goals and commitments interact over time with institutional experiences (the formal and informal academic and social systems of an institution). The extent to which the individual is successful in becoming academically and socially integrated into the systems of an institution determines the individual's departure decision.

Positive experiences and interventions will reinforce persistence by heightening individual intentions and commitments, whereas negative experiences will weaken intentions and commitments. Intentions can include the desire to earn a degree in a particular field of study, whereas commitment is the student's desire to complete that degree and willingness to spend the time and energy necessary to obtain it (Astin, 1985). Therefore, the greater the individual student's levels of integration into the social and academic systems of the college, the greater his or her subsequent commitment to the college (Baumgart & Johnson, 1977; Pascarella, et al., 1986; Terenzini, et al., 1981).

The Tinto (1987, 1993) model has served as the foundation upon which retention programs and services have been based. The Seidman Retention Formula is built on this foundation too, and provides a college with a course of action to follow. The formula states, Retention = Early Identification + (Early + Intensive + Continuous) Intervention (RET = E_{ID} + (E + In +C)$_{IV}$)—that is, RETention = Early $_{IDentification}$ + (Early + Intensive + Continuous) $_{InterVention}$). But it takes this theoretical model a step further with one simple issue and way to solve the issue. It does not provide colleges with a "free ride"; that is, it will not require only scarce funding to implement. Rather, it will be necessary to provide the funds needed to develop and implement the formula "up front," but the payoff will result in enhanced term-to-term retention and graduation rates.

The issue pertains to the academic ability of the student to become academically integrated (we now are using the term *engaged* interchangeably with *integrated*) into a college, whether formally or informally. The undergraduate experience will be used throughout this chapter, but you can apply this to graduate programs as well, and even to the K-12 experience. Suppose a student graduates from high school with a ninth-grade reading and writing skill level. An entry-level college course requires reading and writing skills at the twelfth-grade level, while three other courses the student will enroll in require a college-level reading and writing level. It makes no difference how academically and socially integrated or engaged a student is: if she cannot read, understand, critically assess the material, and/or submit papers of sufficient quality, she will not pass the course; period, end of discussion.

Let's look at another scenario. Many colleges assess students' reading, writing, and mathematical skills prior to enrollment and place a student into a remedial program or course if necessary; that is a good thing. Unfortunately, the student is lacking three of ten skills necessary to successfully complete the foundation course (I define *foundation course* as a first college entry-level required course such as English 101, Psychology 101,

Accounting 101, etc.). Regardless of the missing skills, the student has to take the remedial course from the beginning and stay in the course the full term. No wonder so many students complain that they are enrolled in a remedial course for which they already know the material: they are receiving no college credit for it, and are paying for it to boot. In addition, how many colleges actually know what skill foundations courses are necessary for student success? How many know the reading level of the text, writing skills necessary for success, or mathematical skills necessary for success for these courses?

For argument's sake: many colleges also have early alert systems and will catch the deficiencies early in a term or by midterm. If a student can overcome reading and/or writing deficiencies by midterm, fine; but for the vast majority that will be impossible. For most students who are behind in grade level, to overcome the deficiency in a matter of weeks and then overcome negative grades to date just isn't feasible. Now this student must not only continue in the failing courses, but must also take a skills course, adding to the number of classes to be taken that particular term. And we expect the student not only to take the extra course, but also to overcome the deficiency in a short period of time while taking other courses. No way, it just won't happen.

The Seidman Formula and Success Model takes these situations into account. But prior to delving into the Formula and Success Model, let's back up a bit and look at retention in general. The previous chapters should have given the reader a fairly comprehensive background regarding college student retention. Nonetheless, here is some more background information.

Whenever this author discusses retention at conferences, or when consulting, there are a number of issues that are dealt with prior to discussing the Seidman Formula and Success Model. Not surprisingly, the first is a definition of retention. So what's in a common definition? Accepting or at least having one in mind keeps everyone, so to speak, on the same page. The terms retention, dropout, and attrition have been used synonymously and conjure up different visions in different people. So, first things first. What is the definition to be used in this chapter?

In this chapter, retention will be defined as student attainment of academic and/or personal goal(s). A student may attain academic and/or personal goals prior to graduation or may graduate without meeting those goals. Therefore it is important for a college to ascertain the reason(s) a student enrolls in the first place and whether the reasons for college attendance change over time and whether the goal(s) have been met when a student leaves (prior to graduation and after). Simply graduating within a specified period of time does not mean that the student has met her or his academic and/or personal goals. Chapter 4, "How to Define Retention," deals with this issue from a statistical standpoint, and that is fine if you are looking at pure numbers and relating them to budgetary issues (see chapter 5, "Finances and Retention: Trends and Potential Implications").

Additionally, aligning and defining retention in accordance with college mission is essential. It is a continual source of amazement how long and elaborate some college mission statements are. That isn't bad, as long as everyone knows what the college mission statement is and how it is applied to the curriculum and everyday college life on campus or through cyberspace. This author has dealt with the issue when giving presentations through the two-dollar challenge. A two-dollar bill is given to the first audience member who can recite his or her institution's college mission statement word for word. After at least twelve years of offering this incentive, it was finally given to a very proud faculty member at a very small religious college. Up until that point, college presidents, chancellors, etc., had not been able to recite their college mission statements. This applies to colleges that have it posted all around the campus. It is simply ignored, but should not be.

For the purposes of this chapter, *program, course,* and *student retention* will be used. *Program retention* is the current federal government college definition requirement to measure retention. The U.S. Department of Education requires colleges to report fall term, full-time, first-time student enrollment after the census date and tracks students over a period of time (six years for four-year colleges and three years for two-year colleges) to determine whether the student graduated in this specific time period. Naturally, this definition excludes the millions of students who enroll each fall term part-time, or those who start their college careers in the second term.

Course retention and attrition measures the number of students enrolled in each college course after the course census date and how many students successfully complete the course with an A-D grade at the end of the term. Using the census date, usually the tenth to twentieth day of the term, gives time for a student to determine whether or not to stay in a specific class. After the census date, it is assumed that the student has made a commitment to the class.

Course retention and attrition also gives an overall picture of retention by course, and does not distinguish between the full- and part-time student and year of attendance. Using course retention, a college can look at all sections of the same courses too, regardless of whether the student is enrolled full- or part-time, or is a first-, second-, third-, or fourth-year student. Some course sections (i.e., Accounting 101 in a course that has multiple courses) with higher-than-average retention and attrition rates can be examined to determine the reason(s). Perhaps a greater-than-average attrition rate in a course section is due to inappropriate course placement, or advisement, or course content, etc. A foundation course that prepares a student for the next-level course can also be examined if a larger number of students in the next level course are having difficulty and the students came from a specific previous course section. Case in point: a larger than usual number of students performed poorly in a next-level course, and all came from a specific foundational course section. When queried, the professor in the specific foundational course said that he knew the reason those students did poorly in the next level course. He could not finish the course due to the number of weather-related course cancellations. The students were unable to receive the instruction necessary to be successful in the next-level course. This prompted the administration to change the make-up day policy for weather-related course cancellations.

Student retention and attrition data would discover whether or not the student attained his or her academic and/or personal goal(s) at exit. A student who misses two consecutive terms, excluding summer sessions, would be contacted to try to determine if his or her academic and/or personal goal(s) had been achieved while enrolled. These data can be matched with student goal data collected at college entry. If indeed the student achieved her or his academic and/or personal goals, whether or not a degree was earned, this should not count as attrition; rather, it should count as retention. After all, the student obtained what she or he set out to achieve at college entry.

$$RET = E_{ID} + (E + IN + C)_{IV}$$

The Seidman Retention Formula, Retention = Early Identification + (Early + Intensive + Continuous) Intervention (Seidman, 2004), also needs to be defined. Now that the generic retention term has been defined, what exactly do we mean by early identification, early plus intensive plus continuous intervention? Without common definitions it is difficult to understand exactly what is being discussed.

Early identification is assessment of student skill levels. The assessment of skills can take place at the time of application, through the thorough examination of academic records and types of courses taken in high school, difficulty of courses, grades received, and scores received on standardized assessment (SAT/ACT). The review of written recommendations may reveal non-course-related academic and/or personal issues as well which may hinder student success. A common college-administered assessment prior to enrollment, however, is ideal. The idea is to collect the information necessary to ascertain student readiness for foundational (primary) college level courses or the best placement for a student to remediate a specific deficient skill.

Paradoxically, many colleges already have the information to help identify a "student at risk" for not completing her/his program. Using past student data, a profile of prior unsuccessful students can be developed. When a student applies and is accepted with a similar profile, logic dictates that that student may also have difficulty. If profile information is not readily available either in the college database or through regular data gathering, a file should be started right away. Gathering all necessary student information may require developing or buying a form and database program, or having existing databases linked. But ideally this process should be conducted prior to student enrollment.

Skill assessment can be given over the web with a pledge of authenticity. That is, the student pledges that she actually completed the assessment (no one took it for her). If after enrollment the result of the assessment and course completion is inconsistent, the student can be mandated to retake the assessment. If indeed the student did not take the initial assessment then she should be dismissed for dishonesty. Let's face it; the student will not be successful because of mismatching of assessment results. The student has probably taken a seat from a qualified student, and is not being honest. Those consequences can be part of the pledge of authenticity.

When this issue was mentioned in the first edition of this book it was dismissed out of hand, since there was such a mistrust of a student actually taking the assessment over the web. With the increased use of the web, this type of assessment is becoming more acceptable, especially within non–brick-and-mortar colleges. It is difficult to see a downside to this since assessment can be taken anywhere in the world at any time. The pledge of authenticity holds a student to high standards, but as with anything, it needs to be administered in such a manner that if the student breaches the pledge, consequences are actually applied and upheld.

Early intervention is defined as starting an intervention at the earliest time possible after identification. Intervention programs and services should be available as early in a student's college career as possible. A college does not have to wait until a student enrolls to begin intervention programs and services; rather, it can be a part of the student's acceptance to the college. Intervention(s) can begin while the student is still enrolled in high school and/or during the summer months prior to the beginning of the first term. Admission can be contingent upon the student taking part in the intervention process and successfully completing it prior to actual enrollment. The intervention should continue until the student has demonstrated that the deficiency has been overcome.

Intensive intervention is defined as creating an intervention that is intensive or strong enough to effect the desired change. This can result in a student spending five days per week, two to four (or more) hours per day, in an intervention program. The student must demonstrate that he/she has mastered the skill(s) or social factor(s). Specific deficiencies in skill sets may be identified and the student must demonstrate mastery of each skill set to continue at the college. The intervention program must provide the student with an experience powerful enough to be effective and make the desired change in the student's academic and/or personal behavior.

Continuous intervention is defined as an intervention that persists until the change is effected. The intervention can continue throughout the student's college career (in the case of a social issue) and beyond. No time limit should be established for the student to complete the intervention program and process for personal issues but should be established for academic issues. A relationship with the student becomes a lifelong commitment between the student and the college, and the college and the student.

Here now is an important qualifier for academic intervention. It should be noted that most often a student with a particular deficiency is put into a remedial class for a full term. Suppose your college gives a student a writing assessment and the student demonstrates mastery in ten of fifteen necessary skills needed to be successful in a foundational level class. Instead of putting the student into a class that teaches all fifteen skills, individualize the program and only concentrate on the deficient skills. A student may demonstrate mastery of the five skills in a shorter time than a full term and be able to move back into regular classes more quickly. A student should not have to take a class that repeats skills he or she has already mastered and should be able to attain the needed skills through a flexible program. This may eliminate the student/parent complaint that the college has put the student into a remedial course regimen simply to receive more tuition money.

There is backing for this proposition. In a study of mathematics students at Foothills College on California, Silverman (2010) found that students placed in the Math My Way (MMW) program preformed significantly better than those who were simply placed in classes that repeated already mastered skills. The MMW program combined two remedial courses into ten hierarchical and sequential modules. Using the mastery learning of concepts methods (one module built upon another), students were assessed and could be placed within the ten modules (start at module four for one student, number six for another) depending on assessment results. Spiral assessment was instituted where a student was required to pass two modules per term with 100 percent assignment grade within each module and an 87 percent module grade to advance to the next module. A student spent ten hours per week in the program; there were peer tutors and a 150:5 student-to-faculty ratio.

In sum, the aim of the Seidman formula is to identify a student in need of assistance academically and/or socially as early as possible, assess student needs, prescribe interventions, and monitor, assess, and adjust interventions where necessary. An intervention program can start prior to enrollment, actually having acceptance contingent upon the student successfully completing the intervention. The intervention program must be intensive enough and continue until the desired change is effected.

The medical model can provide an analogy for the Seidman Retention Formula. A physical examination or prescreening for a specific condition can be completed before it becomes a problem. In the case of a student, a prescreening can be instituted before the student enrolls by using the student's past academic and/or social history or using college-specific data (past unsuccessful students) or pre-enrollment student assessment as a diagnostic tool.

If there is a history of a specific health problem in a family, a test can be conducted to determine whether or not a family member or relative is predisposed to the same or similar problem. In some instances, remedial action can be taken if the particular trait is found in the person. A pre-enrollment academic "physical" or assessment can find a potential academic and/or personal problem. A pre-enrollment physical can also uncover potential physical and/or emotional problem(s) before they surface. Neither the medical model nor the retention formula is punitive; rather, they are preventative. As such, students should know up front the reason(s) and purpose(s) for the pre-enrollment assessment and possible outcome(s) thereof. Transparency is important, and a student/college partnership should be developed. It is important that a potential student understand the process, the reason he or she is asked to participate in it, the expected outcomes, and the consequences. Colleges need to be upfront with students at all times and not let "philosophy follow finance, but finance follow philosophy."

A student or parent would think very favorably of a college that truly cares about a student's growth and development. Failing to make the process accessible, understandable, and transparent will only cause anxiety and may drive the student to another college. Letting a student or parent know up front the reasons for the assessment and intervention should help them understand and appreciate what the college is trying to accomplish—to give the best possible services so the student will be successful in his or her academic and social endeavors.

When a person becomes ill, sometimes medical help is not desired because the person may believe the illness will pass or will get better in a short period of time. The illness is slight and the person does not have a temperature, although the throat is sore. Sometimes a person will not seek help because of the cost. When a student gets into academic difficulty, he or she may not seek help because things may get better as the term progresses. The student believes that he or she will study more, or will complete and turn in late homework, or the one big project due next week will earn an A and save the term grade, etc. Educators have heard many excuses, throughout their teaching careers, why a student has not completed work or has done poorly on an examination. Many students have "lost" many family, friends, and relatives at the end of a course or been hospitalized innumerable times, forgetting to tell the professor!

A student's lack of willingness to seek help in college should not be a surprise to college administrators. After all, a student directly out of high school is used to having someone tell him or her that a problem exists and an intervention is needed. This is the high school model. A high school guidance counselor may call a student into his or her office to discuss academic or personal difficulties reported by a teacher, and to suggest and/ or require a specific remedy. In college it is left up to the student to seek help when necessary. Sometimes a student will not seek help for a personal problem that can be embarrassing, although recent research shows that more students are using counseling services on campus than ever before. Other times, the student does not know whom to contact if in difficulty. A college needs to be proactive and facilitate this process.

After a time, the untreated illness lingers and may get worse. A person can tell that she or he is not getting better and that something has to be done to cure the illness. The student may get a D grade or fail the course before the realization sinks in that assistance is necessary. A person with a lingering illness will finally go to the doctor so that the nature of the illness can be diagnosed and a prescription given to help overcome the illness. The student will finally seek help because he or she has been put on academic probation or even dismissed from the college.

Many students will not seek help because they may think that college personnel are keeping close tabs and will come to the rescue. That is far from reality. Students may deal with the problem simply by dropping out of college. The literature illustrates that a student will blame finances as the reason for failure even when it is not. When a student is contacted to find out why he or she has left an institution, research shows that the student is amazed that someone actually has taken the time to call. In some instances the student will talk about the problem, seek help, and re-enroll in a subsequent term.

When a patient goes to the doctor, an examination is given and an assessment is made based on a patient's symptoms (given verbally and by the examination), or sometimes by using tests (blood tests, etc.; and, in the case of students, assessment). The doctor will then make a diagnosis. The diagnosis uses the knowledge gained through years of data-gathering, since the patient with certain symptoms most likely will have a specific illness or ailment. The doctor will then prescribe a course of action or intervention such as bed rest, plenty of fluids, special diet, and non-prescription or prescription drugs. The key is to give the patient an intervention that is powerful enough to make the patient well. That is the reason a doctor will tell patients to take *all* of their medicine. If the patient does not take the medicine for the prescribed period of time, often the illness will come back and may even be prolonged. If the drug that the doctor gives the patient is not powerful enough, or the diagnosis was wrong, the patient will remain ill, and may have to return to the doctor, who will prescribe an alternative medication or course of action.

A similar occurrence may affect a student who is at risk academically and/or socially. The problem may not be caught in time, too late in the term, may be misdiagnosed, and/or the intervention may not be powerful enough to make a difference. The point here is that early identification, proper diagnosis of the problems (both academic and social), and prescription of an intervention(s), over a period of time, with periodic check-ups, is the key to the successful student/college retention program. The diagnosis must be accurate and must use an appropriate assessment. The prescription must be powerful and long enough to effect change.

There is evidence that the preceding approach shows promise. Reisberg (1999) in *The Chronicle of Higher Education*, states, "Ohio State University, for example, has turned to a high-priced consultant to identify incoming freshmen who are most at risk of dropping out before their sophomore year, and to suggest ways to keep them on campus" (p. 54).

Although the increase in retention for this group was slightly greater than for those who were identified as "at-risk" but not given additional services, 75 percent versus 72 percent, the results are promising. Perhaps the interventions were not powerful enough to effect change.

To date there is some research that tests the Seidman formula and its applicability and utility. However, Young (1999) reports some of his findings using the Seidman Retention Formula. He concludes,

> The second research question asked if Seidman's (1996) equation for retention—$R = E(Id) + (E \ \& \ In)(Iv)$ or Retention equals Early Identification and Early and Intensive Intervention—applied to community college students. The TASP [Texas Association of School Psychologists] requires that all Texas public colleges test students using standard exams to determine their readiness for college-level course work. This was the primary method used by all of the colleges to identify students at risk.
>
> Only the two colleges with high retention had any intervention programs that could be called intensive, and both colleges started the interventions early in a student's college career. The two colleges with relatively low retention did not start interventions until students started to miss classes, and the interventions applied were not intensive. Based on this study, it appears that Seidman's (1996) equation of retention did apply to the colleges in the study. In recent correspondence, the researcher learned that Seidman has updated the retention equation to read: "Retention equals Early Identification and Early, Intense, and Continuous Intervention" (A. Seidman, January 15, 1999). Since college A's intervention lasted only one term, and college B's interventions continue until the student completed remediation, college B may more closely have followed this updated model.

Stated earlier, Silverman (2010), using the Seidman formula, found that students have significantly greater retention and grade performance when placed into skill modules and given the skills needed to be successful. She also cited other works that backed up this premise. The Universidad del Este in Puerto Rico has been using the Seidman formula for a number of years with good results (16 percent increase the first year alone).

IMPLEMENTING THE FORMULA

It is a relatively easy process to implement the Seidman Retention Formula. There is a two-pronged approach. First, term course prerequisites and course skill levels need to be identified by the faculty. That is, what are the skills necessary in reading, writing, and mathematics in a foundational or college entry-level class (see Figure 12.1, right side) for a student to be able to perform the work at a satisfactory level?

The second part is the student, or left side, of the model. Student assessment is the key. Once faculty have identified what skills are needed to be successful in the foundational entry-level class they teach, the student skill levels must be determined. The assessment can be given over the web with a pledge of authenticity, that is, a pledge by the student that indeed he or she has taken the assessment. If the student meets all of the skills levels necessary to be successful in the foundational entry-level classes, then he or she should be placed into those courses. If a student is missing any of the skills

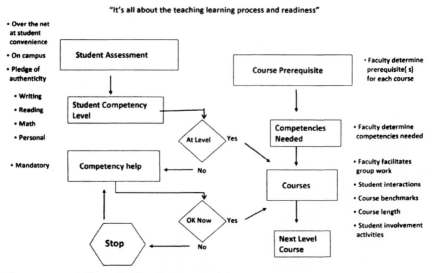

Figure 12.1. Seidman Student Success Model.

necessary to be successful in a foundational course, then the student should be placed in the lowest skill level module to overcome the deficiency. The college needs to determine how many times a student can take or be in a developmental module before the "Ability to Benefit" rule kicks in. The "Ability to Benefit" simply means that the college has given the student the opportunity to overcome the deficient skill and the student simply does not have the ability to overcome the deficiency. This rule has been used often by open admissions colleges (community college) to exclude a student for academic reasons and should be used where necessary.

Figure 12.2 simply is a schematic of the implementation of the Seidman Retention Formula. It is longitudinal and begins with the all-important assessment of student skill levels. The formula starts with the premise that the student comes first. The teaching/learning process is essential for student academic and personal growth and development. The student enters the institution to acquire the academic and personal skills necessary to achieve academic and personal goals. Assessment and interventions are longitudinal processes, commencing at the time of acceptance and continuing throughout the student's career at the institution, and perhaps beyond. Although the formula appears to be for one term, it is, in essence, for all terms a student is at the institution.

Once those deficiencies are determined, the student who needs skill assistance must meet with a professional for skill diagnosis and skill deficiency placement. Students should be monitored on an ongoing basis and reassessed continually. Once a student masters the necessary skills, he should be allowed to enroll in foundational first level college courses. It cannot be stressed enough that each succeeding course should also be built upon the skills acquired from a prior level course. That is, the skills needed for success in Psychology 102 must match up with the skills obtained in Psychology 101. So it is necessary to have each and every course skill needed on file, and build upon the previous level courses. New course development should have prerequisites also.

CONCLUDING REMARKS

Education is a process that should be nurtured, cultivated, and developed. Education should be a lifelong learning process for all citizens. It is a benefit to our nation and society if we can promote and encourage the thirst for knowledge. Anyone should feel comfortable seeking out answers to simple and complex questions using the skills gained through the education process. There are many benefits to the pursuit of lifelong learning opportunities: one is that keeping current in an ever-changing and complicated world is essential. Since job skills continue to evolve, employees should know

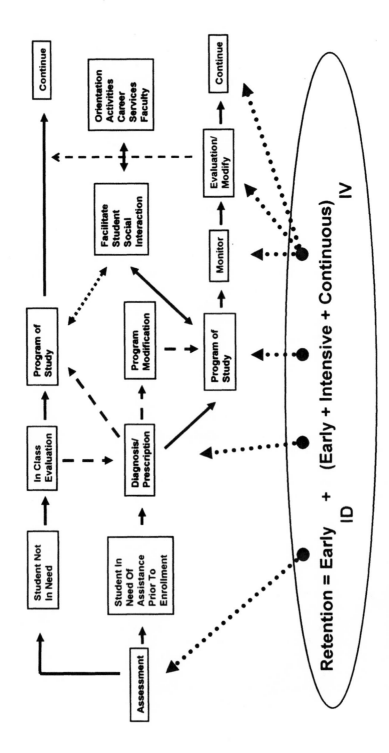

Figure 12.2.   Implementing the Seidman Formula.

how to access a variety of learning experiences. Our society should also encourage its populace to seek out learning simply for the joy of learning. The development of critical thinking skills is essential so that people can filter what they hear and read and make independent judgments.

The programs and services of colleges and universities should afford individuals the opportunity to develop new ideas, mature emotionally, experience the world around them, develop critical thinking skills, and learn to tolerate individual differences. Are colleges meeting the needs of students in this regard? Are programs and services integrated to give students a sense of the world around them and the needed support to be successful? Does a college practice what it preaches in its literature, that a high value is placed on learning? Does a college demonstrate this to its students? Should everyone be given the opportunity for a college education? How much in financial resources should the nation spend to help all students achieve academic and personal goals?

Students need to be able to complete programs that they are interested in pursuing. Students who are recruited and admitted to a college should have a reasonable expectation that programs and services will provide them with a chance for success. How can we ensure that programs offered by a college are excellent and provide students with the needed skills in an area of specialization? To ensure academic program excellence, assessment, of course, and program offerings, and a good "fit" with future courses and programs are necessary. For instance, does the exit skill for a course meet the entry-level skills for the next progressive course? How does a program at the college effectively prepare the student for the next-level program at another college or for a job? Does a community college program in accounting prepare a student to transfer to a four-year college and not lose credit because courses do not match up? Does the community college have transfer agreements and/or developed programs to match the first two years of the four-year college program? Has the four-year college program prepared the student with the skills necessary for the world of work? Have colleges received feedback from employers about whether or not programs have adequately prepared the student for the demands of the workplace? How flexible is a college to alter its curricula to meet changing industry and business needs? Has the four-year college prepared the student to pursue a graduate degree either directly after graduation or later?

The smooth transition and progression of courses and programs will enable the student to better achieve her or his academic and personal goals. Courses should complement each other and work in progression as a student learns about a particular area of interest. Outcome measures of achievement need to be considered along the way to ensure that the student is learning what is supposed to be learned.

The exploration of creating classroom communities for commuter students may enable them to become integrated into the academic and social systems of a college. The research shows that commuters find it harder to become integrated into the social systems of a college. This occurs because, once finished with a class, the student goes home, back to relationships of the past. The transition from high school to college is a lot harder to accomplish in this instance. Developing classroom communities can help to overcome this barrier.

The establishment of learning communities makes a college look at different ways to deliver course content and programs to students. Grouping students with similar interests together in residence halls and classes establishes a bond within the group and should help the student become integrated into the academic and social systems of the college.

Therefore, it is incumbent on colleges and universities to recruit, accept, and enroll students who will be successful at their institution. Colleges should attempt to match student characteristics with those of the college. Accepting a student who does not meet college characteristics academically may be setting up the student for failure. And if a college does accept a student, it is also important to provide the student with the programs and services to help the student succeed.

Over the years, retention rates have not improved in spite of the many and varied programs and services that colleges have instituted. Colleges have spent enormous sums of money and resources to help students become integrated into the academic and social systems of the college. Individual programs, such as orientation and academic counseling, have been shown to have a positive impact on retention, but taken in isolation, they may not provide the most comprehensive and intensive experience to really effect change. It appears, then, that for retention programs and services to make a difference they must be powerful enough to effect change. It is evident from the research that colleges are taking retention seriously. From the money expended and resources committed to retention, it continues to be an important issue on our campuses.

It is time to move forward in the quest to help a student meet his or her academic and personal goals. While the Tinto model provides the foundation, the Seidman Retention Formula provides colleges with a method to achieve retention goals.

$$RETention = Early_{IDentification} + (Early + Intensive + Continuous)_{InterVention}$$

gives a college a formula to help students succeed. Simply, the "student at risk" is identified as early as possible, using a variety of assessment tools, and once identified, the student and a professional meet to discuss the assessment outcome (diagnosis) and plan intervention(s) to remediate any deficiency. An honest discussion of area(s) of concern and how the college will assist the student in overcoming the deficiency is essential. The student needs to know that, as part of the admissions process, the remediation plan is mandatory. The student must follow the prescription specified with periodic assessment to check on progress and adjust the program where necessary. The college will have to commit the resources necessary to monitor and follow up with a student. The program must also be flexible enough to be modified where necessary, and powerful enough to effect change. The college may also want to set time limits allowable to complete the mastery of skills, but give sufficient time to complete them.

Linkages with community agency services should be a part of the assistance offered to the student. The sharing of resources can strengthen the bond between the college and local community, cut costs, and provide a positive exchange between colleges and local and governmental agencies. If a new program or service needs to be developed, these partnerships can help to minimize expenses. Sharing resources may overcome cost issues by providing enough clients to make the program cost effective.

Is this type of program people-intensive? It can very well be. Chapter 5, "Finances and Retention: Trends and Potential Implications," deals with this topic and demonstrates the cost benefit of keeping a student through academic and personal goal attainment.

Preparing a student for the challenges of an ever-changing world in which she or he must live is part of the mission of a college. Providing the student with programs and services to help accomplish academic and personal goals and aspirations is a small price to pay to accomplish this mission. An educated citizenry will keep the United States strong and vibrant. This, in essence, is what makes us a great nation and an example for others to follow and emulate.

REFERENCES

Astin, A. (1985, July/August). Involvement: The cornerstone of excellence. *Change.* 35–39.

Conklin, J. F. (2009) The impact of developmental and intrusive academic advising on grade point average, retention, and satisfaction with advising and the nursing program among first semester nontraditional Associate Degree Nursing students. (Unpublished doctoral dissertation). Walden University, Minneapolis, MN.

Crockett, D. S. (1984). *Advising skills, techniques, and resources.* Iowa City, IA: The ACT National Center for the Advancement of Educational Practices.

Green, E. (1987). At many colleges, orientation has become a serious introduction to campus life. *Chronicle of Higher Education, 34*(6), 41–43.

Reisberg, L. (1999, October). Colleges struggle to keep would-be dropouts enrolled. *The Chronicle of Higher Education, 46,* 54.

Seidman, A. (1992a). Integrated admission counseling: Impact on enrollment. *The Freshman Year Experience Newsletter, 4:6.*

Seidman, A. (1992b). Academic advising can have a positive impact on student enrollment. The results of an integrated admissions and counseling process on student enrollment. *Colleague.* State University of New York, 36–42.

Seidman, A. (1993, April/May). Needed: A research methodology to assess community college effectiveness. *Community College Journal, 63*(5), 36–40.

Seidman, A. (1995, May/June). The community college: A challenge for change. *Community College Journal of Research and Practice, 19*(3), 247–254.

Seidman, A. (2004). *Retention slide show.* Accessed April 12, 2004. Source: www.cscsr.org/docs/RetentionFormula2004a_files/frame.htm.

Seidman, A. (2005). *College student retention: Formula for student success.* Westport, CT: ACE/Praeger.

Silverman, L. (2010). Academic progress in developmental math courses: A comparative study of student retention. (Unpublished doctoral dissertation). Walden University, Minneapolis: MN.

Silverman, L. & Seidman, A. (2011–2012). Academic progress in developmental math courses: A comparative study of student retention. *Journal of College Student Retention: Research, Theory & Practice.*

Tinto, V. (1987). *Leaving college: Rethinking the causes and cures of student attrition.* Chicago: The University of Chicago Press.

Tinto, V. (1993). *Leaving college: Rethinking the causes and cures of student attrition.* 2nd Edition. Chicago: The University of Chicago Press.

Tinto, V. (1997). Classrooms as communities. *Journal of Higher Education. 68*(6), 599–623.

Tinto, V. (1998). Colleges as communities: Taking research on student persistence seriously. *The Review of Higher Education, 21*(2), 167–177.

Tinto, V., Russo, P., & Kadel, S. (1994, February/March). Constructing educational communities: Increasing retention in challenging circumstances. *Community College Journal, 64*(4), 26–29.

Young, R. J. (1999). *An examination of factors influencing retention of developmental education students at selected Texas community colleges.* Unpublished doctoral dissertation. University of Texas at Austin.

Index

Cross, P., 256
Current Population Survey, 50, 58–59
curricular choices, as indicator of degree completion, 180, 187, 236, 241

default, loan, 110–11
degree completion, 119–35; bachelor's vs. other types of, 190–91; beyond first year, 229–46; data analysis concerning, 126–27; determinants of, 175–89, 185t, 201–2t; environmental contingencies and, 123–24, 132–33, 244; gender and, 128–29, 129t; high school grades and, 129; institutional characteristics and, 122–23, 133–34; institutional types and, 127t, 128, 169–70, 171–73f, 174–75; persistence vs., 190, 194; previous research on, 120–24; research definition of, 196; research method applied to, 124–26, 139–43, 194–203; research results on, 127–34, 144–45; significance of, 167; socioeconomic factors in, 167–203; students' academic resources and, 169–70, 171–73f, 174–75; students' pre-college characteristics and, 121–22, 130, 132. *See also* pathways to degree attainment; persistence; student success
denominators, in persistence data, 37
departure. *See* early departure
DesJardins, S. L., 239, 240, 242, 243, 244
developmental courses. *See* remedial courses
Dey, E. L., 122
diffuse socialization, 69–70
digital immigrants, 212, 216, 219, 223
digital natives, 212, 216, 219
disabilities, students with, 222
disadvantaged students, 167–203; academic resources of, 169–70, 171–73f, 174–75, 177–78, 178f, 184, 186, 192–93, 197; attainment aspirations of, 178–79, 179f, 186,

197; challenges faced by, 167–68; college experiences of, 180–81, 181t; determinants of degree completion for, 175–89; financial aid for, 182–83, 182t, 193; pathways to degree of, 169–75; programs for, 168; suggestions for helping, 192–94. *See also* underrepresented student populations
discipline retention, 92
dismissal, 12
distance learning, 30, 84. *See also* online learning
diversity. *See* student diversity
Dowd, A. C., 241
dropout, 12, 83–85
dual enrollment programs, 155–56
DuBrock, C. P., 241, 244
Durkheim, Emile, 69, 71–73, 86

early departure: defining, 251–53; financial consequences of, 2; institutional costs of, 96; negative consequences of, 1–3; persistence of, 4; programs to address, 3–4, 75–76, 267, 282; Tinto on, 71–73
early identification, of student deficiencies, 75–76, 270, 272–73, 278. *See also* assessment and feedback, as contributor to student success
early intervention, 76, 273
Eaton, J. S., 148
economy: community colleges and, 151; retention and, 3, 96
educational attainment, and employment, 102
e-learning. *See* distance learning; online learning
Emergency Relief Appropriations Act (1935), 63
employment: community colleges and, 151–52; educational attainment and, 102; preparation for, 1–2, 96; student, 111
engagement. *See* integration, academic and social; involvement

About the Editor and Contributors

Alan Seidman is a core (full-time) faculty member and the General & Self-Designed Specialization Coordinator with the Richard W. Riley College of Education & Leadership at Walden University, Minnesota. In addition, he is the executive director of the Center for the Study of College Student Retention (www.cscsr.org). The Center provides retention resources to individuals and educational institutions including the *Journal of College Student Retention: Research, Theory & Practice* which Dr. Seidman founded and edits. It is the only scholarly journal devoted exclusively to college student retention issues. Seidman has also published articles in scholarly journals in the areas of retention and attrition, student services, and enrollment management, and has given presentations on these topics at local, state, regional, national, and international conferences as well as presentations/workshops to college and university administrators, faculty, and staff. Dr. Seidman appeared on *Fox News Live Weekend* to talk about college student retention.

In addition to his professional responsibilities, Dr. Seidman is a member of the New Hampshire Judicial Council, appointed by the governor of New Hampshire, confirmed by the Executive Council; was an examiner, US Department of Commerce Malcolm Baldrige National Quality Award (MBNQA); has been a grant reader for the US Department of Education; was the alternate, State of New Hampshire Taxpayer Advocacy Panel, Internal Revenue Service, US Department of the Treasury; has been an Instructor Trainer, American Red Cross; and AARP Volunteer Income Tax Assistance program volunteer.

Dr. Seidman has over thirty years of experience in education as a college administrator, educational consultant, and elementary school teacher. He earned his BA and MA from Glassboro State College (Rowan University), New Jersey, and his EdD from Syracuse University, New York.

Alexander W. Astin is the Allan M. Cartter Distinguished Professor of Higher Education, Emeritus, at the University of California at Los Angeles (UCLA). He is also the founding director of the Higher Education Research Institute at UCLA and the author of twenty-one books and more than four hundred other publications. His research and writing in the field of higher education has earned him awards from thirteen different national associations.

Dr. Astin has been identified as the most frequently cited author in the higher education field, and his book *Four Critical Years* as the most frequently cited book in the field. Astin has served as a fellow at the Center for Advanced Study in the Behavioral Sciences at Stanford University, been elected to membership in the National Academy of Education, and is the recipient of eleven honorary degrees.

Joseph B. Berger is professor of education and associate dean for research and engagement in the School of Education at the University of Massachusetts Amherst. Dr. Berger's scholarly interests focus on the impacts of leadership, policy, and organizational structures on higher education outcomes with a particular emphasis on student retention. In recent years, much of his work focuses on improving higher education in a variety of national contexts including Malawi, China, Russia, Afghanistan, Egypt, and the Philippines. He has authored dozens of journal articles, book chapters, and research reports, and his work has been funded by agencies and foundations such as the Nellie Mae Education Foundation, National Science Foundation (NSF), and United States Agency for International Development (USAID). He has won several national awards for his scholarship from associations such as the Association for the Study of Higher Education (ASHE), American College Personnel Association (ACPA), and National Association of Student Personnel Administrators (NASPA). He earned his PhD in education and human development, specializing in higher education administration, from Vanderbilt University.

Erin W. Bibo is a doctoral candidate in the Education Policy and Leadership Program at the University of Maryland, College Park. Her research interests focus on the role middle schools play in the college choice process, parental involvement, and low-income and first-generation student populations.

Kurt R. Burkum is principal research associate at ACT. He has spent the last fifteen years working with colleges and education nonprofits on education policy issues. His research interests focus on education policy formation and implementation, college and career readiness, and data visualization.

Alberto F. Cabrera is professor of higher education at the University of Maryland, College Park. He specializes in college choice, the impact of college on students, classroom experiences, minorities in higher education, and college outcomes. He has served on the advisory boards of Pathways to College Network, the National Postsecondary Education Cooperative (NPEC)'s Student Outcomes, the GEAR UP Evaluation Council of the National Council for Community and Education Partnerships (NCCEP), and the Pell Institute and Higher Education Accreditation Agency of the Provincial Government of Aragon, Spain, as well as on the editorial boards of *Journal of Higher Education, Review of Higher Education, Research in Higher Education,* and *Revista Complutense de Educación.* His work on classroom practices, the role of finances on college persistence, alumni, and determinants of default behavior has received several awards. He was also co-principal investigator for the IES grant titled "Dream Deferred," which provided a most comprehensive review of the impact of GEAR UP on awareness and readiness for college among low-income middle school students. He was the co-leader of the Diversity Institute, a project funded by NSF seeking to create inclusive teaching practices in STEM fields.

Gloria Crisp is assistant professor in the Educational Leadership and Policy Studies Department at The University of Texas at San Antonio (UTSA). The focus of her scholarship includes understanding how mentoring is perceived and experienced by college students, the factors that influence the success of community college and/or Hispanic students, and the impact of institutional and state policy on student transfer and persistence. She is an associate editor of *The Review of Higher Education.* Her work has been published in many top journals including *Research in Higher Education, The American Educational Research Journal,* and the *Journal of College Student Development.* She has also contributed to numerous book chapters including a recent volume of *Higher Education: Handbook of Theory and Research.*

Ann Gansemer-Topf is the associate director of research for the Office of Admissions at Iowa State University and a lecturer in the Department of Educational Leadership and Policy Studies at Iowa State University. She has worked in residence life, campus ministry, conference services, academic advising, and institutional research. She has presented at several national conferences and her areas of interest include educational policy related to strategic enrollment management, assessment of student learning, and effective teaching/learning pedagogies. She holds a PhD in Educational Leadership and Policy Studies from Iowa State University, an MS degree in Higher Education from Iowa State University, and a BA in Psychology from Loras College in Dubuque, Iowa.

Linda Serra Hagedorn serves Iowa State University as the associate dean of undergraduate programs; diversity, equity and community; and student services in the College of Human Sciences. She also directs the international programs in the college. Hagedorn is also professor and the current interim chair of the Department of Educational Leadership and Policy Studies. Hagedorn is currently working on expanding the College's international outreach and offerings with increased international partnerships and study abroad experiences.

Dr. Hagedorn's research focuses on community college student success, retention, and transfer. She is especially interested in issues pertaining to underrepresented student groups and equity. Prior to joining the faculty at Iowa State University, she directed the Institute of Higher Education at the University of Florida. She was also the director of the Transfer and Retention of Urban Community College Students Project (TRUCCS), a longitudinal study of over five thousand students enrolled in the Los Angeles Community College District. Although Dr. Hagedorn performs both quantitative and qualitative research, she is especially known for developing techniques to analyze enrollment and other college files. She has created new rubrics and designs for the longitudinal analyses of transcript data (transcript analysis). Her most recent published works include: *Looking in the Rearview Mirror: Factors Affecting Transfer for Urban Community College Students; An Investigation of Critical Mass: The Role of Latino Representation in the Success of Urban Community College Students;* and *Hispanic Community College Students and the Transfer Game: Strikes, Misses, and Grand Experiences.*

Steven M. La Nasa is president of Donnelly College, in Kansas City, Kansas, an institution exclusively focused on post-secondary access and success for underserved students. He has served in various administrative and academic roles for almost twenty years. His research interests deal with assessment, college-going decisions, student persistence, and faculty roles.

Susan Lyons is the associate dean of academic affairs at Bard College at Simon's Rock, where she is responsible for student success and faculty development. Her work focuses on issues of student retention in higher education, with a particular emphasis on women and underrepresented groups. Other areas of interest and expertise include issues in higher education related to early college programs, academic support services for students, and the impact of study abroad and civic engagement on retention. Dr. Lyons earned her doctorate at the University of Massachusetts Amherst in 2009.

Liliana Mina has over twenty-five years of experience in college student development, administration of adult education programs, and student support services for underrepresented populations in post-secondary education. Her scholarship, teaching, and service have three primary foci: college student affairs administration, student development, and teaching and learning in the online environment. Other research interests include community college education and ethnic identity development. She is assistant professor at the University of Wisconsin-Milwaukee, School of Education, Department of Administrative Leadership. Dr. Mina earned both her master's degree in Student Affairs Administration and her PhD in Higher Adult and Lifelong Education from Michigan State University.

Lonnie Morrison is director of Metropolitan Admissions Programs at Syracuse University and adjunct associate professor at the Maxwell School of Citizenship and Public Affairs. He is responsible for the planning, development, and implementation of the university's recruitment, admissions, and financial aid activities in the New York Metropolitan area. Among the administrative positions held during his career, he was assistant director of the office of special programs at the State University of New York at Oswego, assistant dean of the College of Arts and Sciences at the State University of New York at Oswego, and director of the Educational Opportunity Fund Program at New Jersey Institute of Technology.

Dr. Morrison received his Bachelor of Science degree from the State University of New York at Albany, his Master of Science degree from the State University of New York at Oswego, and PhD degree in Higher Education from Syracuse University. He has a strong interest in public policy issues that pertain to urban public education.

Thomas G. Mortenson is senior scholar at The Pell Institute for the Study of Opportunity in Higher Education in Washington, DC, and an independent higher education policy analyst living in Oskaloosa, Iowa.

Mortenson's policy research focuses on opportunity for postsecondary education and training and the ways public policy fosters or impedes access to that opportunity. He has special concern for populations that are underrepresented in higher education. His studies have addressed academic and financial preparation for college, access, choice, persistence, attainment, and labor force entry of college graduates. He is particularly interested in public and private finance of higher education opportunity and the enrollment consequences of the cost-shift from taxpayers to students that has been underway since 1980. He has been employed in policy research and budget analysis roles for the University of Minnesota, Illinois Board of Higher Education, Illinois State Scholarship Commission, and the American College Testing Program.

Currently Mortenson is editor and publisher of *Postsecondary Education OPPORTUNITY*, a monthly research letter devoted to analysis and reporting on the demographics, sociology, history, politics, and economics of educational opportunity after high school. He provides consulting services on higher educational opportunity policy to state and national organizations, and makes presentations on educational opportunity throughout the country and in Europe.

Amaury Nora is professor of higher education and associate dean for research in the College of Education and Human Development at the University of Texas at San Antonio. His research has focused on student persistence, engagement, and degree attainment; the impact of psychosocial factors on academic and social integration in college; and differential social support systems for undergraduates at two- and four-year institutions.

Dr. Nora has been selected as an AERA Fellow (Class of 2010) by the American Educational Research Association; appointed to the Texas Higher Education Coordinating Board Think Tank on Developmental Education; appointed to the AERA/NCES Think Tank to improve national databases produced by the National Center for Education Statistics; named as senior scholar for the American College Personnel Association (ACPA); and nominated for the position of vice-chair of the Scientific Committee for Europe and North America, Scientific Committees of the UNESCO Forum on Higher Education, Research and Knowledge. Currently, he is the chief editor for *The Review of Higher Education*, the journal of the Association for the Study of Higher Education.

Leticia Oseguera is assistant professor and research associate in the Department of Education Policy Studies and the Center for the Study of Higher Education at Pennsylvania State University. She received her PhD from UCLA. Her work focuses on college access and completion for low-income students and other marginalized populations. Her research has been published in *The Review of Higher Education*, *Research in Higher Education*, and *Youth and Society*. She was recently named a Ford Foundation Fellow.

Gerardo Blanco Ramírez is a doctoral candidate in the educational policy and leadership program at the University of Massachusetts Amherst, with a concentration in higher education administration. His work focuses on the study of international higher education, incorporating postcolonial, critical, and intercultural perspectives. His interests also include leadership, management, and organization; diversity in higher education; and qualitative inquiry. He has experience in Mexican higher education working on institutional accreditation and faculty development initiatives. Blanco Ramírez also has experience as a student affairs practitioner and earned a master's degree in student development in higher education from the University of Maine.

Daniel W. Salter is currently director of Strategic Research Initiatives in the Center for Research Support and a member of the doctoral faculty in The Richard W. Riley College of Education and Leadership at Walden University. He came to Walden in 2004, after serving on the graduate faculty at Pennsylvania State University for eight years. Dr. Salter has a PhD in higher education and student affairs from The Ohio State University. His research interests include a focus on assuring student success, especially in the increasingly distributed environment of higher education.

John H. Schuh is Distinguished Professor of Educational Leadership and Policy Studies Emeritus at Iowa State University. Previously he held administrative and faculty appointments at Wichita State University, Indiana University (Bloomington), and Arizona State University. Among his books are *Student Services: A Handbook for the Profession* (edited with Susan Jones and Shaun Harper), *Student Success in College* (with George D. Kuh, Jillian Kinzie, and Elizabeth Whitt), and *Assessment Methods in Student Affairs.* Dr. Schuh has been recognized by several professional organizations including the Association for the Study of Higher Education, from which he received the Research Achievement Award. Currently he is associate editor of the *New Directions for Student Services* sourcebook series.

Loretta Silverman received her PhD in education specializing in community college leadership from Walden University, her master's in mathematics from San Jose State University, and her baccalaureate degree in mathematics from the University of California, San Diego. She is currently teaching mathematics, both developmental and college-level, at Foothill College. She is involved with and has conducted research on developmental math student retention in two-year institutions. Her article titled "Academic Progress in Developmental Math Courses: A Comparative Study of Student Retention" was published in the fall of 2011 in the *Journal of College Student Retention: Research, Theory and Practice.* She has won teaching awards and belonged to an international educational honor society.

Vincent Tinto received his PhD in education and sociology from the University of Chicago. He is currently Distinguished University Professor at Syracuse University. He has carried out research and has written extensively on higher education, particularly on student retention and the impact of learning communities on student growth and attainment. He has consulted widely with federal and state agencies, independent research firms, foundations, and two- and four-year institutions of higher education on a broad range of higher educational issues, including the retention and education of students in higher education. He serves on the editorial boards of several journals and with various organizations and professional associations concerned with higher education. He chaired the national panel responsible for awarding $5 million to establish the first national center for research on teaching and learning in higher education and served as associate director of the $6 million National Center on Postsecondary Teaching, Learning, and Assessment funded by the US Office of Education. He is involved in a number of national initiatives to improve college completion including Completion by Design funded by the Bill and Melinda Gates Foundation; the Roadmap Project of the American Association of Colleges and Universities; the Institute of Higher Education's Pathways to College Network project funded by the Lumina Foundation for Education; and the American Association of Community Colleges' Community Colleges: 21st Century Initiative. Dr. Tinto also serves as a Senior Scholar for the Pell Institute for the Study of Opportunity in Education and the Council for Opportunity in Education. His new book forthcoming from The University of Chicago Press, entitled *Completing College*, lays out a framework for institutional action and shows how it can be applied to enhance the success of students in both two- and four-year institutions.

CPSIA information can be obtained at www.ICGtesting.com
Printed in the USA
BVOW030000300412

288958BV00001B/2/P